Setting research priorities

J. Douwe Meindertsma, editor

Setting research priorities

Towards effective farmer-oriented research

DEVELOPMENT ORIENTED RESEARCH IN AGRICULTURE

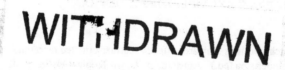

ROYAL TROPICAL INSTITUTE - THE NETHERLANDS

DEVELOPMENT ORIENTED RESEARCH IN AGRICULTURE
A Royal Tropical Institute Series

I L.O. Fresco. *Cassava in shifting cultivation: A systems approach to agricultural technology development in Africa (1986)*
II H. Savenije and A. Huijsman. *Making haste slowly: Strengthening local environmental management in agricultural development (1991)*
III A. Budelman. *Woody species in auxiliary roles: Live stakes in yam cultivation (1993)*
IV J. de Graaff. *Soil conservation and sustainable land use: An economic approach (1993)*

CIP-DATA KONINKLIJKE BIBLIOTHEEK, DEN HAAG
Setting

Setting research priorities : towards effective farmer-oriented research /
J. Douwe Meindertsma (ed.) - Amsterdam : Royal Tropical Institute. - Ill. -
(Development oriented research in agriculture ; 5)
With ref.
ISBN 90-6832-084-X
NUGI 835
Subject headings; research management ; agriculture / farming systems research.

© 1994 Royal Tropical Institute - Amsterdam
Cover design: Nederlands Ontwerp bv
Cartography: Kees Prins
Printer: ICG Printing, Dordrecht
ISBN 90 6832 084 X

Table of contents

II Project experiences

Preface

This new volume in the *Development Oriented Research in Agriculture,* or DORA, series originated in an international workshop on research management, *Priority setting in farming systems research and development* (December 9-13, 1991, in Amsterdam). Field experiences of projects in which KIT participates were taken as a starting point; several resource people also contributed to the exchange. The objective was to learn from each other and to assess management problems for which further support would be needed. Participating projects and programmes – MARIF, ATA-272, in Indonesia; Lake Zone, in Tanzania; DRSPR, in Mali; ARPT-Western Province, in Zambia; RAMR, in Benin; PROFED, in Mali; PLAE, Mali; and PRIAG, in Central America – recorded how their priority setting is done in practice, and these documents served as a basis for discussion. Most of these projects and programmes operate at regional or district level; consequently, the focus of the book is mainly on the local processes and actors involved.

This book has been made possible by many years of fruitful collaboration between the Royal Tropical Institute (KIT) and its partners in the countries concerned, years in which not only good institutional relationships but also many good personal relationships have developed. The aim of the publication is to systematize the experiences of the projects and make the results more widely accessible. In particular, priority setting at programme and project level is seen as one key to research management: a well-structured priority setting process can help teams, working in collaboration with other actors, to make the best use of their potential and to produce relevant, sustainable results. We hope the conclusions and recommendations found here will be a step towards making research priority setting more efficient, effective, and transparent, thereby strengthening the research management and thus the performance of farmer-oriented research, our common development endeavour.

N.H. Vink
Director General, Royal Tropical Institute (KIT)

Acknowledgements

The international workshop in Amsterdam that formed the basis for this publication flowed from discussions within the Department of Agricultural Development at the KIT. The editor would like to acknowledge and thank those involved in conceptualizing and organizing the workshop, in particular Bram Huijsman, Stephan Seegers and Willem Stoop. We would also like to express our appreciation to Deborah Merrill-Sands and her colleagues at ISNAR. There were frequent contacts during preparation; further, ISNAR staff members were among the resource people at the workshop, and their participation was important to the discussions.

Above all, I would like to thank the authors of the chapters. The decision to highlight particular phases of the process, made at the workshop, meant that many papers (particularly the project experiences) had to be rewritten and refocused. This process has taken time; I hope the final product will be satisfying, both to authors and contributors; and above all, that it will be useful to practitioners in the field. I would also like to thank those who have read and commented upon draft versions. Further, KIT Press, in addition to their work in producing the book, has played an integral part in the give and take involved in improving and finalizing the manuscript.

Introduction

Fewer than 10 years ago, many donor agencies regarded FSR&D – farming systems research and development – as a revolutionary approach to agricultural research.[1] Farming systems research programmes were seen as vehicles for revitalizing the process of technology development and transfer, giving a voice to farmers and involving social scientists in agricultural research. The concept of FSR&D was very simple and rational – and easy to sell. Unfortunately, it was too attractive. Like a good wine, it needed time to mature, but donors jumped on the bandwagon before this could occur.[2]

In recent years the glow of the farming systems movement has clearly waned. Many FSR&D programmes have not lived up to expectations, but these expectations had clearly been set too high. We would assert that the fundamental problem lies not with the principles of the FSR&D approach, but with the way it has been implemented and managed. When on-farm research began to receive more emphasis from researchers and donors (in the early seventies), a rather simplistic view of its role and potential prevailed. Over the years, on-farm research has increasingly evolved towards 'systems research', thereby providing an essential link between real-world agriculture – including the socioeconomic and institutional environment in which farmers operate – and the specialized thematic and commodity research conducted on experiment stations. The complexities that accompanied this shift now confront FSR&D teams doing what used to be considered simple on-farm testing. Not surprisingly, programmes have had difficulty coming to grips with managing this research; yet needs for training in FSR&D management, and for the development of new methodologies, have remained largely unrecognized. Rather than side-stepping the complexities, it is necessary to face up to them, and perhaps even to change them into opportunities.

Attention to research management is not entirely new. Many national agricultural research systems (NARS) are engaged in strengthening their management capabilities. Various organizations are involved in related training courses, and funding agencies such as the World Bank support projects on agricultural research management, covering aspects such as institution building, research planning and programming, and management of human, physical, and financial resources. Most attention, however, has been directed at the national level; little of the literature on research management covers operational issues at programme and project levels.[3]

Increasing professionalism in the research management aspects of FSR&D is needed. With donor and government support to agricultural research declining, this is especially important: it is imperative to demonstrate that FSR&D can make an essential, cost-effective contribution to agricultural development. This will require increased awareness of managerial and organizational issues, and of the methods and tools that can be used to involve various actors in the process of setting priorities. Sufficient experience is now available to begin to provide some guidance on aspects such as planning, priority setting, evaluation, and monitoring of research for managers within FSR&D programmes and projects. Tools and procedures for incorporating participation of stakeholders, diagnosis of local situations, and methods for establishing priorities among research themes, research questions, and research activities are becoming available, and it is time to begin consolidating the experience of projects in the field.

Research management is seen as a way to improve both the effectiveness of research – the extent to which objectives are achieved, and efficiency – the use of resources, including personnel (expertise, experience), facilities (building, laboratories) and finances (investment and recurrent). Achieving effectiveness and efficiency in FSR&D requires a great variety of skills. Organization and management within the team are of course necessary, to assure coordination and proper management of physical and human resources; issues within the team – particularly interdisciplinary issues – are an important part of the complexity. But also there must be linkages to other individuals and organizations, ranging from the national government to the farmer; and choices must be made involving the intervention area, the target group and the activities to be carried out (ranging from diagnosis to research to pre-extension), all of which are closely related to the varied interests of the many stakeholders. Research management in this environment requires the ability to recognize conflicting interests, to communicate with many actors and find ways to strike a balance that results in productive research. Setting priorities – whether among research themes, research questions, or activities to be carried out – is the key to successful research management.

Outline of the book

The following chapters are divided into two parts. Chapter 1 introduces the material to be covered; the remainder of Part I further explores many of the issues, methods and tools involved in research management, beginning with a closer look at priority setting as a part of the FSR&D process. The project experiences in Part II highlight phases of the research process and specific groups of actors, exemplifying diverse research approaches. The last project described, PRIAG, involves a project for regional cooperation among six Central American countries. Regionalization of research and extension can be particularly important in small countries with diverse agroecological environments, where pooling resources can be a way to obtain relevant research results efficiently. The final chapter highlights the lessons of the preceding material and gives an agenda: issues that FSR&D research management must begin to address, if systems-oriented research and development is to remain a force for change.

Notes

1   For simplicity, we use FSR&D (farming systems research and development) as a generic term throughout this book. The discussion applies equally to a broad variety of activities, including those known under a variety of other acronyms, such as FSR&E (farming systems research and extension); FSRAD (farming systems research and agricultural development; OFCOR (on-farm client-oriented research); OFR/FSR (on-farm research with a farming systems perspective); and the francophone R-D (recherche développement); RSP (recherche sur les systèmes de production); and RAMR (recherche appliquée en milieu réel).

2   David Norman, in his concluding remarks for the international workshop on *Priority Setting in Farming Systems Research and Development.*

3   In the bibliography of the On-Farm Client-Oriented Research Study (OFCOR) produced by ISNAR (1989), only 9% of references are of special relevance to the management of the research process and of field operations.

1 Issues and approaches

1 Setting research priorities in FSR&D programmes

Stephan Seegers, J. Douwe Meindertsma and Willem Stoop

Setting priorities for FSR&D programmes is a complex process. This complexity has two major sources: the nature and characteristics of FSR&D work; and the large number of actors who – in one way or another – need to be involved. FSR&D, in contrast with much other agricultural research, must deal with systems and processes that are dynamic. They are affected simultaneously by both technical and human elements, so that FSR&D must continuously refocus its efforts on a 'moving target' (Maxwell, 1986). Nevertheless, there must be continuity in research; this obviously requires close interdisciplinary cooperation within the research team. At the same time, real participation of clients (particularly farmers) and other stakeholders is needed. They are interested in getting results. Participation therefore encourages a focus on real problems, and helps to assure that the research programme is regularly adjusted in response to changing needs.

The target areas and target groups of farmers concerned are, however, far from uniform. Further, actors at all levels have quite varied concerns. In setting priorities for FSR&D programmes, it is often necessary to try to reconcile conflicting demands and objectives: for example, short term production versus long term conservation/sustainability; location specificity versus results that can be applied more generally; or the interests of various groups of farmers – small scale, large scale, male, female and so forth. Thus it is not surprising that priority setting in FSR&D tends to be 'messy'.

Given this situation, FSR&D teams have typically attempted to set priorities by involving primarily researchers, who have made use of rather 'intuitive' processes. Making decisions intuitively has a number of disadvantages, both for the team and for its relationships with other individuals and groups. It makes readjustment in the face of changing conditions difficult. The lack of transparency inherent in intuitive decision making also stands in the way of communication, blocking both good interdisciplinary relationships within the team and participation from others. A more structured approach to priority setting is the key to strengthening FSR&D programmes. It can increase the relevance of FSR&D, improving not only the likelihood that results will be implemented, but also that sustainability will be achieved.

This book illustrates three major elements of a structured approach, which are briefly introduced in this chapter:

- the process of setting priorities, including questions such as what research, for whom, and where research will be carried out;
- the related decision making with respect to planning and methods: when and how the programme will be implemented;
- the actors who need to be involved in decision making.

A more structured approach alone is not enough. An important aspect of management is to become more aware of the environment in which research takes place and to work to shape this environment, rather than simply reacting to it. The relevance and importance of research results must be evident to others; this too is essential to sustainability. As proposed in the final chapter, FSR&D teams need to adopt an open, proactive attitude, seeking linkages with other actors and opportunities for collaboration – working, as Bingen says (Chapter 6), 'as partners, not as adversaries.'

Priority setting and research

Priority setting can be described as an exercise in identifying key problems, then selecting among a number of possible courses of action, seeking the best ways to address these problems. The decisions that must be made in the analysis and definition of problems, the identification and screening of possible solutions, and the matching of problems with solutions are the core of any priority setting process.

Research, including FSR&D, is an iterative process. This process is characterized by a number of phases which together constitute the research cycle (Box 1). Priority setting is necessary in each phase of the research cycle, helping to gradually zoom in on key problem areas and most appropriate solutions: this is crucial in ensuring that scarce research resources are used effectively and efficiently.

The research cycle outlined in Box 1 obviously represents a model situation. In practice, neither the research cycle nor the associated priority setting are necessarily followed sequentially. Shortcuts or crossovers among phases are often possible. For example, diagnostic studies and monitoring usually continue even after on-farm experiments have started. This allows fine-tuning of the initial analysis and better appreciation of the dynamics of farming systems (for example, the annual adjustments made in farming practices in response to variable weather and changing market conditions). The information gained during a project may also suggest that additional diagnosis is necessary.

Box 1. The major phases of the FSR&D research cycle[a]

1. Area selection: both the geographical area and the target group that are to be the subjects of the research must be chosen.

2. Diagnosis: involves examination of farming systems in the context of the total environment, identifying limiting factors (constraints) and screening for opportunities (potential technical changes or potential flexibility) for the target groups. This requires knowing the goals and motivations of farmers, but also understanding the external, contextual factors and the causes of constraints. To simplify this process, the target groups defined (the domain definition) often consist of homogeneous categories of farmers, with comparable access to resources and markets and comparable farming systems.

3. Design: includes matching of constraints and possible solutions. Choices among research activities are made on the basis of selection criteria, plus resource availability. Identification of alternative intervention strategies and/or recommendations is based on the existing body of knowledge (from research conducted elsewhere, plus past research on station and by farmers) but could also involve new experimentation at the research station or on farms.

4. Testing: involves assessment of technologies and of potential recommendations under farm conditions with respect to their technical feasibility, economic viability and social acceptability. For some research themes, it may be necessary to turn to on-station research.

5. Dissemination and feedback: dissemination makes successful technologies available to farmers in the same or similar recommendation domains, initially through pre-extension; feedback provides researchers and other actors with information on the performance and impact of decisions and results. Farming systems programmes are usually committed to ensuring implementation: either directly (e.g. seed multiplication) or indirectly, by working with the extension service.

6. Impact assessment: evaluation of reasons for adoption or rejection of technologies. This may lead to the reappraisal of a technology and a new cycle of adaptation and testing.

---

[a] The research cycle is described here without indicating when specific actors, including farmers, are involved.

While this theoretical sequence of phases and activities often cannot be followed in practice, keeping the sequence in mind can help the research manager to determine at which phase a programme has arrived and where to take shortcuts or go back to an earlier phase. Management needs to ask questions – have the appropriate actors been involved in defining key problems; has there been sufficient diagnosis to move on to the design phase; does the planned research address the primary problems; have research results been sufficiently verified to be disseminated; and so on. Most importantly, the research team should recognize that the various phases of the research cycle are interdependent, and that there must be linkages between them. For example, the fact that dissemination will occur has definite implications for the earlier diagnostic and design phases.

The FSR&D process

Each phase of the research cycle requires some degree of priority setting with respect to the activities to be carried out and the actors to be involved.

Area selection

The very first priority setting issue is the selection of the research area and target groups. This initial choice is often not in the hands of the FSR&D team, but lies instead with policymakers and donors. Decisions made at the national level before a team begins its work often play a predominant role in the FSR&D initiatives to come, by defining:
- the institutional setting of the FSR&D team (that is, the national counterpart organization to which it will be attached, where the team will be based, and how it will operate and be managed);
- the geographic area the project is to cover, and thus the agricultural constraints that will be the primary focus;
- the particular target group to be addressed, broadly formulated (e.g. 'resource-poor farmers' or 'small farmers');
- the broad research programme issues to be emphasized, which clearly will reflect current national and/or donor policy objectives.

The objectives of most FSR&D programmes involve vast, extremely diverse areas. Even when these objectives include a preliminary definition of area and target groups, it is generally impossible for one team to cover their area in detail and work with development and/or extension agents throughout the entire district or region. Typically, the FSR&D team will also be unable to develop standard recommendations that are valid across the entire district or region, even though development/extension services would prefer this. Thus, the team must, at an early stage, come to terms with the question of how it will cope with the great diversity in agroecological and socioeconomic conditions commonly seen within project areas.

To minimize these problems, strategic choices must be made. For example, it may be preferable to focus on a limited number of target areas or villages for interventions. This may require negotiations with policymakers, who may be under political pressure to see that the entire region profits from FSR&D services. Making choices with respect to intervention areas and target groups is crucial not only to increasing the potential for establishing coherent research themes, but also to project success. In making choices, an understanding of both agroecological and socioeconomic conditions in the local setting is critical; technical information is obviously important, but socioeconomic information, including the role of women, is equally so. This brings us to the diagnostic phase.

Diagnosis

Background information, whether it comes from the literature or from new research, should be fully used in determining constraints and opportunities as well as in deciding which problems should have the highest priority and which approaches are most likely to succeed. Diagnosis also helps to sharpen the definition of the target group. The involvement of actors other than researchers should be considered early in the diagnostic phase. However, as illustrated by the project experiences in Part II, it is quite common to simply present the final results of a diagnosis to other stakeholders, once researchers have completed the analysis. This is a tempting procedure; it seems faster and simpler. In the long term, however, involving others – including farmers, extension workers, thematic researchers, policymakers and donors – in even the earliest stages of FSR&D is a way to build understanding and commitment. In the end, this can be expected to lead to more sustainable solutions to local problems. When researchers work alone, others may feel that a major part of the priority setting has already been done without them, during analysis and reporting. Moreover, even when researchers are trying hard to be objective, their disciplinary backgrounds and personal interests, as well as lack of a local perspective, can lead to a narrow focus. Integrating local knowledge helps to avoid such biases.

Data collection decisions must also be made early in the diagnostic phase. Issues related to data collection come up throughout this process: which data are essential to an initial characterization of existing systems and their constraints, and to subsequent definition of research questions and recommendation domains?[1] A common experience in FSR&D programmes has been a heavy investment of time and manpower – both in the initial phase and later – in developing massive collections of data. Although it is important to have good and sufficient baseline data available, existing information should be properly exploited first (see Chapter 15). The most commonly used data collection tools are reviews of background literature; informal surveys; rapid rural appraisals and related methods; formal surveys (using questionnaires); and the farm-monitoring systems often used by economists. In practice, FSR&D programmes will not rely on just one of these tools, but will use a combination. This information then becomes the basis for defining on-farm trials and socioeconomic research issues. (These research activities also have diagnostic value: unsuspected causes of problems or even additional problems may be identified, requiring a return to the activities of the diagnostic phase.)

While a detailed discussion of data collection methods is beyond the scope of this book, in Chapter 7 Meindertsma et al. focus on the use of rapid rural appraisals. In addition, several alternative diagnostic tools have been developed recently. A selection of these 'farmer participatory research methods' are discussed by Rhoades (Chapter 4); they serve to integrate a wealth of farmer experience and knowledge into subsequent research activities. (For further discussion of the diagnostic phase, see Roeleveld and van den Broek, forthcoming; and Mettrick, 1993). Whichever data are used, a thorough analysis (not an intuitive interpretation) is needed, to translate the results of diagnostic activities into research programmes. This increases the likelihood that the resulting research programme will be clearly related to the initial problem diagnosis.

Design: from diagnosis to research themes

FSR&D programmes are only beginning to learn how to use formal procedures to manage decision making regarding priority research themes, and the subsequent translation into a programme of activities. Diagnosis generally results in a long and often interrelated list of problems. These may be related directly to production (for example, diseases, varieties, or response to fertilizers); to marketing and support services (falling prices at harvest time, lack of credit facilities and so forth); or to agricultural policies (e.g. a cropping pattern prescribed by the government).

Stakeholders (those whose interests may be affected) are apt to have different ideas about which problems are most important, and what causes them; thus, it is essential to work toward consensus regarding the relative importance of problems. Especially when projects are in their early phases, such decisions are often made intuitively, with few people involved. Later, when more information is available, the process becomes more structured. A more structured process not only allows more people to participate; it also encourages a critical review of on-going research programmes.

In a more structured approach, use is made of more formal decision making criteria: first come those which immediately eliminate themes or research questions (boundary criteria). These may include questions that cannot be resolved through research, but require other types of intervention; a theme that is outside the mandate for research; a research question that cannot be answered within the project time span; items for which the required expertise is not available (not present in the research team, and too difficult or expensive to contract out); politically sensitive issues or logistical problems of various kinds. After this, other criteria are used to rank problems in order of importance. Examples are the number of farm households affected; whether the problem is related to a priority activity of farm households; and who within households is involved, with respect to gender and other factors.
   This critical examination of problems and the accompanying consensus building regarding their relative importance is a key part of the process. This is particularly evident in the next phase, when solutions are examined and matched to problems. Sometimes known problems and solutions assume new significance, either because their relevance is recognized or because a given problem is found to be a 'leverage point', for which a solution would have a broad impact.

Setting priorities among themes or research questions is a stepwise, iterative process. Ideally, the research programme should not be too broad, but also not too narrowly focused, covering only a single crop or a few components. The programme should include a mixture of problems: some which can be addressed in the short term, using available solutions; some for the medium term; and others that require research over a period of years. Achieving this sort of balance is not easy. Among the issues brought out clearly by the project experiences is the notorious tendency of FSR&D teams to be over-ambitious in designing their research programmes (Barker and Lightfoot, 1985), while underestimating the time required for interpreting data and reporting. Programmes end up with too many activities covering too many sites, thereby jeopardizing not only the successful completion of the research programme but also a key asset of FSR: the opportunity for real farmer participation! On the other hand, a programme that is too narrow may use up too many of the available human and financial resources, leaving little room for new initiatives, refined diagnoses, or changing interests of stakeholders.

Chapters 7 and 8, experiences from Indonesia and Tanzania, in particular, give examples of the process of translating identified problems into research programmes. Enserink et al. show how themes are eliminated in the process of formulating the research programme, and how interventions are designed, emphasizing different types of farm trials. Woolley and Tripp (Chapter 3) stress cause–effect relationships and develop an approach towards priority setting of problems and solutions. Chapter 9 (Kooijman et al.) provides one example of dealing with an excess of research activities, while establishing a programme that was feasible in terms of researchers' time. This and other projects made use of the OOPP technique. The strength of this method lies in clarifying cause–effect relationships. Alternative techniques for reviewing a programme, including 'state of the art' papers, were used by the KAOMA maize programme of ARPT in Western Province, Zambia (Vierstra and Ndiyoi, Chapter 10).

Testing: from priority themes to field activities

On-farm field trials are conducted for several reasons:
- to improve a diagnosis, thereby clarifying the causes of a problem;
- to explore additional solutions;
- to test a solution for acceptability to farmers.

Depending on the objectives of a trial, responsibility for its design and management may lie with researchers and/or farmers (Matlon, 1984).

In general, field trials provide an excellent tool for generating feedback from farmers and extension agents about the advantages and shortcomings of various interventions, when carried out in farmers' fields. This is the primary objective. Collection of detailed technical data is secondary; high coefficients of variation (due to the impossibility of controlling the many non-experimental variables) make on-farm data less precise than those collected under the more controlled conditions of experiment stations.

FSR&D researchers have often failed to understand and explain this complementarity between their on-farm trials and conventional on-station experiments. Consequently, on-station researchers have often dismissed the results of on-farm trials as inaccurate or inconclusive; while on-farm researchers have attempted in vain to use on-station methods and trial designs – which are inappropriate to their needs – to improve the credibility of their research. In fact, as long as the nature, purpose and expectations of on-farm trials are properly understood, including the trade-offs to be obtained by testing under real-world conditions and incorporating farmer-related factors, such trials can contribute greatly to satisfying the needs of the various FSR&D clients. Norman (Chapter 2) spells out differences by type and characteristics of trials, with some implications for management.

Recommendations and feedback

Annual interpretation and reporting of results, as well as periodic syntheses, are important in several ways. Feedback can strengthen the team's linkages with other stakeholders – farmers, extension and on-station research, policymakers and donors – and increase their involvement and commitment. Here it is necessary to develop different reporting mechanisms, suited to the various major actors. Equally important is the use of these mechanisms to strengthen the internal consensus of the team regarding the future direction of the programme.

Data interpretation and reporting are often squeezed in, coming at the end of the season's research programme, when reports must be written and a new research period is about to begin. Consequently, analysis and reporting may be limited to data from the season that has just ended; further interpretation (based on a comparison to results from past seasons and/or other areas or countries) is often neglected. As a result, no recommendations are formulated, and on-going research may drag on for years. Meanwhile, the possibility of adopting new research themes or approaches that might be more promising, or more relevant to the problems at hand, are inadequately considered. Bingen deals with these aspects in greater detail in Chapter 6, as do Chapters 7 and 10.

Actors in the process

Priority setting within an FSR&D programme is, ideally, the result of a consultative process. Negotiation within the team focuses on achieving agreement among team members and disciplines; external consultations provide information about the interests of other relevant stakeholders, plus the possibility of collaboration. The process often takes place under direct pressure from some stakeholders (whether internal or external) to pay attention to their specific interests. The team needs to strike a balance among external and internal interests. Since it will never be possible to fully satisfy all, compromises will have to be made; when other actors are incorporated in the process, they will be more likely to realize the broad range of factors involved and accept this. The central stakeholders or actors, and their roles in this process, are discussed briefly below. We begin with the researchers: a team's ability to work together is a vital base for collaboration.

Researchers

Within team linkages. If an FSR&D team wants greater involvement of other actors, it must begin with good communication and coherence among its own members. The team needs to be clear about its approach, objectives and strategies; obviously, such matters as geographical spread, size of the programme, and the need to avoid fragmentation must be resolved early on. Team building and team management, effective collaboration among disciplines, and establishing and achieving continuity in research themes are therefore imperative. Interdisciplinarity is a key element of FSR&D.[2] It is not automatic, but must be built in, encouraged and managed. Opportunities for interactions between researchers, for confronting differences in approaches and terminology, and for conducting joint research activities must be established by FSR&D management. This is particularly important where disciplines are organized in separate sections (agronomy, socio-economics, etc.), since this may lead to a situation in which sections formulate plans and operate independently. Even in the absence of formal sections, disciplinary barriers can be substantial, requiring strong team management to hold the team together.

As FSR&D programmes and projects are often externally funded and reinforced with expatriate scientists, intercultural interactions can also be problematic. Expatriates and resident researchers often have different objectives and perceptions, which must be reconciled. Norman (Chapter 2) and Vierstra and Ndiyoi (Chapter 10) deal specifically with these aspects.

Linkages between on-farm and on-station researchers. Special reference is made here to linkages of the FSR&D team to on-station commodity and/or disciplinary research, but linkages to other sectoral institutes and universities are often important as well. The field experiences in this book all involve FSR&D projects that are integrated into national agricultural research structures. Two major means of integration can be distinguished:
- FSR&D programmes in which researchers are also involved in thematic or commodity research programmes (as is the case for the MARIF FSR&D team, Indonesia, Chapter 7);
- specialized FSR&D teams made up of technical and socioeconomic disciplines, which are exclusively responsible for on-farm research. Such teams have generally been created as externally funded projects (e.g. the FSR&D

teams from Tanzania, Mali, Zambia and Benin, in Chapters 8 through 11).
Both solutions have advantages and disadvantages. There is no ideal
model for organizing on-farm research (Merrill-Sands et al., 1991). In the
first case an attempt is made to maintain the systems approach of FSR&D
programmes within a research institute, with an organizational structure
based on commodity and thematic research. This requires strong coordination to ensure interaction among the various disciplines and commodities.
However, integration and linkage problems are also inherent in the second
model. These have been analyzed in detail by Faye and Bingen (1989) for
Senegal. The discussion on how to minimize linkage constraints is relatively advanced as a result of the OFCOR study (Merrill-Sands et al., 1991).
Where FSR&D is well-connected to other research, its design and diagnosis
phases can be instrumental in reorienting commodity/thematic research
programmes. While we discuss primarily on-farm trials, most projects
described in this book emphasize interaction with on-station researchers,
including the need for feedback of priorities to on-station research. In any
case, linkages between these two types of research are essential.

Chapter 2 presents an overview of researcher-researcher linkages, and
explores the importance of functional two-way links between farm-based
FSR&D and station-based thematic research. On-station research can
provide potential solutions to problems identified at farm level by FSR&D
teams. Thematic research should be complementary to FSR&D. If FSR&D
teams fail to feed new research topics back to on-station researchers, and
thus to have them included in subsequent on-station research agendas,
FSR&D programmes will be deprived of their 'lifeblood'. Thematic research
profits from this exchange too, by gaining information that can lead to
more relevant research.

Farmers

Farmer participation in FSR&D has received much attention, in both projects
and publications (for instance, the ILEIA newsletter). It is extremely important to recognize that not all 'farmers' have similar interests. Some examples: first, crops exclusively grown by women are often considered to be
'minor crops' and therefore are not given priority. Nevertheless, these crops
may well be crucial in avoiding food shortages at certain times of year.
Second, farmers with large holdings will view issues like mechanization,
intensification and sustainability differently from those with small plots.
Such differences make it important to ensure that all sorts of farmers
participate. Few of the projects represented in this book, however, state

explicitly how farmers are involved in setting priorities, or the extent to which their participation has had a direct impact on the orientation of research and research activities.

When farmers favour particular technologies, FSR&D has the task of properly understanding their rationale (Meertens et al., forthcoming). With respect to intensification and sustainability issues, there is apt to be considerable distance between farmers' and researchers' viewpoints. Participation should be a way of narrowing such differences, making it more likely that farmers will readily adopt research results and recommendations; if they do not, it calls into question the effectiveness of FSR&D. The goal should not be farmer participation for its own sake, but participation that incorporates local knowledge and leads to research focused on real problems and conditions, so that the results will meet farmers' needs.

Rhoades (Chapter 4) points out that real farmer participation has rarely been achieved; he suggests tools to increase participation, recommending increased use of non-conventional methods. Koudokpon and Sprey (Chapter 11) describe a process by which farmer participation was gradually increased over time; Zuidberg and Kortbeek (Chapter 12) discuss the difficulty of taking into account the priorities of women in FSR&D programmes.

Extension, development and technology transfer agents

Extension agencies and other development and technology transfer agencies need to be involved in FSR&D programmes for a number of reasons. (For simplicity we will refer only to extension.) Extension agents will also have useful local information; and extension programmes should be among the primary users of research results. Further, extension agencies should be aware of the implications of FSR-developed technologies and approaches for their future work programme. Clearly, they should be a natural partner in FSR&D activities.

The effectiveness of involving extension depends to a large extent on the type of participation the FSR&D team expects. Among the possibilities mentioned in Chapter 6 are an effective partnership; informal participation; seeking specific information; or a one-way relationship in which FSR researchers simply keep the extension agency informed. However, as Eponou points out in Chapter 5, even with intensive involvement of extension there may be a number of problems. Thus, while a partnership between the FSR&D team and the local extension organization appears a logical feature, it rarely comes about automatically. For instance, extension programmes may have an interest in maintaining the status quo. They are accustomed to working with the local population in their own ways; staff may feel they are the experts, and may not see any need for changing to a more participative approach. In particular, where extension follows the conventional linear model (in which research and extension are seen as sequential), extension agencies can easily perceive research as cumbersome and dangerous, and as invading their territory. While the qualities of individual participants certainly play an important role in establishing linkages, limitations due to the overall institutional structure of research and extension often cannot be overcome by well-motivated individuals alone.

A further issue is that extension institutions often lack the information they need to carry out their activities, yet they are not expected to conduct research themselves; requests must be made to other agencies. These demands are often only partially met, and/or it may take a long time to get results. Two implementation projects, the anti-erosion project PLAE (Chapter 13) and the women and development project PROFED (Chapter 12), analyze the response of an FSR&D programme (DRSPR, Chapter 9) to their research demands. As demonstrated in Chapter 9, research programmes on the other hand may feel that too many research topics are being proposed for their agenda (perhaps reflecting a lack of priority setting on the part of the requesting party); and that they are overloaded (perhaps reflecting a lack of priorities on their part). This points to the need not only for priorities, but also for participation of implementing agencies – whether extension or others – in the priority setting process. Ideally, there will be consensus; if not, there should at least be understanding regarding the priorities chosen.

Policymakers, planners and donors

As illustrated by the project experiences in Part II, the organizational setting within a country and the local situation determine to a large extent the boundaries within which priority setting takes place. These boundaries are strongly affected by the initial formulation of a programme or project. Even though FSR&D projects often take place within national systems, they are frequently only loosely connected to these systems. At the height of the 'FSR&D boom' in the mid-eighties, projects were often funded by donors without due concern for how they would fit into the national research structure. Van Sluys and Silva (Chapter 14) signal the institutional weakness in some Central American NARS and note the limited impact of such projects. A study of on-farm client-oriented research (OFCOR) conducted by ISNAR analyzed institutional factors influencing effectiveness, and the integration of such research within NARS (Merrill-Sands et al., 1991). For FSR&D teams to be functional and remain effective in the long term (even when donor support runs out), it is generally essential to have full integration into the national system from the beginning. Such integration creates the potential for development of long-term, effective linkages between principal actors, while simultaneously increasing research capacity.[3]

As demonstrated by various ISNAR publications (see e.g. Dagg and Haworth, 1988), priority setting and research programme formulation at national level initially involve a top–down resource allocation process. This process is guided by considerations of national resource availability and its macro-allocation and distribution over various priorities, related for example to particular commodities or geographic regions. However, distortions in the distribution of resources are common. These originate from donor support to specific regions or a specific research theme or commodity; and often also from governments themselves, due to their market and subsidy policies. Both distortions are serious; sooner or later they will have to be rectified, either by terminating projects and programmes or by changing policies. This can have many consequences: for instance in Zambia, lifting subsidies on major food grain crops and chemical fertilizers caused major shocks to farmers and consumers, as well as to FSR researchers whose programmes had been focused too narrowly (Chapter 10).

The time span of funding is another area in which donors have a significant impact. The projected time span should play a major role in defining a strategy regarding the type and number of activities to be undertaken, because donors expect tangible results by the end of a project phase. Often it is not feasible to achieve results regarding desired objectives in a three-year period. Donor willingness to make a commitment for a relatively long period (say six years or more) can thus greatly influence the success of the project.

Political choices can have both direct and indirect effects on priorities. External pressure from policymakers, including their desire to add new topics or objectives, may be an important factor in planning. Also, many technological innovations tested by FSR&D teams are dependent on the availability and quality of agricultural support services (inputs, credits, markets, storage and other infrastructure) and on the organizational strength of rural communities (including village groups and cooperatives) for success. These can be fundamental constraints to the success of an FSR&D programme. In several countries these have been politically sensitive issues; for that reason they have long been considered unalterable conditions of local farm environments. Consequently, FSR&D has tended, certainly in its earlier days, to bypass such issues. It is now generally accepted, however, that FSR&D should address non-technical issues pertaining to local agricultural support services and local farmer organizations. Considerable progress has been made in countries like Mali and Benin (Chapters 9 and 11–13).

The central issues related to linkages with policymakers involve finding ways, first, to balance national and regional policies with demands from rural communities, and from target groups within these communities; and second, to achieve feedback to national and regional levels regarding the rural situation. This includes the need to establish and maintain information flows regarding research results. FSR&D teams must play an active role in initiating these linkages as early as possible and, beyond this, in seeking ways to make the insights and opinions of the team a part of the policy debate, thus creating possibilities to influence policy formulation. Feedback to policymakers and donors can also serve as an important means of assuring continuing support.

Bingen (Chapter 6) reviews ways in which policymakers, planners and donors could be more intensively involved and effective in the FSR&D priority setting process. He distinguishes between strategic and non-strategic interests, and argues that an FSR&D team can work to accommodate these various interests positively into their priority setting. In addition, FSR&D teams should be actively involved in developing institutional linkages on their own initiative. Moreover, an FSR team can shape such linkages by taking an active role in formulating the project documents submitted to the host government and to donors. Eponou, in Chapter 5, suggests that since rural extension services and other development agencies often have better links to policymakers than does FSR&D, effective collaboration with these organizations can further the success of FSR&D not only directly but also indirectly, by opening new channels for information.

The following sections make clear the need to find appropriate times to involve these central actors, from farmers to policymakers. In the final chapter, the importance to FSR&D of working collaboratively is discussed further.

Notes

1   In simplified outline, a 'recommendation domain' defines a group of farmers who are similar enough that the same recommendations can be expected to be relevant for all in the group. When this concept is in use, an attempt must be made during the diagnosis to specify the variables that differentiate between one recommendation domain and another: that is, whether it is size of holdings, land type, availability of draught power, labour, water or other resources – and so forth – that differentiates between farmers who will need separate recommendations.

2   As Norman emphasizes in Chapter 2, a multidisciplinary programme – simply having a variety of disciplines present – is not enough. Interdisciplinarity implies a programme that is cohesive enough for various disciplines to join together in working on one or more research topics.

3   This potential, however, is not generally realized. For example, a common response to a desire to improve coordination and continuity has been to establish a national coordinating unit for FSR&D within the national agricultural research institute. These national units mainly play a role in maintaining and strengthening linkages with other actors at national and regional levels (that is, above programme/project level): national commodity and thematic research; policymakers and donors; national and provincial or regional research structures. However, the role of these national coordinating units is often limited, as regional or zonal FSR programmes usually operate fairly autonomously. This is often enhanced by the location-specificity of research and the fact that many FSR programmes are donor funded. Similarly, the potential role of technical backstopping for regional or zonal teams by the national unit is often rather modest, due to limitations of funds and personnel.

Bibliography

BARKER R AND LIGHTFOOT C (1985) Farm experiments on trial. Paper presented at the farming systems research and extension: management and methodology symposium, 13–16 October 1985. Manhattan, Kansas: Kansas State University

DAGG M AND HAWORTH F (1988) Program formulation in national agricultural research. ISNAR Working Paper no. 17. The Hague: ISNAR

EICHER CK (1989) Sustainable institutions for African agricultural development. ISNAR Working Paper no. 19. The Hague: ISNAR

FAYE J AND BINGEN RJ (1989) Senegal. Organisation et gestion de la recherche sur les systèmes de production. OFCOR Case Study no. 6. The Hague: ISNAR

MATLON PJ (1984) Technology evaluation: five case studies from West Africa. In: Coming full circle: farmers' participation in the development of technology. Ottawa, Canada: IDRC

MAXWELL S (1986) Farming systems research: hitting a moving target. World Development 14: no. 1, 65-77

MEERTENS HCC, NDEGE LJ AND ENSERINK HJ (forthcoming) Dynamics in farming systems: changes in space and time in Sukumaland, Tanzania. Amsterdam: Royal Tropical Institute

MERRILL-SANDS D, BIGGS SD, BINGEN RJ, EWELL PT, MCALLISTER JL AND POATS SV (1991) Institutional considerations in strengthening on-farm client-oriented research in national agricultural research systems: lessons from a nine-country study. Experimental Agriculture 27: 343–373

METTRICK H (1993) Development oriented research in agriculture: an ICRA textbook. Wageningen: ICRA

ROELEVELD L AND BROEK VAN DEN A (forthcoming) On-farm research on livestock systems. The diagnostic phase. Amsterdam: Royal Tropical Institute

STOOP WA AND BINGEN RJ (1991) 'Systems research' or 'research with a systems perspective' in Africa. Some organizational and technical issues. Agricultural Systems 35: 235–249

2 The research–research interface[1]

David Norman

Collaboration among researchers plays a critically important role – along with effective farmer participation – in determining the success of FSR. This chapter attempts to set out the conditions within which such interaction will be fruitful, particularly for priority setting. Research–research interaction, as interpreted in this chapter, has two dimensions: first, interaction within the team; and second, the relationship between FSR&D farm-based research and thematic (commodity and factor) research. Successful collaboration among researchers provides the basis for the work with farmers and other actors that is needed to arrive at solutions which will work and are sustainable.

A key determinant of effective interaction among FSR&D team members is whether they function in a truly interdisciplinary manner. This not only influences the choice of research priorities, but also helps to determine the way in which research is carried out and the value of the potential results. Interdisciplinarity is important because, while the constraints/problems identified by farmers are often technical in nature, the relevance of solutions is heavily influenced by socioeconomic factors. Thus, within-team relationships can play very significant roles in selecting relevant research priorities and assessing solutions to the problems identified earlier, in a relevant manner.

Functional two-way links between farm-based FSR&D research and station-based thematic research are a necessity if the research organization is to be truly effective, results-oriented, and efficient. Given the right supporting circumstances, the reductionist thrust of station-based research provides an efficient way of developing technologies that can be considered as potential solutions to farmer problems/constraints identified through FSR&D team activities. FSR&D activities, with their farmer-based orientation and systems perspective, provide a suitable milieu for testing potential solutions. Potential solutions emanating from the research station in response to problems identified at farm level therefore play an important role in determining the research priorities of the FSR&D team. At the same time, when they identify problems for which no immediate solution is available, FSR&D teams can play an important role in feeding research topics back to thematic researchers. Thus, thematic research is complementary to FSR&D; in essence, it is the lifeblood of FSR&D.

Strategies for ensuring that such a two-dimensional research–research interaction takes place are considered in the following two sections. A brief concluding section addresses the role of interaction among researchers in determining the research priorities of the FSR&D team. The KIT associated FSR&D projects described in this book, as well as experiences elsewhere, provided ideas and examples for these sections.

Internal team issues

What factors are important in creating conditions that encourage an interdisciplinary approach? Obviously a necessary, though not a sufficient, condition is that the FSR&D team include representatives of more than one discipline – preferably both technical and social scientists. The choice of specific disciplines to be represented should be influenced by factors such as the major enterprises in the farming system, the major problems/constraints to be addressed (which sometimes will be related to the mandate of the institution in which the team is located), etc. However, in fact, more practical constraints such as limits on resources for research, staff availability and so forth are often the major determinants. Most FSR&D teams consist of crop-oriented scientists (that is, agronomists in particular) and agricultural economists. Disciplines sometimes, but not always, present include animal scientists and sociologists. Representation from other disciplines is often provided on a part-time basis, as and when required, from thematic researchers.

Multidisciplinary teams obviously enable the use of a multidisciplinary approach: that is, individuals of different disciplines work independently on the same or different research topics. But having a *multidisciplinary* team does not, without further action, ensure that an *interdisciplinary* approach will be adopted, with individuals from different disciplines working together on the same research topic. Three major groups of factors are important in determining whether a team will be cohesive enough to contribute to the effective implementation of an interdisciplinary, rather than simply a multidisciplinary, approach: personal characteristics, organizational considerations, and joint team activities.

Personal characteristics. To be potentially effective in an interdisciplinary setting, team members must first have compatible personalities (Vierstra and Ndiyoi, Chapter 10). They also need to have confidence in using the analytical tools of their own disciplines, together with a healthy respect for the role of other disciplines, and be willing and able to be team players (Norman et al., 1982). Above all, as Rincon (1987) has emphasized, they need to be able to listen, understand and accept other viewpoints, and be prepared to modify their own views when this is appropriate. Finally, whoever the team leader is, it is important that he/she tries to exploit the strong parts of each team member's personality and to minimize the negative impact of the weak points we all possess (Norman, 1989). On balance, competence and personality are more important in selecting a suitable team leader than is their specific discipline.

Organizational considerations. In part, the harmony within an interdisciplinary team is determined by the degree of transparency between all team members in job descriptions, communication, responsibilities, distribution of research resources, and reward systems. Important strategies that can help create a basis for harmony include:
• frequent and open dialogue in formal (Chapter 10) and informal settings (Esslinger and McCorkle, 1986). It is highly desirable to strive for relaxed situations in which dialogue about both administrative and technical matters can take place;
• clear and equitable distribution of responsibilities and research resources (e.g. monthly allocation of transport allowances). Research resources, particularly when they become more limited, can create discord. Also, in the current research climate, there is undoubtedly a need to maximize the return from the increasingly limited research resources available to FSR&D teams. Several FSR&D teams allude to this; for example, Enserink et al. (Chapter 8) advocate limiting research activities to a few representative locations. Another possibility is to carry out joint research activities and/or to use surveys that, whenever possible, require only single interviews, are sharply focused, do not over-emphasize the collection of quantitative information, and provide a quick turnaround in terms of results (Worman et al., 1990). This is in contrast to the much more expensive 'traditional' approach, which involved multiple purpose surveys and required frequent interviews and the collection of large amounts of quantitative data. With such surveys, there are inevitably long delays in getting results;
• good documentation. This should include clear and realistic research protocols (Chapter 10), whenever possible using an interdisciplinary approach, and the production of multi-authored papers reflecting the

contributions of different members of the interdisciplinary team. When researchers write research protocols, it is important that they concisely justify the research and list objectives. The anticipated length of the research proposal should be indicated, and the approach to be used should be outlined. In an FSR&D project in Botswana, continuity was enhanced by dividing the research programme into themes. In addition, documentation always indicated links with research done in previous years (usually by means of a numbering system) and, if appropriate, when and why specific research projects were discontinued, even when they yielded useful results.

Joint team activities. In the case studies, several FSR&D teams emphasize the value of rapid rural appraisal (RRA) or 'sondeo' techniques, not only for descriptive/diagnostic purposes, but also as a means of ensuring interaction among disciplines (Meindertsma et al., Chapter 7; Koudokpon and Sprey, Chapter 11). However, joint activities are potentially important at each stage of the FSR&D process – not only during description/diagnosis but also in the design, testing, and even dissemination stages. Nevertheless, there may be some differentiation in terms of relative emphasis (Worman et al., 1990). If there is to be a sound understanding of the relationship and inter-action between physical/biological (technical) and socioeconomic (human) variables, then it is critically important to involve both technical and social scientists in the design, implementation, and analysis of mutually agreed surveys and trials. The systems, and therefore the farmer, perspective often tends to be lost when insufficient attention is paid to the relationships between these two types of variables.

Special problems can arise in donor-funded FSR&D projects that include both local and foreign researchers. Problems can often be avoided or re-solved by having leadership in the hands of able nationals, with expatriates acting in advising/implementing roles (Chapter 10). It is important to try and cement relationships between national and expatriate researchers. Joint activities to which both can contribute in a complementary manner can be very helpful in establishing harmonious and productive working relation-ships. Moussie (1987), for example, has suggested that the use of an RRA provides opportunities for national researchers, with their greater local knowledge, to establish their credibility.

Efforts to derive research priorities that are realistic and will result in useful and relevant technologies for farmers in the future are likely to be enhanced if a true interdisciplinary approach, taking into consideration the factors discussed above, is realised. These factors can also help to ensure efficient team management and leadership.

Interaction with thematic research

In spite of the need described above for a two-way, interactive linkage between thematic and FSR&D research, this often does not operate in an optimal manner. Reasons given by FSR&D teams in the case studies include the long distances between experiment stations and areas where FSR&D teams are located, and deficiencies in the staffing of thematic research (Chapters 8, 10, 11). Consequently, at least in the short run, the impact of FSR&D research is severely inhibited in two ways:

- potential solutions to problems/constraints identified by the FSR&D team are not immediately available;
- research resources may be diverted and used to carry out applied research (which otherwise would be undertaken by thematic researchers) and develop the necessary potential solutions; this is done at the expense of adaptive research, in which FSR&D teams have a comparative advantage.

When a quick impact is demanded of FSR&D-type activities, there can be little justification for implementing an FSR&D approach in an area where few potential technologies can be made available (that is, where there is no experiment station suitable for the ecological niche in question). However, when funding agencies are prepared to take a longer time perspective in terms of expecting results, circumstances may justify implementing an FSR&D approach – for example, where resources are made available, first, for the needed applied research, to be undertaken by the FSR&D team itself or in collaboration with thematic researchers; and second, for on-station research that represents the natural environment where the FSR&D team is operating.

In general, it is desirable to have an operational FSR&D team when thematic research is to be done: the team's activities have the potential for a positive impact on the efficiency of thematic research. That is, the potential relevance of such research is improved, because FSR&D can help to provide priorities based on constraints/problems identified under actual farming conditions. This feedback loop to thematic research is also, as indicated, important in maximizing the impact (both actual and potential) of FSR&D work. However, it continues to be more difficult to establish than that in the reverse direction (Merrill-Sands et al., 1989). While logistical problems primarily account for problems in the link from thematic research to FSR&D activities, in the reverse direction, feedback may have a much more direct effect on the activities of those responsible for thematic research; this may be perceived as threatening.

Another important dimension lies in helping thematic researchers to think through experimental design issues related to experimental and non-experimental variables. With reference to this issue, two points are potentially important in improving the practical relevance of thematic research (Norman and Modiakgotla, 1990): first, the results of thematic (i.e., usually cause–effect type) research are more relevant if variables that farmers may actually be able to implement are included by researchers among their experimental variables. If the level of input required is too high for farmers to adopt, then the research may have little relevance, unless special support programs for farmers are provided. This applies not only to external inputs, like improved seed or fertilizer, but also to internal inputs such as household labour availability.[2]

A second, closely related consideration is what the experimental and non-experimental variables in thematic or technology development type work should be. Generally, it is not possible to assume that the non-experimental variables will be the same under on-station and farmers' conditions. For example, seed-beds are often better prepared on experiment stations. Varietal testing under such conditions can provide very different results from what would occur if the seed-bed preparation more nearly approximated that generally used by farmers. It is important, *ex ante*, to evaluate whether the levels of the non-experimental variables are likely to influence the relationships being examined between the experimental variables. In other words, will there be cross-over effects, such that the experimental variables will have significantly different relationships under different levels of non-experimental variables. Special care should be taken if the levels of the non-experimental variables differ significantly from what the farmer is likely to be able to achieve.

Finally, whether thematic research is more efficiently undertaken on experiment stations or actual farms is an issue. In general, trials designed to answer questions about cause–effect relationships should, whenever possible, be carried out on experiment stations. The reasons include lower implementation costs (in terms of logistics, time, and so forth) and potentially better control (in terms of easier supervision, easier maintenance of *ceteris paribus* conditions, etc.). However, there are occasions when conducting such trials on actual farms is highly desirable; sometimes it is even essential. Such a situation arises if it is believed that the special environmental situation of the experiment station does not provide a sufficiently realistic environment for testing a technology. Will the technology fail completely if it is transferred to farmers' fields? For example, a great deal of herbicide work probably needs to be done with respect to farmers' fields – where the weed complex is likely to be different from that on the experiment station. This could be seen in a research-managed and implemented trial undertaken in Botswana, mainly on farmers' fields. The objective was to systematically compare tillage treatments for a number of soil types, designed to improve water availability to the plants. Because this trial was designed to determine cause–effect relationships, a decision was made to keep the treatments as weed-free as possible, so this would not complicate the analysis of differences between tillage treatments. It was recognized, however, that farmers would not be able to create a weed-free environment. Therefore, the time required in each treatment to keep the plot weed-free was measured.

Achieving constructive interaction

Given the obvious complementarity between thematic and FSR&D research activities, how can constructive interaction be assured? There are many ways to help in creating the credibility necessary for the FSR&D team to stimulate such interaction. Building effective communication, trust and credibility are key factors.

Effective communication between thematic and FSR&D researchers is an important basis for creating credibility. A precondition for this is recognition of the complementarity between station and farm-based research. Some of the relevant factors are shown in Table 1. It is very important to be specific about FSR trials. Not all types of trials appeal equally to the multiple clients of FSR. Trials can be differentiated on the basis of who manages and who implements them – that is, the researcher (technician) or the farmer. Thus, three types of trials are possible:
- researcher managed and researcher implemented (RMRI);
- researcher managed and farmer implemented (RMFI);
- farmer managed and farmer implemented (FMFI).

RMRI trials are the equivalent of those conducted on experiment stations by thematic researchers. Therefore, the level of testing meets the standards demanded by experiment-station-based researchers. Due to management and resource constraints of farmers, yields or returns will diminish when moving from the RMRI to the FMFI level. Table 2 presents the major differences between RMRI work – mainly the preserve of experiment station research – and RMFI and FMFI trials, which emphasize on-farm work. Once the differences in roles suggested by the table are acknowledged, it is easier to recognize the complementarity of the different types of trials, and the appropriate criteria for evaluating the value of research.

Table 1. Characteristics of thematic and FSR&D research

Characteristic	Thematic research	FSR&D research
Major emphasis of research	Applied	Adaptive
Location of trial	Usually experiment station	Usually on-farm
Disciplines involved	Often single Mostly technical	Usually several Technical and social
Priority setting for trial done by		
Researcher	More involved	Less involved
Farmer	Less involved	More involved
Experimental design		
Complexity	Usually more	Usually less
Management	Researcher	Researcher or farmer
Implementation	Researcher	Researcher or farmer
Degree of experimental control	More	Usually less
Ability to establish cause–effect relationships	Easier	Harder
Factors taken into account in evaluating trial results		
Systems perspective	Less likely	More likely
Technical feasibility	Yes	Yes
Economic viability/reliability	Less likely	More likely
Social acceptability	Less likely	More likely
Farmer opinion	Not likely	More likely
Expense of experimental programme		
Fixed (overhead) costs	Likely to be higher	Likely to be lower
Variable (recurrent) costs	Likely to be lower	Likely to be higher

Adapted from: Norman and Modiakgotla, 1990.

Table 2. Characteristics of different types of trials[a]

	Researcher managed and researcher implemented (RMRI)	Researcher managed and farmer implemented (RMFI)	Farmer managed and farmer implemented (FMFI)
Experimental			
Stage	Design[b]	1st stage testing	2nd stage testing
Design			
Complexity	Most	Less	Least
Type	Standard	With and without	With and without
Replication	Within and between sites	Usually only between sites but can also be within	Between sites only
Who selects technology?	Researcher	Researcher/farmer	Farmer
Participation			
Farmer	Least	More	Most
Researcher	Most	Less	Least
Numbers of farmers	None	Some	Most
Farmer groups	Least	More	Most
Potential			
'Yield'	Most	Less	Least
Measurement errors	Least	Greater	Most
Degree of precision	Highest	Less	Least
Data			
Hard (objective)	Most	Less	Least
Soft (subjective)	Least	More	Most
Determination of cause–effect relationships	Easiest	Less easy	Least easy
Incorporation into farming system	Least	More	Most
Evaluation			
By whom?	Mainly researcher	Researcher/farmer	Mainly farmer
Nature of test	Assesses technical feasibility	Features of RMRI and FMFI, plus economic evaluation	Validity for farmers: practical, acceptable
Appeal to			
Researchers	Most	Less	Least
Extension staff	Usually least	More	Most
Farmers	Least	More	Most
Ease of acceptance of trial results	Researcher/ extension	Researcher/ farmer	Farmer

a. There is a degree of subjectivity in some entries in this table, but in general they do reflect the usual situation. In a sense, these characteristics – that is, what is expected in each case – also reflect the reasons for undertaking the different types of trials.
b. Standard multi-locational trials are also RMRI.
Adapted from: Norman, 1989.

As long as the nature, purpose and expectations of the different types of trials are properly understood, they can help satisfy the needs of the different clients of FSR&D research (e.g. thematic researchers, extension workers, and farmers). In fact, a lack of specifications regarding trials is to my mind often one of the factors that contribute to misunderstandings between FSR&D teams and thematic researchers, and to a lack of respect for farm-level research on the part of the latter.

Several types of activities can be useful in building complementarities between thematic and FSR&D researchers:

- Organizing station-based research programmes around commodities and subject areas that involve all interested parties, including representation from the FSR&D teams. Such interdisciplinary groups can assist in planning and evaluating the results of the research.
- Having some form of national coordination of FSR&D activities and having all teams use similar methodologies. For example, Tanzania (Merrill-Sands, 1990) and Zambia both have national coordinating units, and Botswana has made strenuous efforts to develop a common methodology for use by all FSR&D teams (Worman et al., 1990).
- Organizing field days on farms (Chapter 7) and visits to trials both at the experiment station and in farmers' fields. These can provide very useful forums for informal interaction between farmers, extension and developmental staff, thematic and FSR&D researchers and, potentially, planners.
- A somewhat related issue is the need for thematic researchers to develop an understanding and appreciation of the methodologies used by FSR&D researchers. Trial designs and formats used by FSR&D researchers are often a focus for criticisms by thematic researchers. This can usually be diffused if FSR&D researchers classify trials as to who is managing and implementing them (i.e. farmers or the researcher) and clearly indicate the expectations and purposes of the different types (Norman and Modiakgotla, 1990).

Another facet of the credibility equation is that, in their work, FSR&D teams need to be seen as taking into account information and results from earlier thematic work, as doing work that is potentially useful for thematic researchers, and as producing a continuous stream of results. The following can be helpful in ensuring these points:

- State-of-the-art papers on past and recently completed research can be particularly useful in systematic consideration of the work of others, especially thematic research on cause–effect relationships. Producing such papers provides a firm foundation on which future work programmes can be based (Chapter 10).
- Workshops on specific topics (e.g. soil fertility issues), attended by both

thematic and FSR&D researchers, can provide a very useful forum for reviewing past work and deciding on future research priorities (Chapter 8).

- Obviously, the adaptive farm-level testing by FSR&D teams of technologies (developed earlier by thematic researchers – see Chapter 7) that are expected to solve identified problems/constraints is viewed as a useful outcome of thematic research.

- The primary (that is, direct) role of FSR&D research is to design and test technologies with farmers, to address constraints/problems that have been identified. However, as implied earlier, it can have a secondary (indirect) supportive role in helping thematic researchers design new, potentially relevant technologies. In Botswana it proved to be important for FSR&D teams to respond, as far as possible, to requests from thematic researchers for surveys and farm level trials on topics for which they needed help. Especially when a response is likely to involve considerable disruption in normal FSR&D-type activities, it is important to collaborate insofar possible in undertaking the activities and, if necessary, arrange for a joint commitment of the necessary research resources.[3] However, such requests for help have often involved interventions with low- or non-leverage-type characteristics (Heinrich et al., 1990). High-leverage interventions involve introducing changes in an operation or enterprise in a part of the farming system that is a major absorber of farm resources and/or where timing of those resources is restricted. All other things being equal, the adoption of technologies that improve the productivity of such resources is likely to maximize improvement in the productivity of the farming system as a whole. Low or non-leverage interventions, on the other hand, may not have a major impact on the productivity of the farming system as a whole, but may help in improving the productivity of a particular enterprise. Farmers are quite likely to mention problems/constraints whose solutions have potentially high-leverage characteristics. This does not mean, however, that low-leverage interventions have no place. For example, they could be part of a technological package that has high-leverage potential, could use resources at times of the year when these are underutilized, could help fulfil equity objectives (e.g. improving the welfare of women within households), and/or could encourage ecological sustainability.

- A proven record for producing results is, of course, the best means for FSR&D teams to obtain credibility and create an atmosphere for constructive interaction with thematic researchers (Chapter 11). Widespread farmer adoption of technologies – originally developed by thematic researchers – that have passed through adaptive testing via FSR&D teams obviously reflects well on the research organization as a whole.[4] Here again (for thematic researchers in particular), good documentation of results, whether successes or failures, of FSR&D teams is important. This includes timely production of various papers, including preliminary results; these can help to stimulate thinking and discussion among researchers.[5]

A further important point with respect to achieving constructive interaction is that it is very desirable, if possible, to have some form of joint activity involving both thematic and FSR&D researchers.[6] For example, the value of using thematic and FSR&D researchers together in RRA activities is often noted (Chapters 7 and 11). Once such descriptive/diagnostic exercises have been undertaken, what about other joint activities? One possibility is to have the same individuals engaged in both thematic and FSR&D activities (Chapter 7). This is potentially possible in restricted geographical areas (for example, in small countries or where the natural environment represented by an experiment station is limited and close to the station). A possible variant of this would be to have thematic researchers based on research stations undertake some research activities on actual farms in the applied research area, in conjunction with FSR&D researchers (Chapter 8). Conditions for such cooperation are particularly favourable when FSR&D teams operate from regional research stations or substations. Cooperation becomes more difficult to organize when countries are bigger, greater distances are involved, more personnel are employed in the research organization, and the FSR&D team has a high degree of autonomy (as is currently often the case in FSR&D activities, which are frequently funded in part by donors). Therefore, obviously, there is no optimal model for cooperation (Norman and Collinson, 1986), but it is important to strive for a link between thematic and FSR&D research that involves joint activities. Unlike separate activities, which can often engender a feeling of competitiveness, working jointly can foster a symbiotic relationship. Competition is particularly likely to develop when separate activities have to be funded from one limited research resource 'cake' (Chapter 11), which is becoming progressively smaller. Further, results and conclusions arrived at cooperatively do not require transmission from one party to the other. This minimizes feedback problems arising from the receipt of unwelcome information. Where research resources are very limited, other collaborative work becomes even more critically important, because FSR&D researchers are likely to be less qualified and experienced. In such situations, collaboration has the potential to improve the credibility and potential productivity of FSR&D-type research.[7]

Concluding remarks

What constitutes relevant research prioritization is determined by many factors. Some of these relate back to the guidelines laid down in the strategic plan, and some to later modifications of this plan. Modifications are apt to arise, for example, as a result of improved understanding of the causes and magnitude of the problems/constraints; better information about the time required to obtain potential solutions; assessment of the availability and potential relevance of potential solutions offered by thematic research (e.g. from the farmer's viewpoint; or with respect to intra-household relationships, including impact on women; inter-household relationships, including equitability; ecological sustainability; the likelihood that policy/support systems necessary to adoption will be available; etc.); and finally, indications with respect to the degree of leverage offered by a potential solution. Many of these factors are largely outside the realm of the dynamics of the research–research interactive process. However, effective research–research interaction can provide a favourable environment for satisfactory resolution of the issues involved. Further, research–research interaction plays a critically important role in determining the success of short term or annual adjustment of research priorities: the priorities within the broad themes laid down in the strategic plan.

Notes

1   This chapter is a revised version of KSU Agricultural Experiment Station Contribution Number 92-301-A.
2   There is, of course, justification for having a range of levels of experimental variables that go beyond what farmers are likely to adopt. This is particularly relevant in a design-type experiment used to estimate response curves. The approach can also be justified if is apt to be possible to use the results from responses at the higher levels in an attempt to influence planners to change support systems, and thus enable farmers to use the specific inputs at a higher level. As suggested in other chapters, FSR&D teams are now trying a more interventionist approach to influence the policy/support system. This is in contrast to the former, more conventional approach, which was more submissive in accepting the policy/support system as parameters, rather than as variables that could be changed.
3   In addition to verifying the interest and commitment of thematic researchers in the need for such work, their involvement will probably make the results more acceptable to them, even if these are unpalatable.
4   It is important that FSR&D teams do not claim all the credit for such adoption. FSR&D in its most efficient form facilitates a process rather than producing a product.

5   In Botswana, a number of different types of papers have been produced, geared to different audiences: annual reports, including results and work plans; major research reports summarizing major results; working papers containing final results of specific studies, surveys, and trials; progress reports presenting preliminary findings; miscellaneous papers containing material presented at conferences and workshops; and externally published papers. Numbering each series permits easy identification and retrieval.

6   One spin-off of such activities is the possibility of incorporating more of a systems perspective into thematic research. Thematic research, as indicated earlier, usually has a strong reductionist orientation.

7   Admittedly, while as a result the relationship between on-station and on-farm research is not a 'mutually exclusive' or 'uneasy' one, it is likely to be 'leading-supporting' (Simmons, no date). Although some FSR&D researchers may find it difficult to accept such a relationship, it could be argued that Simmons is quite right in concluding that this type of relationship is likely to have the biggest pay-off in the long run. However, in such a relationship it is important to ensure that thematic research is not emphasized at the expense of adaptive research.

Bibliography

ESSLINGER D AND MCCORKLE C (1986) Communications in FSR team building: the inter-disciplinary research team. In: Flora C and Tomecek M, eds, Selected proceedings of Kansas State University's 1985 Farming Systems Research symposium. Farming Systems Research Paper no. 11. Fayetteville: University of Arkansas and Winrock International Institute for Agricultural Development, pp 158–175

HEINRICH G, SIEBERT J, MODIAKGOTLA E, NORMAN D AND WARE-SNYDER J, eds (1990) Technical summary of ATIP's activities, 1982–90: Research results. ATIP RP 5. Gaborone: Department of Agricultural Research

MERRILL-SANDS D (1990) Project document: Project for strengthening the national development and coordination of Farming Systems Research in Tanzania. The Hague, Netherlands: ISNAR

MERRILL-SANDS D, EWELL P, BIGGS S, AND MCALLISTER J (1989) Issues in institutionalizing on-farm, client-oriented research: a review of experiences from nine national agricultural research systems. Staff Note no. 89–57. The Hague, Netherlands: ISNAR

MOUSSIE M (1987) Impact of diagnostic survey on strengthening linkages – Burundi experience. Paper given at the 1987 Farming Systems Research symposium. Fayetteville, Arkansas: University of Arkansas, 18–21 October

NORMAN D (1989) Communication and information systems in Farming Systems work: an overview. In: University of Arkansas, ed, Proceedings of Farming Research symposium 1987: How Systems Work, Farming Systems Research Paper No. 15. Fayetteville: University of Arkansas and Winrock International Institute for Agricultural Development, pp 287–303

NORMAN D (1991) Soil conservation: using Farming Systems development as an AID. Report produced for the Food and Agriculture Organisation

NORMAN D AND COLLINSON M (1986) Farming Systems Research in theory and practice. In: Remenyi J, ed, Agricultural systems research for developing countries, ACIAR Proceedings no. 11. Canberra, Australia: Australian Council for International Agricultural Research

NORMAN D AND MODIAKGOTLA E (1990) Ensuring farmer input into the research process within an institutional setting: the case of semi-arid Botswana. Agricultural Administration Network Paper no. 16. London, UK: Overseas Development Institute

NORMAN D, SIMMONS E AND HAYS H (1982) Farming Systems in the Nigerian savanna: research and strategies for development. Boulder: Westview Press

RINCON H (1987) Listening abilities and the communication of information among groups of agricultural experts in Peru. Paper given at the 1987 Farming Systems Research symposium, Fayetteville, Arkansas: University of Arkansas, 18–21 October

SIMMONS E (no date, mimeograph) A tour d'horizon: some observations on doing Farming Systems Research in the Sahel. Bamako, Mali: USAID/Mali

WORMAN F, NORMAN D AND WARE-SNYDER J, eds (1990) Farming Systems Research Handbook for Botswana. ATIP RP 3. Gaborone: Department of Agricultural Research

3 Priority setting tools for research groups

Jonathan Woolley and Robert Tripp[1]

Planning tools are tools and nothing more. They are not a substitute for experience, intuition, intelligence or hard work. No tool is likely to produce the 'best possible' plan the first time it is used in an area. However, planning tools do increase the chance that a) the widest possible range of suitable hypotheses and solutions is generated, and in a logical manner; and b) that the hypotheses and assumptions used are recorded in a written summary. A written summary provides a way to readjust the research programme in each future year, as assumptions and hypotheses change (for example, due to new research results, policy changes or social changes). In other words, this is a way to keep research honest and prevent it from getting 'in a rut'.

This chapter reviews research planning methods useful for local or regional (i.e. sub-national) research groups. It draws on our own experiences and on the literature to suggest tools and techniques to cope with the factors involved in planning. Planning includes setting various types of priorities: geographical area selection (which we shall not cover in detail), selection of priority crops or other enterprises, problem selection, selection of possible solutions, selection of research activities. Our major concerns are:
- planning should be properly integrated with diagnosis and data gathering;
- problems should be described in sufficient detail so that the programme can discuss and research them effectively;
- the nature or causality of problems must be hypothesized and tested before potential solutions can be proposed;
- FSR programmes should work through the sequence diagnosis–planning–adaptive research–recommendation–promotion, by gradually filtering the options. However, the flow is not linear, but iterative, with feedback loops;
- shared diagnosis and planning exercises are valuable integrators of teams and/or actors.

Tools and techniques

Much has been written about project planning, but without specific reference to agricultural research and extension. Delp et al. (1977) is a concise and useful handbook. A brief overview of methods follows.

Project planning matrices are a tool commonly used in setting up the inputs, outputs, means of verification and assumptions of projects. Donor organizations often require the use of project planning matrices as a pre-condition for project acceptance. The 'logical framework' (described in Delp et al. 1977) is widely used by the United States Agency for International Development; it is also a part of the objective oriented project planning (OOPP) or 'ZOPP' methodology (GTZ, 1988), which is used by a number of development agencies. Chapter 9 gives an example of the use of OOPP by DRSPR.

OOPP also uses problem trees, building them around a 'core problem'. A hierarchy of effects is built upwards, and a hierarchy of causes spreads downwards to lower levels. The rules for constructing these diagrams are quite rigid. OOPP is particularly useful for setting up and analysing rural development projects. Useful ideas for agricultural research planning can be drawn from it. However, neither it nor the logical framework was developed for agricultural research planning at micro level; they should not be expected to be completely applicable to topics covered in this chapter.

Other tools are specifically aimed at agricultural research planning, in particular OFR and FSR&D. Early contributions to systematizing the evaluation of problems and solutions can be found in publications from IITA (Mutsaers, 1985), IRRI (Van der Veen, 1984), ICRAF (Huxley and Wood, n.d.) and CIMMYT (Collinson, 1984). More recent contributions include a method published by CIMMYT and CIAT for identifying factors for experimentation (Tripp and Woolley, 1989) and recent work by Clive Lightfoot of ICLARM and others on farming systems diagnosis (Lightfoot et al., 1988, 1990).

We can identify three main types of these tools, used separately or in combination: tools for ranking the relative importance of production problems faced by farmers; for examining the causality of problems; and for screening potential solutions (this last factor is discussed below, under planning). To rank the importance of problems or solutions, scales using various criteria are a fairly obvious step; examples can be found in all the publications mentioned. The main challenge is choosing sufficient, suitable criteria and deciding how to weight them, and whether to attempt a summary by scores or by descriptive melding of criteria.

Understanding causality

The examination of causality is the most fertile area for innovation. This is not intuitive – many plans that are otherwise logically constructed completely miss out this step. In teaching planning, we find this is what most excites the imagination of participants: solutions depend on the correct identification of causes. For example, low plant population in beans was diagnosed as a problem in a sole-crop production system in the Altos de Jalisco area of Mexico. Farmers were planting plenty of bean seed, but few plants emerged. Potential causes, all of which were reasonable hypotheses for this area, were: root rots, soil insect damage, poor seed viability, soil crust formation, sporadic blockage of the planting machine, and fertilizer burning of seedlings. Sampling, further interviews with farmers and experimentation were needed to determine which cause or causes were truly important. Obviously, if root rots were the cause, the solution would be very different than if it were soil crusting.

The tools for analysing causes considered here all analyse system hierarchies, using flow diagrams to show cause–effect relationships. They are similar to the 'oval diagrams' described by Delp et al. (1977).[2] The tools differ with respect to the levels of the hierarchy they designate as problems, causes and effects (or symptoms) (Figure 1). At the highest system level in this figure, there are only two problems: 'low yield' and 'inefficient resource use'. Tripp and Woolley (1989) do not use the concept of effects or symptoms, but aim to consider all effects on level 2 of the hierarchy as 'problems'. Those on level 3 or below would usually be considered 'causes'. Some flexibility is needed: problems can in their turn be causes of other problems; items originally considered as problems may turn into causes as analysis proceeds. The systems analysis is not rigid; the hierarchy works itself out. The whole purpose of the exercise is to organize or create evidence, and guide research towards realistic options.

Lightfoot uses a problem tree similar to the problem–cause diagrams. However, he separates biophysical and socioeconomic causes into two halves of the diagram. The novel step is that the causes are then organized into a circular systems diagram (following Spedding, 1979) in which the size of each segment shows its relative contribution (Figure 2). Although such diagrams look difficult to construct, Lightfoot's papers give interesting and positive reports about the use of this method by farmers as well as researchers. He also uses problem–cause diagrams quite extensively.

An example from Woolley (1990) illustrates causality in multiple cropping systems: in the tropical valley of La Fraylesca in southern Mexico, farmers grow beans in relay with maize. To reduce the problem of

Figure 1. Schematic representation of relationships between problems and causes

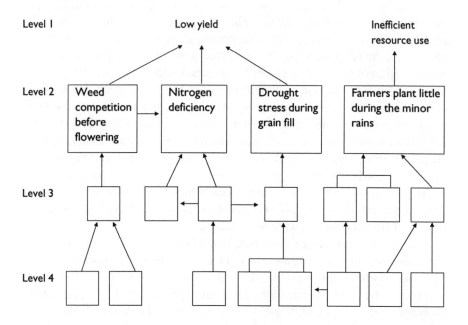

end-of-season drought in beans, the obvious solutions appear to be an earlier maize variety or an earlier bean variety (Figure 3). Both are unsatisfactory, because yield potential would be lost in one crop or the other. A more careful examination of causes suggested that beans could be planted earlier, before maize maturity, if a less leafy maize variety of equal maturity and yield potential were used. Experiments have confirmed that this is feasible.

A procedure for diagnosis and planning

Tripp and Woolley (1989) work through a detailed example of planning using their techniques. Other useful published examples of diagnosis and planning, which follow the same method of analysing causes, include Dahlan et al. (1987) and Hobbs et al. (1991). Harrington (1990) has prepared sets of training materials to use in training courses which follow the approach described in this section. Since Tripp and Woolley (1989) is the basis of most published examples, we will summarize the way we use the method at present.

Figure 2. Example of a systems diagnosis

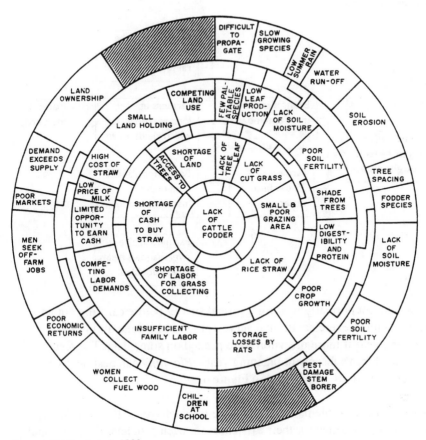

Source: Lightfoot et al., 1990

Diagnosis includes the study of secondary data, and an informal survey (around 30–50 farmers are interviewed, and their fields are visited for agronomic observations). The team is divided into groups of 2–3 if it is large enough. Each evening there is a discussion of the day's findings, and new guidelines are drawn up for the following day. Discussion can require as much or more time than that spent in the field. After perhaps one-third of the visits, we may be listing priority cropping systems and searching for evidence about priority problems; after two-thirds of visits we might be listing apparent problems. Our guidelines for the remaining visits will then include searching for evidence to try to narrow down the number of causes hypothesized. It is rather difficult to prove hypotheses about causes at this stage, but some hypothesized causes can be eliminated.

Figure 3. Causes of drought stress on beans in a maize–bean relay, La Fraylesca, Mexico

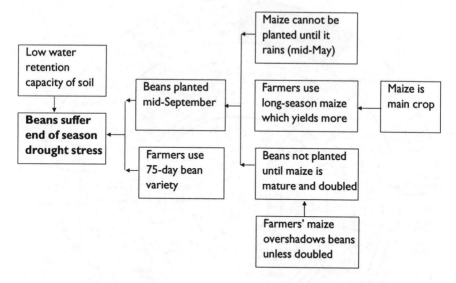

We would not normally wait for a formal survey before carrying out an initial planning exercise. Formal survey(s) might be done during the following year if more precision were needed on some data. The results would feed into subsequent planning years. *Planning* can best be discussed as a series of steps, as pictured in Figure 4.

Step 1. List the problems which limit the productivity of the farming system, and the evidence for their existence; for each problem, list additional data, if any, that would be required to confirm that the problem exists.

Step 2. Rank problems with respect to their distribution (who suffers from them); importance of the crop enterprise; and severity (on average, for those who suffer).

Step 3. Identify the causes of each problem and construct a flow diagram for each one.

Step 4. Fit together the various problem–cause diagrams, if they have points in common. This serves to identify 'leverage points' or 'special research opportunities', for which tackling one cause may directly or indirectly affect several problems at once. But, truth be told, it is rather rare to find really convincing 'special research opportunities'.

Figure 4. Steps in the planning process

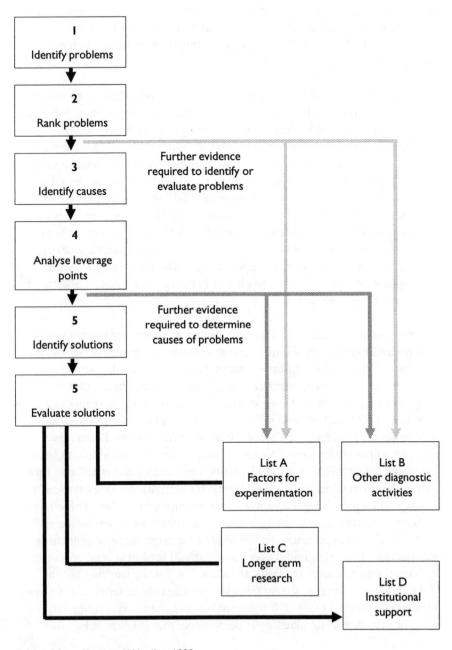

Adapted from Tripp and Woolley, 1989

Step 5. Identify possible solutions to the research problems. We have found that working through the causes of each problem (using the diagrams from either step 3 or step 4) is the best way to generate solutions. For each cause or group of causes, a small brainstorming session is conducted. We filter out only obviously implausible solutions before passing to the next step.

Step 6. Evaluate possible solutions. Criteria have been adjusted by other users to fit their circumstances, but we find the following robust: probability that the technology to be tested will function (a purely technical criterion); profitability; compatibility with the farming system; contribution to reducing risk (in economic terms, not just yield); need for institutional support; ease of testing by farmers (possibility of small-scale testing and number of components); and ease of experimentation. For a solution to pass initial screening, it must rate well on the first two criteria. If a large number of solutions to a particular problem are to be tested, these first two criteria alone might be used as an initial filter. The next three criteria are desirable characteristics of a solution, but not essential. The final two are usually only used when it is necessary to choose between solutions that otherwise have been rated similarly.

Products of the six steps. As shown in Figure 4, factors for experimentation (including possible solutions and diagnostic experimental factors) are only one of the products of the six steps. Needs for other diagnostic activities, longer term research (on-station or on-farm, but not directly adaptive) and institutional support are also identified. Other diagnostic activities might include field sampling of soil or plants; field surveys to determine the incidence of a problem; or informal or formal interviews focused on particular topics. Needs for longer term research have to be evaluated for probable costs and benefits, time scale and possibilities for extrapolation to other target areas. Needs for institutional support usually emerge when promising technologies are nearing verification. These might include supplying inputs, credit, and/or special extension campaigns.

As we gained experience, we discovered the importance of generating information during the initial diagnosis that will feed in at least up to step 3. Sometimes it is useful to think ahead to step 6 while carrying out the field diagnosis. Usually, the information gathered about farmers' resources is enough to conduct step 6. If the team has a chance to stay in the target area, or to return while planning is being done, that is better still.

A list of factors for experimentation and a list of needs for further diagnosis do not make a research programme. To achieve an efficiently designed programme, we carry out three more steps. These are described in more detail in a draft working document (Woolley, 1987).

Step 7. Prepare outlines of trials and diagnostic studies and estimate the resources (human and operational) required for each. Outlines attempt to place factors that interact and/or can be grouped together in the same trial or study, to save research resources. In the planning meeting, subgroups can brainstorm to find alternative ways of using resources efficiently. The best aspects from the work of each subgroup can be combined. Exact treatment details are not prepared at this point.

Step 8. Trial and diagnostic study outlines are adjusted to fit the resources available. Since we do not have full details of each activity at this stage, we use estimates of professional time required for different stages of experimentation and common trial sizes, taking into account that there are fixed costs (travel time, farmer contact) for each trial site. Thus, two sites of 16 plots each take more total research time than one site of 32 plots.

Step 9. For each activity that passes step 8, the experimental design, treatments (or survey observations) and management are defined in detail.

The sequence followed in steps 7 to 9 keeps open the possibility that one trial or diagnostic study could include several different themes. This increases the efficiency of resource use. It also reduces the resistance of each team member to having his/her special interest cut from the programme, since less time has been invested in preparing details (and anticipating hoped-for results).

Just how fast the numbers of available problems, solutions or factors are reduced from one step to the next depends on the group's style. We used to favour keeping many problems up to step 6, to increase the chance of finding 'highly attractive solutions to medium-priority problems' instead of just 'difficult solutions to the most important problems'. Now we tend to be stricter, beginning in an earlier stage, to better focus the group to look at the serious problems.

Although group work in diagnosis and planning has been discussed here, we have seen this process successfully carried out by individuals, provided resource people from different disciplines are 'on call'.

Actors in the planning process

The method described above was designed because it appeared that researchers did not know how to move effectively from a field diagnosis to research plans. Although often long and costly, many diagnoses were quite superficial. This tool was therefore originally designed to help researchers interpret and apply what they saw and heard about farmers, whether from the farmers themselves, from field observations or from other actors (technology transfer agents, policymakers and so forth). As we gained experience, we gradually realized how other actors should be incorporated.

Thematic researchers. This group can both contribute to the diagnosis and gain benefits (putting their own research in context and receiving motivation). They can participate in planning for similar reasons. Because of the time required, this may not be practical for all thematic researchers every year. However, they should definitely be 'on-call' during the planning in case more information is needed about specialist subjects or available technology. If the study area is not remote from their base, they might also be 'on-call' to identify problems encountered during the diagnosis. The previous agenda of thematic researchers will tend to dominate testing at the start, because those are the technologies that will be available, while other solutions, however desirable, may not be. Despite this, previous research decisions should not be allowed to dominate the planning process. For this reason, it is important to build up an information network to obtain solutions from other regions or countries, not just the target region.

Technology transfer workers. While technology transfer workers should participate in making the diagnosis, those who organize the planning must be aware of the possible bias they may introduce in farmer selection or farmer responses. We also attempt to have representatives of extension services present during the planning sessions.

Farmers. Farmers have not, as far as we know, been directly involved in the planning approach presented here as a whole, but we see few barriers to this. Clive Lightfoot has used step 2 directly with farmers. Defoer, Erenstein and Hussain (1992) describe how farmer groups can participate in identifying causes, construct causal diagrams and jointly plan experimental work with researchers. We understand that Lightfoot has recently used problem–cause diagrams similar to those in steps 3 and 4 of Tripp and Woolley (1989) with farmers. World Neighbours has asked farm families to rate solutions on multiple criteria (Bunch, 1985). Making research designs more complex or innovative to obtain maximum research efficiency (step 7) might be more difficult to handle when working with farmers. On the other hand, greater farmer involvement would itself reduce some research costs, by helping to pre-screen the wide range of potential and complex solutions with respect to criteria relevant to farmers before beginning experimentation. Although outside the scope of this paper, we would like to draw attention to developments in participatory rural appraisal (e.g. Mascarenhas et al., 1991).

The policy environment. This is usually assumed to be an external variable, outside the control of this planning approach. Interactions with policy are contemplated in Figure 4, but we acknowledge that this may be too limited when aggregating the results of planning from different micro-regions. The value of finding ways to keep policymakers informed and encourage mutual feedback is discussed in Chapters 2 and 5.

Issues in the use of planning tools

Unimaginative use. As with all tools, there is a danger that once information has been systematized in tables or diagrams, the discussions and doubts that preceded the systematization are forgotten. For example, researchers may lose sight of the fact that hypotheses on problems and causes are just that – hypotheses: guesses tend to be merged with firmly supported conclusions. Similarly, in screening solutions, researchers may be tempted to assign scores for each criterion and sum them; and then to compare the sums to select the 'most promising' solutions, without making appropriate contrasts between the evaluations of similar solutions.

Integrating diagnosis and planning. Our experience is that the initial diagnosis should be relatively brief but deep. It must go deep enough to be able to define the relative importance of problems, provide information on causes, and provide information that permits the evaluation of possible solutions. Although the initial diagnosis should be brief, diagnosis should be an ongoing activity which responds to questions raised during planning and, alongside testing of solutions, leads stepwise to a clearer understanding.
    Problem lists are often rather general and superficial. This is a common problem with rapid rural appraisals and informal surveys, when insufficient attention is paid to reworking the guidelines several times during the survey. If problems are not explained precisely, it is difficult to identify their causes and, hence, their solutions.

Diagnosis is often conducted without specific reference to the information needs created by planning. In fact, diagnosis must seek out the information likely to be needed in planning. To do this, a quick draft of the earlier steps in planning must be made before the first year's diagnostic activity is concluded.

Agronomic monitoring is a way of testing hypotheses about problems and causes at a lower cost than experimentation. A good example is provided by Bukoba district, Tanzania (Chapter 8). A recent summary of agronomic monitoring as a tool can be found in Byerlee et al. (1991).

A further point is the need for clarity in linking problems and solutions. Without a clear link, it is difficult to identify solutions, focus research themes and speed up research.

Efficient design of experimentation. We think that the need for efficient research design usually outweighs the danger of confusing farmers by handling more than one factor or objective in a single trial. This contrasts with the desire for simplicity of some on-farm researchers. If researchers know what and how to show them, farmers can see concrete results even in more complex designs; it helps if the farmers were present at planting. It is not clear why more complex designs are thought to produce more ambiguous results. Most produce greater experimental precision and hence less ambiguity!

A good example of efficient design is the clustering of trials in contrasting but neighbouring sites (e.g. Chapter 8), as a way of economizing research resources. It is, however, necessary to ensure that the neighbouring sites differ in significant characteristics; these may initially appear unimportant but later turn out to differentiate recommendation domains (see Tripp, 1982 and Mead, 1990b for discussions of site selection).

Linkages between micro-level planning and broad-based projects. As seen in Chapter 14, designing a priority setting process for a regional or sub-national programme or project involves specific issues. These include the extent to which priorities can be built up as the sum of a series of micro-level exercises in priority setting and whether different tools are needed.

Initially, selection of potential work areas for a sub-national project is apt to be done using criteria based on national development policy, indicators of social welfare, logistics and the like: political/logistic choices. The choice of one or two representative geographical research areas for the initial work could be made using data from simple field diagnoses. Each could be quite short, perhaps two days' work for a team of two to four people. Principal farming systems, apparent problems and possible research opportunities should be identified. Having diagnostic information beyond the geographical areas chosen for field research trials is useful, to remind researchers that their programme must generate information that can be extrapolated to similar agroecological areas. KIT projects in Tanzania (Chapter 8) and Benin (Chapter 11) are taking action on this issue.

National research priorities are usually set top–down, using national indicators (foreign exchange savings, value of production), social and biological indicators (cultural importance, nutritional value), research criteria (availability of trained professionals, likely time scale) and so on: we find the papers for ISNAR by Norton and Pardey (1987) and Collion and Kissi (1991) a clear exposition. Harrington (1991) reviews the links between the literature on national research resource allocation and micro-level planning. He suggests (personal communication) as a first step that a few screening criteria common to both levels could be identified. Can and should local research priorities be built up into national priorities? Except in a small country, it is difficult to imagine how information on problems and most suitable solutions could be built from the local level upwards. Even though this may not be generally feasible for national level planning, the importance of communication among different planning levels, incorporating local groups, cannot be overemphasized. One of the greatest problems confronted by local level planning is its inability to direct a critical mass of resources at priority problems. This requires that local groups be able to compare notes and collaborate on research.[3] Such a synthesis not only guarantees consistency within the larger research organization, but helps direct scarce resources to high priority problems at local level.

The micro level, on the other hand, is a good place (though not the only place) to integrate people, drawing on friendships between actors at the local level. We have found that the shared experience of diagnostic fieldwork, followed by evening discussions, really unites FSR researchers, thematic researchers (these two may not always be different people) and transfer agents. Where diagnosis has a strong participatory flavour, strong mutual respect and sharing with farmers also evolve. We don't think it impractical for a research director or employee of the ministry of planning to participate in this experience for a day or two (there are examples, of this, for the research leaders).

Priority setting within a broad systems mandate

The priority setting methods discussed here are rather crop oriented. The concept of rapid, deep diagnosis (farmer interviews plus field observations) integrated with stepwise planning should work for livestock and perennial crops as well, but there are not many examples to date.

A number of methods assume work on a narrow range of commodities. Some researchers are unhappy about this; they state that one should work on 'the whole system'. They have misunderstood how diagnosis and planning work in practice. A project with a 'geographical area mandate' rather than a 'commodity mandate' will identify the principal farming systems early in the informal stage of diagnosis. The farming systems that have the most problems and more research opportunities will also become apparent. The following stage is setting priorities with respect to the various crop and animal activities of the farmer. Not all that the farmer does necessarily provides a research opportunity, and not all that the farm family does is of highest priority. Thus, a 'whole system' mandate soon reduces to a series of priority subsystems. For each of these we must maintain a 'farming systems perspective' and be aware of interactions – which may or may not be important – with other subsystems. But most of the analysis is conducted within single subsystems. The tools proposed are perfectly adequate for that.

It is possible that methods for redesigning complete farming systems will be developed in the future, such as the 'new farming systems development' proposed by Simmonds (1986). Farmer participation would almost certainly be necessary. Present barriers are lack of knowledge about innovations possible for different commodities and limitations in systems analysis. Too many projects that diagnosed 'whole farming systems' at great expense have ended up unable to formulate research plans worthy of the time and money invested.

For the moment, all the FSR workers we know of have severe problems achieving simultaneous adoption of more than one or two components. The largest changes we have obtained in farming systems have occurred via a series of component changes (e.g. the introduction of an extra crop in highland southern Colombia, by using earlier beans or bean–maize associations: Woolley and Davis, 1991, pp 710-711). However, in our own experimentation on zero tillage to conserve soil fertility and reduce costs in a highland area of Mexico, several simultaneous changes (land preparation, residue use, time of planting, varietal type) would be necessary. The organizations that are nearest to obtaining widespread adoption of new farming systems appear to be NGOs (non-governmental organizations); one example is work on soil conservation and integrated farm management in Indonesia (World Neighbours, n.d.).

Necessary future evolution of planning tools

We believe that the method described in this chapter is robust and flexible, and hope for further evolution in the hands of other practitioners. Among the points of further evolution needed in cause-based planning tools are:
* an improved description of steps 7 to 9. As an input to this, working papers have been developed (Mead, 1990a and b) under CIMMYT's auspices to help improve the efficiency of on-farm trial design;
* methods to indicate clearly the relative confidence in different hypotheses about problems and causes, and to show the relative importance of causes when causal chains split;
* a method of assigning higher weight to long-term research. Typically, it is hard to make concrete estimates of yield decline or damage to the resource base. Additionally, solutions that are more sustainable in the medium to long term may show up badly in assessments based on the short term. To overcome this, we sometimes evaluate the same solution on both time scales and incorporate one or both into the research plan;
* greater emphasis on the iterative nature of diagnosis and planning and the need to continue both throughout the life of a project. In Tripp and Woolley (1989) we chose a running example to illustrate methods, in which two years' research had already been conducted. It is common to find diagnosis conceived only as an initial activity, and not uncommon for planning to suffer the same fate;
* the method described above might be adapted for use by extension services considering using existing research results, rather than new research. Allan Low (personal communication) has explored this with one or two National Agricultural Research and Extension Systems in Southern Africa. Peuse and Mmbaga (1987) have worked in Tanzania on problem and solution definition for extension workers;
* adaptation of the method could also be done by those who wish more farmer participation. We would add the caveat that FSR must draw on a synthesis of researcher and farmer knowledge if it is to be successful. Putting new tools of analysis in farmers' hands will not in itself make possible a change in their welfare. Lightfoot et al. (1990) and Mascarenhas et al. (1991) have made important contributions to this topic, but still focus more on diagnosis than on planning. Participation in planning, by farmers

or researchers, implies a commitment to follow through, to monitor and to adjust: it is necessary to keep returning to the plan over several years, revising as more information is gathered. At present, this step appears to be missing from many participatory techniques. Several years after diagnostic techniques for OFR had been established and documented, planning techniques were described. Participatory diagnosis is now established, but participatory planning methods still need to be developed and clearly documented. Something like the participatory evaluation manual prepared by Ashby (1990) is needed for planning.

Notes

1   We are grateful to colleagues at the workshop *Priority Setting in Farming Systems Research and Development* and to Larry Harrington for suggestions incorporated in this paper.
2   Harrington (personal communication) suggests that 'inefficient resource use' is clearer if divided into 'inefficient use of purchased inputs', 'inefficient use of farm resources' (leading to cropping pattern changes and broad system interventions) and 'problems associated with sustainability'.
3   Byerlee et al. (1986) pieced together a view of national wheat research priorities in Pakistan by carrying out on-farm research in areas representative of the major farming systems for that crop.

Bibliography

ASHBY GOY (1990) Evaluating technology with farmers: a handbook. Jar, Colombia: CIAT

BUNCH R (1985) Two ears of corn: a guide to people-centered agricultural improvement. Oklahoma City, USA: World Neighbors

BYERLEE D, GO B AND JAY M (1991) Integrating agronomic and economic perspectives into the diagnostic stage of on-farm research. Experimental Agriculture 27: 95-114

BYERLEE D, HOBBS PR, KHAN BR, MAJID A, AKHTAR MR AND HASHMI NI (1986) Increasing wheat productivity in the context of Pakistan's irrigated cropping systems: a view from the farmers' field. PARC/CIMMYT Paper 86-7. Islamabad, Pakistan: PARC

COLLINSON MP (1984) From problems to possible interventions: key stage in the design sequence. Farming Systems Support Project Newsletter 2(2): 10-12

COLLION MH AND KISSI A (1991) An approach to long-term programme design: Including priority setting and human resource allocation. ISNAR Working Paper no. 37. The Hague: ISNAR

DAHLAN M, HERIYANTO, SUNARSEDYONO, SRI WAHYUNI, SANTEN CE VAN, STAVEREN JP VAN, AND HARRINGTON LW (1987) Maize on-farm research in the district of Malang. MARIF Monograph no. 3. Malang, Indonesia: MARIF

DEFOER T, ERENSTEIN O AND HUSSAIN SS (1992) From consultative to collaborative on-farm experimentation in the Agricultural Development Programme in northern Pakistan. (Unpublished draft paper)

DELP P, THESEN A, MOTIWALLA J AND SESHADRI N (1977) System tools for project planning. Bloomington, Indiana: PASITAM

GTZ (1988) ZOPP (an introduction to the method). Eschborn, Germany: GTZ

HARRINGTON LW (1990) Adaptive research training manuals (set of three). Bangkok, Thailand: CIMMYT Economics Program

HARRINGTON LW (1991) Setting research priorities: concepts and applications to on-farm adaptive research. Presented at the Training Course on Agricultural Research Operations, Bangkok, Thailand, July 1991

HOBBS PR, HETTEL GP, SINGH RP, SINGH Y, HARRINGTON L AND FUJISAKA S (1991) Rice-wheat cropping systems in the tarai areas of Nainital, Rampur, and Pilibhit districts in Uttar Pradesh, India: diagnostic surveys of farmers' practices and problems, and needs for further research. Mexico DF: CIMMYT

HUXLEY PA AND WOOD PJ (no date) Technology and research considerations in ICRAF's 'Diagnosis and Design' procedures. ICRAF Working Paper 26. Nairobi, Kenya: ICRAF

KIRKBY RA (1986) On-farm trials for crop improvement: explaining their potential. IAR/IDRC Third Oilcrops Network Workshop, Addis Ababa, Ethiopia, October 1986

LIGHTFOOT C, GUIA JR O DE AND OCADO F (1988) A participatory method for systems-problem research; rehabilitating marginal uplands in the Philippines. Experimental Agriculture 24: 301-309

LIGHTFOOT C, SINGH VP, PARIS T, MISHRA P AND SALMAN A (1990) Training resource book for farming systems diagnosis. Manila, Philippines: IRRI/ICLARM

MASCARENHAS J, SHAH P, JOSEPH S, JAYAKARAN R, DEVAVARAM J, RAMACHANDRAN V, FERNANDEZ A, CHAMBERS R AND PRETTY J (1991) Participatory rural appraisal. Rapid Rural Appraisal Notes 13. London/Bangalore: IIED/MYARDA

MEAD R (1990a) Development of designs to improve efficiency of OFR. Training Working Document 3. Mexico DF: CIMMYT

MEAD R (1990b) Choice of on-farm trial sites. Training Working Document 5. Mexico DF: CIMMYT

MUTSAERS HJW (1985) An approach to the organization of on-farm research training workshops. IITA OFR Bulletin 3. Ibadan, Nigeria: IITA

NORTON GW AND PARDEY PG (1987) Priority-setting mechanisms for national agricultural research systems: present experience and future needs. ISNAR Working Paper no 7. The Hague, Netherlands: ISNAR

PEUSE HG AND MMBAGA WDS (1987) Helping farmer groups problem-solve: a workshop macrodesign for extension workers. Agricultural Administration and Extension 26: 17-26

SIMMONDS NW (1986) A short review of farming systems research in the tropics. Experimental Agriculture 22: 1-13

SPEDDING CRW (1979) An introduction to agricultural systems. London: Applied Science Publishers

TRIPP R (1982) Data collection, site selection and farmer participation in on-farm experimentation. CIMMYT Economics Program Working Paper 82/1. Mexico DF: CIMMYT

TRIPP R AND WOOLLEY J (1989) The planning stage of on-farm research: identifying factors for experimentation. Mexico DF and Cali, Colombia: CIMMYT and CIAT

VEEN MG VAN DER (1984) Setting research priorities: a review. IRRI Training Paper D06. Manila, Philippines: IRRI

WOOLLEY J (1987) The design of experiments in on-farm research. Draft working document. Cali, Colombia: CIAT

WOOLLEY J (1990) The diagnosis of intercropping problems in farmers' fields and its relation to planning research. In: Waddington SR, Palmer AFE and Edje OT, eds, Research methods for cereal/legume intercropping, pp 19–26. Mexico DF: CIMMYT

WOOLLEY JN AND DAVIS JHC (1991) The agronomy of intercropping with beans. In: Schoonhoven A van and Voysest O (eds) Common beans: research for crop improvement, pp 710–711. Wallingford, UK: CAB International/CIAT

WORLD NEIGHBORS (no date) Integrated farm management (Practical guide to dryland farming series). Oklahoma City, USA

4 Farmer participation in priority setting

Robert E. Rhoades

Farmer participation in FSR&D

Active participation by farmers creates several advantages for FSR&D. First, by definition the purpose of FSR&D is to improve farming systems by working directly with farmers to generate workable and economically feasible solutions to farm problems. If farmers are not active participants in that process, if they do not feel a part of the solution to their own problems, then it is unlikely that they will adopt the technologies recommended by the FSR programme. Scientists do not have to live with the results of their technologies, but farmers do. By involving farmers from the beginning as 'watchdogs' for the research process, success is enhanced. Farmers, therefore, are central to the process and must not be relegated to a minor role.

Second, farmers possess substantial local knowledge about problems and resources, including the plants, soils, and animals in their regions. The old assumption that scientists' knowledge is unequivocally superior to that of farmers has been abandoned in the past few years. No longer do we look upon traditional agriculture as a primitive, backward production system destined to be replaced by modern farming before 'progress' can advance. Scientists have now realized that it is cost-effective to build on this indigenous knowledge, rather than trying to supplant it altogether. In many tropical areas, traditional agriculture has persisted for centuries, allowing human groups to meet their basic physical and social needs. Often such traditional systems operate with minimal energy inputs, are capable of withstanding major external disturbances (both ecological and economic), and are managed by people who have the goal of integrating complex biological and social components, rather than simply increasing the yield of single crop or animal components.

Third, farmers are known to be active innovators, experimenters, and seekers of new knowledge in their own right. Prehistoric farmers invented agriculture itself; in the process they selected and domesticated all the major and minor food crops which humankind still uses to survive today.

Even in the modern era, farmers continue to contribute to science – not only specific technologies (e.g. agronomic techniques) but sustainable systems (for example, farmers have practised agroforestry for centuries). Many 'improved' technologies being promoted by international agriculture research centres are in fact farmer-derived. A study in the 1970s documented that most of IRRI's rice technologies were in this category (Goodell, 1981). The classic case of diffused light storage was a technique CIP scientists learned from farmers and then helped spread to other farmers.

Fourth, only farmers can bring realistic 'holism' to a research project. FSR scientists and extension workers are often justifiably focused on the technical matters at hand. However, 'technology' is only part of the story. Important political, social, and even religious concerns affect farmers, who must weigh technologies within a broader framework of 'life'. Higher farmer productivity and economic efficiency may be the goal of an FSR team, but may not be the highest ranking priority of farm households.

Roles of farmers

A farmer can serve in many roles: advisor, colleague, student, and extension agent (farmer-to-farmer, or farmer-to-scientist). FSR teams that are open to farmers will benefit, because they approach the research process in an honest and direct manner. Farmers are no fools; they are quick to see through superficiality, and detect when scientists are missing the point or promoting ill-conceived technologies. On the other hand, farmers respond positively to open, direct researchers who make it crystal clear what they know (e.g. disease) and what they do not know (e.g. local conditions). In such an open dialogue, the role of the farmer will vary in relation to the knowledge and expertise of the FSR team. Clearly, though, farmers may not understand that an aphid in the stored seeds is the vector of a virus that hits in the field several months later. The theory, or even the concept, of disease may not be understood. In this case, the farmer is a student, usually eager to learn and try new ideas. In another case, perhaps the FSR team will be unaware of the complex field rotation system in a community, but they need to know how a new practice would fit in. This time the farmer becomes the teacher, the one who gives knowledge. Finally, the farmer can be a colleague: the parties may join each other in trying new technologies or researching a question of common interest. This partner relationship is perhaps the most fruitful possibility, but is the one mutual role that is least fostered. Scientists may have a difficult time accepting 'uneducated' farmers as equals or as 'experts' in their own right.

Organizing farmer participation

Strategies for understanding farmers' problems

Admitting that a team needs to understand farmers' problems is only the first step; arriving at an operational and effective strategy is a more difficult issue. In my opinion, it is not only the research tools that must be relevant (see next section), but also the overall model of research guiding the interaction between the FSR team and farmers.

One of the most widely used models for farmer-scientist interaction is 'farmer-back-to-farmer', which was formulated at the International Potato Center in the early 1980s (Figure 1). This model was based on the premise that agricultural research and development must both begin and end with farmers – that they must be involved at all stages, from diagnosis to evaluation of results. Variants of this model have been proposed over the past decade, including farmer first (Chambers et al., 1989), farmer participatory research, and people first (Cernea, 1985). However, the underlying assumption – that farmers are active participants, not passive, in the technology generation process – remains the same. The model requires a 'psychological flip' in which the scientists' standard philosophy of 'techno-scientific salvationism' (that is, the idea that scientific technology alone will solve our problems) gives way to a more humanistically based orientation that accords respect and appreciation to traditional indigenous knowledge and practices. If an FSR team is able to make this shift, then the next steps of research execution will be manageable, although never easy.

Appreciating farmers' priorities

Priority means 'precedence in order or rank'. However, it should be realized that there are several dimensions to farmers' priorities. First of all, for farm households around the world farming is a means to an end, not the end in itself. Therefore, the aim of farming is to provide needed food for the family or cash to buy items or services not produced on the farm. The basic priorities of farm households are happiness, health, and hope, especially for their children. Farming systems research teams sometimes overestimate the importance of technical priorities (increasing production) believing that farmers are likewise equally concerned. Sometimes a village would rather hold a festival than attend to a series of experiments.

A second point is that, even within the farming enterprise, there are difficult priorities for each major activity (e.g. herding, cultivation, irrigation, marketing, etc.). The few studies that have compared farmers'

Figure I. Farmer-back-to-farmer

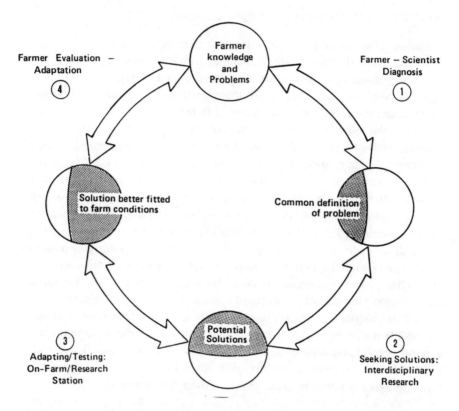

The farmer-back-to-farmer model begins and ends with the farmer. It involves four major activities, each with a goal. The hatched areas in the circle indicate an increasing understanding of the technological problem area as research progresses. Note that research may constantly recycle.

Activities	Goals
I Diagnosis	Common definition of problem by farmers and scientists
2 Interdisciplinary team research	Identify and develop a potential solution to the problem
3 On-farm testing and adaptation	Better adapt the proposed solution to farmer's conditions
4 Farmer evaluation/adaptation	Modify technology to fit local conditions: understand farmer adoption

Adapted from Rhoades and Booth (1982)

priorities with those of agricultural researcher/extension agents illustrate that their perceptions of the problems differ significantly. Farmers asked to respond to an open-ended question by ranking their problems generally begin with items such as low prices, lack of credit, shortage of labour, and drought; and end with technical problems of disease, poor soils, etc. Agricultural scientists, however, generally reverse this order, placing technical issues high while undervaluing the other items. This is one of the reasons the farmer-back-to-farmer model is so important; it requires that a 'common definition' of the problem be mutually identified from the start (stage 1 in the figure).

Finally, a third dimension is that even if farmers and FSR scientists agree on a list of priorities, it must be realized that economically feasible solutions do not exist for all problems. Furthermore, problems and hence priorities shift through time, and priorities are systematically linked to each other. In the light of this complexity, the key to getting a better understanding of farmers' priorities lies in a process of continuous feedback. Again, this is the essence of the farmer-back-to-farmer model. At any point in the research cycle, it may be necessary to return to a previous stage (for example, moving from experimentation back to diagnosis) if the research activity is not producing new results or testable hypotheses. It is this willingness to be flexible, humble, and tenacious that will lead to a proper understanding of ever-changing priorities.

Involving farmers in all stages

Farmers will enthusiastically be involved at all stages if they have a vested interest in the outcome. Fostering this strong interest will only be possible if researchers stay close enough to farm conditions to work on well-defined problems that are truly priorities for the farmers themselves. There are many interesting research questions that are fascinating to scientists, but which are of limited interest to farmers (e.g. chemical fertilizer trials where the fertilizers are unavailable or too expensive). Scientists frequently design technologies (often in laboratories or experiment stations) and then send the technologies out (through an extension agency) in search of farmers and their problems. Such technologies rarely find the problem they were designed to solve.

A research team that wants to guarantee that farmers will be involved in all stages, from diagnosis through evaluation – that is, to guarantee continuous farmer input – should ask themselves the following seven key questions:

- Is the problem(s) to be solved important to farmers?
- Do farmers understand the farming systems project and its goals?
- Do farmers have the time, inputs, and labour required by the improved technology?
- Does the proposed technology fit the present farming system?
- Is the mood in a region favourable to investing in new technologies or crops?
- Is the proposed change compatible with local preferences, beliefs, and/or community sanctions?
- Do farmers believe the technology will hold up over the long term?

By checking off these seven questions as they go through the research–diagnosis process, the team will get a general idea as to whether farmers will be interested. For example, if a large shipment of wheat from a foreign country has just been dumped in the country's port city, so that prices have been depressed, it is not likely farmers will be putting a great deal of emphasis on wheat technologies.

In addition to asking the seven key questions, the research team must become acquainted with local customs and social habits. Although it is not necessary to 'go native', the team must be willing to participate in village festivals. Team members should learn the local language, live as close to rural conditions as possible, and get to know the farmers as individuals. In the FSR process, there can be no substitute for 'missionary zeal' and close contact with clients.

Deciding which farmers should participate

No farming community in the world is homogeneous. There are rich and poor farmers, young and old, men and women, and even ethnic differences within a single region. There are farmers who are well educated and others who are illiterate. Some live near a road or village, while others are far away in the hinterland. Deciding with whom one should work is a major early decision for the FSR team.

The target group of farmers depends on the objectives of the FSR project. The objective may be, for example, to work only with the poorest of the poor. Other projects may focus more specifically on particular 'components' or 'subsystems' (livestock, poultry, home gardens, and so forth). In most cases, the general problem will have been predefined by the donor agency, which is apt to have special interests. They will provide funds for an FSR team that will address, for example, poverty among rural households in the Sahel; or low productivity in a shifting cultivation system in the Amazon Basin. Rarely do FSR projects go into the field first, inquiring into the problem and asking farmers to define their needs.

However, once the general constraints on farmer selection are set, the team needs to consider carefully with which individuals and with which groups of farmers they should participate. In some areas of the world where farmers are organized into tightly knit groups, the farmers (or their leaders) will decide where and with whom the team will work. Normally, however, the team – after working through the local governmental bureaucracy – will be faced with the choice of which household and communities will be their research field.

At this point in the diagnostic phase, it must be realized that each set of farmers (however delineated) will have its own priorities. This diversity can be understood and minimized by selecting research topics that will affect the majority of farmers (focusing, for example, on marketing or a common cropping pattern). Or a sort of sociogram can be constructed for the village, which can be used to describe different points of view.

One technique I have commonly used to set priorities is to study a community in terms of agroecological analysis. Social groupings frequently correspond to specific agroecological zones. For example, large, wealthy farmers may live in the centre of a valley, while poor, resource-limited farmers live on the margins. A team can look at how much production comes from the valley centre, how many farmers will be impacted by potential research, and how their livelihoods will be affected. There may be trade-offs: one can produce more food volume in the valley centre (and thus lower consumer prices in the town), but income and nutrition might be enhanced more if you work on the margins. These are tough questions, and they can only be answered if one knows the social dynamic and the environmental relationships.

As may be apparent, the final decision about which farmers or groups of farmers an FSR team is to work with will nearly always be based on myriad factors, including convenience, funds, outside constraints, farmer willingness, and researchers' needs.

Tools for achieving farmer participation

For the conventional approach, there is an established sequence of methods that has been outlined in FSR manuals (the CIMMYT manual being the most famous). This sequence, which has advantages and disadvantages, involves collecting background literature and reviews about the region; an informal

Table 1. Strengths and weaknesses of information gathering tools for use in applied agricultural research

Tool	Strength	Weakness
Literature review	Helps prevent 're-inventing the wheel'	Requires time and access to good libraries
Maps, meteorological data, statistical publications	Provide background data on agricultural sector	May be inaccurate or too 'macro'
Informal surveys	Provide rapid overview of land use and farming practices	Allow little quantification; outsiders may consider data 'soft'
Direct observation	Helps avoid problems such as farmer recall, and need to interpret verbal responses	Logistical (transport) problems and small sample size
Formal surveys	Quantification; large sample size	Costly; time consuming; and computer-intensive
On-farm experiments	Allow technologies to be tested under farmers' conditions	Very costly; small sample size; require at least one full crop season; logistical problems

survey; a formal questionnaire; on-farm trials; recommendations; and follow-up and evaluation of adoption. In reality, teams do not always follow this sequence exactly. However, the 'on-farm trial' is typically the heart of the sequence, and most of the research process is dedicated to finding out what on-farm trial or technology should be tested with farmers. The strengths and weaknesses of some frequently used information gathering tools for use in applied agricultural research are shown in Table 1.

A new approach

Although we declare that farmers have always been central to FSR, and we are philosophically committed to the ethics of farmer involvement, I believe that the bankruptcy of social science methods used by FSR teams has defeated the reality of true farmer participation. Elsewhere, I have written about what I call the coming revolution in agricultural research methods (Rhoades, 1990). In this chapter, I argue that FSR has based its work on the philosophical position of 'empiricism', and more specifically on 'scientific positivism', which posits that human social and economic actions can be studied using the models of the physical sciences. This means that we must count and measure just as in chemistry and physics. 'Positivism' can be traced back to the French sociologist Auguste Comte, who wanted to reduce human behaviour to scientific principles so that it would become predictable. The questionnaire-based survey was the instrument designed to capture and quantify human behaviour. Jackie Ashby of CIAT has noted that the use of the questionnaire has become a major 'industry' in Third World agriculture. However, by its very nature, the questionnaire (and even the single shot survey or the informal survey) and the desire to assign numbers to things plant major barriers between scientists and farmers.

What are the options if the old, linear sequence (informal survey ⇨ formal survey ⇨ on-farm trial ⇨ evaluation ⇨ recommendation/feedback) is no longer viable. First, I argue that we need to make a 'psychological flip' in the way we look at research with farmers. Second, I argue that we need to expand our tool kit of methods, drawing on a vast array of methods beyond the survey questionnaire.

The idea that we scientists do 'research' while farmers 'farm' is only partially true. Farmers also do research, and although these priorities may change quickly, they set priorities and determine priority problems. The evidence is overwhelming that farmers are excellent experimenters and researchers in their own right. After all, farmers have created the world's complex farming systems, domesticated all major crops, invented most farming tools, and designed intricate irrigation facilities. The problem has been that we scientists have not been very creative in learning how to harness the research potential of farmers.

At the base of FSR's lack of imagination in dealing with farmers is a lack of awareness of the differences between farmers' research methods and 'scientific' research. Farmers have their own ways of calculating, counting, recording, remembering, and predicting. These, however, often do not involve pencil and paper, two items farmers may be uncomfortable with. Modern, urbanized ('Westernized') humans lost many important skills of their ancestors as they began to place greater value on rational and empirical abilities, while emotional and other capabilities have lost their sharpness. Tribal and rural populations in Africa and Asia, however, have not lost these abilities. Moreover, detailed, unwritten oral histories stretching back 10 generations can be related with great precision. Market women can estimate the weight of produce down almost to the gram without weighing it. Indonesian waiters in town restaurants, who may be illiterate, can take and remember precise meal orders for dozens of people without

Table 2. Strengths and weaknesses of selected methods of participatory research

Method	Strength	Weakness
Participatory mapping - resource mapping - social mapping	Provides local view of spatial relationships; fast, inexpensive	Context specific; not 'scientific'; scale problems
Physical models	Gives local understanding of spatial relationships	Expensive; time consuming; scale problems
Interactive visual aids (insect box, sack of seeds)	Uses context; no misunderstanding of discourse item	Limited use
Farmer flow diagrams and pie charts	User-generated; non-traditional concept	Recall difficulties; not precise
Matrix and preference ranking	Insider precision	
Group interviews	Group dynamics and correction of individual bias	Logistics; group control
Time lines and oral histories	Time depth; qualitative data; context	Requires time; questions of generalizability
Group treks	Direct observation; open interaction	Logistics, time required
Traditional games	Easy interaction; openness; culturally sensitive	Outsiders' lack of knowledge; difficult to interpret

writing down a single item. This is not to argue that these capabilities are 'superior' to our own pencil (now computer) and paper skills, but to note that they are different; and once tapped they can yield enormous insights and 'data' about farmers' problems and priorities.

The best way to portray the new methodology of farmer-participatory research is to imagine a cafeteria of tools and skills. The cafeteria is a rich one with many and varied techniques to select from, but they are not in any particular order. Among the dozens of selections you will find a conventional questionnaire or on-farm trial, but they will be no more special than the rest. What more will we find? The sampling given in Table 2 points out a few of the techniques that can be used with farmers to set priorities (for more details see Rhoades, 1990).

While it is clear that no one of the techniques alone will provide enough information to establish FSR priorities, this list illustrates that the survey questionnaire is only one tool among many. The majority of the techniques in Table 2 aim to involve the farmer in the research *and* to capture the farmers' point of view. In reality, it will be necessary to use a combination of these techniques. Contrary to popular belief, most of the techniques can rather quickly yield quantifiable data covering large numbers of farmers. Furthermore, it has been my experience that once FSR teams start to use these techniques, they rarely go back to the old FSR sequence.

We must be realistic, however, and admit that farmers' ranking of priorities may not be the only basis for determining the priorities for an FSR team. Clearly, farmers' priorities may not be in the best interests of the national government (all farmers want higher prices, governments rarely want expensive food). Institutional and donor demands may signal a need for compromise. Farmers in Peru may want to grow coca or Thai farmers may opt for poppy production, but few FSR teams will be encouraged to work on these priorities. Indeed, farmers' goals may not be favourable to long term sustainable food production. Teams will also have their own priorities; this needs to be recognized, so that the question of how to integrate farmer priorities and team priorities can be openly discussed.

The only major disadvantage of these participatory methods arises when a team is concerned with strict, quantifiable science. These participatory approaches do not begin with hypotheses formulated outside the data set, but are in fact generated while the research process is under way. Often it will not be easy to reduce these generated data to 'numbers'. In addition, many conventional researchers will at first feel uneasy using these techniques, which admittedly stray from convention.

Balancing farmers' and researchers' priorities

The basic principle of the farmer-back-to-farmer model is that FSR projects have only one objective: to generate affordable, sustainable, and appropriate technologies or solutions (though not always technical solutions). Farmer-back-to-farmer (now rephrased by some as farmer first) is an applied action model, not a basic, pure research model. Researchers can pursue their own priorities on the experiment station (although this, too, is ethically questionable), but once research is to be justified on development grounds, then the research priorities of scientists and farmers must be melded together. It may be that farmers have priority problems that lie beyond the mandate of an FSR team (e.g. land inequity or racial discrimination). However, within the areas where FSR can be operationalized, it is essential to find common ground.

The only route to matching priorities is to follow an interactive, participatory method such as the farmer-back-to-farmer model, an approach that insists on constant interaction and maintenance of common definitions. If research strays from the real problems, it must be brought back and even recycled through the steps (that is, by returning to joint farmer–scientist diagnosis). The final decision rests with farmers. If they adopt the changes based on FSR and maintain them, then the FSR approach is working. If not, the cycle must be repeated.

Bibliography

CERNEA M (published for the World Bank, 1985) Putting people first. New York and London: Oxford University Press

CHAMBERS R, PACEY A AND THRUPP LA (1989) Farmer first. London: Intermediate Technology Publications

GOODELL G (Unpublished paper, 1981) Communication from Farmer to Scientist. Los Baños, Philippines: International Rice Research Institute

RHOADES R (1990) The coming revolution in methods for rural development research. User's perspective with agricultural research and development (UPWARD). Proceedings of the Inaugural Workshop, April 3–5, 1990. Los Baños, Philippines, pp 196–210

RHOADES R AND BOOTH R (1982) Farmer-back-to-farmer: a model for generating acceptable agricultural technology. Agricultural Administration 11: 127–137

5 Linking research to technology dissemination

Thomas Eponou[1]

To ensure the relevance and broader dissemination of agricultural tech
nologies to resource-poor farmers, strong linkages are needed between
research and other stakeholders and actors in the system: this includes
technology transfer institutions at various levels. Linkages are needed for
the exchange of information and resources; collaboration; sharing of
responsibilities and agreement on priority areas for coordinated allocation
of resources. Technology transfer agencies and agents, their role in FSR
programmes and their links with FSR teams are the focus of this chapter.
Linkages at local level receive most of the attention, but the importance of
links to other levels is also recognized.

While almost everyone advocates participation of technology transfer
agents, and many FSR teams recognize the need for effective linkages with
technology transfer, establishing and managing these linkages have often
been problematic (Ewell, 1990; Merrill-Sands and Kaimowitz, 1990;
Russell, 1991). The usefulness and intensity of their participation are often
questioned, and in fact the contribution to priority setting has often been
minimal, even where mechanisms such as committees and meetings have
been set up. Nevertheless, while some FSR teams have limited the participation of technology transfer in priority setting, others have sought and
found an effective partnership.

Throughout this chapter, there is an important underlying message:
linkages are a key element of success. Effective linkages to technology
transfer – involving users in the process, seeking coordination and synergy,
and finding partners for technology development activities – can increase
the potential for programme success, including effects on leverage with
respect to decision making. When a team has its objectives with respect to
linkages firmly in mind, it becomes possible to design an approach that
will work toward the achievement of these objectives. Such a design
includes the choice of an appropriate degree of participation, and proper

use of both formal and informal mechanisms. One important example – the use of meetings and committees – will be covered in more detail.

The function of links to technology transfer

If research is to be relevant, effective and sustainable, it must be complementary to other instruments of agricultural development such as extension, delivery of inputs and distribution of credit. Participation by technology transfer agents is thus necessary to the success of a research programme. In the discussion below, extension (the 'old' terminology) is sometimes used interchangeably with technology transfer. While relations to the extension service are critical, the latter term seems more appropriate. It is important to keep in mind that not only the extension service, but also representatives of other government bodies, NGOs, or other donor-funded projects, may be important to the transfer of technology. When several such individuals or groups are operating in one area, a lack of coordination can be an additional challenge to a FSR&D team interested in a systems approach.

The key steps in priority setting involve analysing development objectives; analysing constraints on the achievement of objectives (including a review of past research results dealing with these constraints); determining research strategies and objectives; evaluating alternative solutions; selecting solutions to be tested; and designing experiments (including choice of site). Such steps imply that priority setting will require information on national policies, agricultural credits, production conditions, marketing problems, past experiences with certain types of technologies, and much other local knowledge. Especially in complex and heterogenous farming systems, most of this information may not be available to the research team. It seems likely that the shorter the experience of the FSR team in the region, the wider the information gap will be. Extension and other development organizations have been there longer and, especially at the outset, may be closer to farmers. Thus their contribution can be important, particularly for steps in the middle of the process, from analysis of constraints through evaluation of alternatives. Moreover, their knowledge of the area can also be very useful in choosing sites. As the FSR team's knowledge of local farming conditions improves, the need for more structured involvement of technology transfer agents may decline. This is replaced, however, by a need for communication and involvement to make sure that the on-going research is understood and supported, and to generate commitment to implementation of the results. Later, mutual involvement in examining the impact of the project is beneficial. Several of these facets are considered below.

Involving 'users' in the technology generation process. The need for participation of users in the development of relevant technologies is recognized far beyond the agricultural sector (Souder, 1980; Kanter, 1983). Extension clearly should be seen as a user of technology; as an intermediary between research and farmers, it often expresses what can be called the 'derived demand' for new or adapted techniques. Further, if extension agencies and workers are not convinced of the relevance of technologies developed by the FSR team, they may not invest the energy and resources required to transfer them to farmers. Many FSR teams have had such experiences: technologies have simply been ignored by extension. The earlier extension is involved, and the greater the extent to which there is a feeling that its input has been heard and taken into account – in fact the greater the ongoing communication and understanding of the research – the more likely it is that extension will endorse and help to implement the results, because these will be perceived as joint products.

Seeking coordination and synergy. Coordinating research priorities with those for technology transfer has the potential to create synergies, thus increasing the programme's impact. It is important that extension be aware of the implications of the technologies that are under development, as well as the likely timeframe. This will make it possible to coordinate its own programme, leading to better planning and a timely transfer of new technol-ogies. Lack of coordination in programming and prioritizing of the efforts of the various actors is a key factor in the low performance of technology systems (Quisumbing, 1984). Some of the technologies generated by FSR teams have not been widely disseminated simply because extension could not accommodate them in its own programme. It may also be helpful to FSR teams to have information about forthcoming extension activities, and to coordinate with extension about what will happen when.

Partners in technology development activities. FSR&D and extension can be natural partners in technology development activities. Involving extension in FSR&D priority setting may improve linkages during the experimentation phase: for example, it may diminish the impression extension agents often have when they are used as supervisors of trials – that they are being used as cheap labour by FSR teams. Participation may give a feeling of being part of the new approach, and boost the morale of extensionists (Ewell, 1990). The risk that extension will see the FSR team as a competitor or as a threat to its direct contacts with farmers may also be reduced. When extension is made a part of the process, and recognizes its common goals, it can become a help rather than a constraint, in both research and implementation of results.

Participation of technology transfer in FSR priority setting can have additional positive results, by providing incentives and opportunities for technology transfer agencies to think about and perhaps revise their own programmes. For example, revision of extension programmes and policies may broaden the scope and relevance of technologies offered to farmers; or provide training of agents in participatory techniques. Such changes will increase the effectiveness of FSR programmes. Joint planning may also be a way of institutionalizing feedback from linkages (Russell, 1991; Meindertsma et al., Chapter 7; van Campen, Chapter 13): that is, of making feedback a normal part of the process, not only accepted but also *expected* by participants.

Increased leverage over policy decision making. In addition to direct benefits at local level, linkages can be helpful elsewhere. The need of FSR for increased leverage over policy decision making is an important reason for seeking linkages. The need for extension is widely recognized, and extension agencies (like thematic research) are often better embedded in the national structure than is farming systems research. Thus, if FSR&D is supported at all levels by extension, it may gain not only important immediate practical help, but also vital political support. In many instances, extension managers have a greater chance of influencing policymakers than do research managers. When they are a part of the research priority setting process, they can sometimes channel information on needs, constraints and results to policymakers more easily than researchers. Joint implementation and impact assessment support this process.

One disadvantage of increased linkage should be mentioned: linkages can increase the possibility that FSR programmes will be diverted to serve the personal goals of particular actors. This is especially evident with, but not limited to, politicians. The FSR team must take this possibility into account. However, the trade-off in potential benefits is generally worth the risk. Further, the greater the variety of actors involved, and the better the circulation of information among them, the smaller the chance of such a diversion.

Factors affecting linkages

An FSR team that is interested in creating linkages must carefully consider its approach, first making a key decision: what sort of participation do they want and expect from technology transfer agents? There are many possible degrees of participation; the team must decide what is appropriate to the situation. This determines the sort of linkages that can be established. To make this decision, the team must first examine its own interest, willingness and capacity for working in a participative manner (which must be grounded in good internal functioning of the team). For example, does the team really believe a mutual exchange will be worthwhile? If decisions are to be made jointly, are they willing to live with the outcome of the group process?

Degree of participation

One reason the team itself needs to be clear about the degree of participation expected is that this must be transparent for others: participants need to understand ahead of time just what is being offered. Otherwise – if they are led to expect that their contributions will have a major impact, or that they will be seen as partners, when this is not the case – the results can be more negative than if no 'participation' had been requested. This is especially true when mutual expectations are based on the sorts of long-held stereotypes discussed below. Asking extension agencies and agents to participate in more limited ways may be appropriate in some situations, but this, too, increases the need for clarity. Never promise prerogatives that you cannot deliver; instead, state the boundaries within which participants are being asked to make decisions or suggestions.

In the following sections, some possible variations in the degree of participation are examined, followed by additional factors to be considered in designing an approach: which technology transfer personnel can be involved; the extension model in use; and the intergroup climate, including potential conflicts.

Effective partnership. When researchers recognize that technology transfer agents are close to farmers, an effective partnership can be developed. These agents have a good knowledge of farmer conditions, and the capacity to identify or contribute to the identification of constraints; they can also help in formulating plans to deal with constraints. On the other side, technology transfer agents can come to see FSR as an opportunity, rather than a threat. FSR objectives are relevant to those of technology transfer agencies; FSR can contribute to better conditions for farmers, by making new tools and extension messages available. In an effective partnership, researchers are (and are seen as) understanding and interested in on-going technology transfer. In this situation, diagnosis, programme formulation and priority setting can be carried out jointly by research and technology transfer. Such partnerships can develop both with respect to strategic or policy issues, such as location and scope of programmes; and at the micro-level, with priority setting carried out by a combined team, including both FSR researchers and technology transfer agents.

Developing a true partnership is often difficult. There are many reasons; researcher attitudes are one element. Often non-scientists are not really trusted enough to be involved in the identification of research problems. This is an aftereffect of the conventional linear model of technology transfer research, which has not been fully overcome by scientists working in FSR teams. For example, Palmieri reports a case in Costa Rica in which the operational plan for research and extension was to be discussed at a negotiation meeting between researchers and technology transfer agents dealing with the same commodity in the same region. Each transfer agent was requested to provide a list of problems that could be included in the trial programme. However, researchers rejected these lists because, in their opinion, the problems had been identified without the use of a scientific method (Palmieri, 1990). Reviewing the nine country case studies of OFCOR, Ewell (1989) reports that extension workers are seldom treated as partners or given co-responsibility for setting priorities or channelling detailed information as feedback into the research system.

Information exchange/informal participation. Even when a real partnership is not immediately possible, sometimes a mutually beneficial relationship can be established. The FSR team can look for opportunities, whether formal or informal, to involve technology transfer agents and to better understand their work. This might include providing information on planning, feedback of results, or incorporation in some phase of the priority setting process. Technology transfer can be encouraged to do the same. This may lead, over time, to partnership.

In the early stages of some programmes (particularly when activities are limited to on-farm trials of varieties, to determine how they react in different agroecological zones), researchers may use information gathered through informal contacts with extension agents, in addition to other information they have collected, in formulating their research programmes. (The On-Farm Research Project, OFRIC, financed by the Ford Foundation in Côte d'Ivoire used this approach in its early stages.) Informal participation of e.g. extension may also take place alongside a formal priority setting process.

Seeking specific inputs. In many cases, the research team has already elaborated a basic programme and proposals before scheduling a formal meeting in which input is sought from technology transfer agents. What is really wanted from technology transfer is additional information to be used in fine-tuning the proposals or programmes; and/or their seal of approval may be desired. Or technology transfer may be asked to take part in choosing among alternative proposals. But the alternatives generally have to do with e.g. resource allocation or choice of sites, or factors that will enhance implementation or affect socioeconomic circumstances of farmers, rather than a real choice among programmes or a chance to discuss the relevance of the proposal itself. The greatest impact extension can expect to have is to see some proposals abandoned or postponed; the problems they raise are not likely to be added to the programme.

Research 'informs' technology transfer. This is the traditional situation: a one-way flow of information from research to technology transfer agencies and agents. In this case, when technology transfer personnel are invited to a meeting, the motive is not to have a discussion or even to draw information from them, but rather to provide them with sufficient nicely packaged information – which has been generated by FSR – for them to take the next steps in the generation and transfer process. No priority setting, effective participation, or other feedback relevant to priority setting is expected to take place at this meeting.

Type and ability of participants

Assuring that the appropriate technology transfer personnel take part in the various aspects of interaction with researchers is a key to success. When researchers depend on the information they get from extension, quality depends on having extension workers who really know the problems and needs of the target group. Those involved may range from national directors of technology transfer to village level extension workers. Each agent, at all levels, may have a role to play in the process. The problem is to have the right agent involved at the right time. For example, top managers of technology transfer systems may be those most appropriate for setting broader strategies and policies, but are usually not the most relevant for discussing technological questions specific to one region or district – here the officers operating at that level are needed.

The most effective strategy seems to be setting different sorts of priorities at different levels, as described by van Sluys and Silva (Chapter 14). This, however, implies effective coordination mechanisms between the different levels and some form of decentralization in the decision-making process. Where effective decentralization and coordination mechanisms do not exist or do not function properly, there will be problems.

A second issue involves the ability of individuals to participate effectively. Sometimes the basic argument for participation of technology transfer agents – their knowledge of farmer conditions – is challenged by researchers. In Sri Lanka, for example, researchers did not seek information from extension workers because they felt these agents knew less about the farmers than they did themselves (Seegers, 1990). This is also seen in a case in Guatemala (Ruano and Fumagalli, 1988).

In some instances, it is not the knowledge of technology transfer agents that is questioned, but their ability to transform that knowledge into information that can be useful in formulating research questions. Either of these assertions can of course be true. Unfortunately, they can also be part of a stereotyped view of extension workers. FSR team members need to keep their minds open! Such stereotypes can negate all of the potential for effective interaction between FSR and technology transfer.

The capacity of technology transfer agents to participate effectively may vary with their level of training and with the model used for priority setting. The more formal the approach, the more difficult it will be for lower level extension workers to be part of the process. Also, when more quantitative methods of priority setting are used, extension workers may also be cut out. (And even some researchers may not be effective participants.) Informal mechanisms may be the best way to ensure input from village level agents. The limitation on approaches that involve individuals, however, is that they are not always apt to be sustainable in the long run. Thus it is necessary to seek ways to assure an evolution toward more sustainable methods.

Extension model

The effectiveness of participation may also be influenced by the approach being used for technology transfer. In theory, the 'training and visit' (T&V) approach to extension seems quite complementary to FSR: both use an upstream approach, put farmers at the centre of the system, and use the diagnosis of farmers' problems as a key instrument. In an ideal situation, the FSR team can operate as the 'engine' of the system. Its members gather, process and dispatch information and knowledge from and to farmers, extension and on-station research, with subject-matter specialists and contact farmers as their strategic allies.

Problems of duplication of effort, competition, tensions and communication difficulties have, however, been reported where the T&V approach is used (Byerlee, 1988). These problems are often due to a lack of effective leadership at the apex of the national research system. Research and extension may not be perceived as components of the same system; or there may be no monitoring of their performance. Poor coordination among donors can also lead to problems, especially when the FSR programme and the T&V project are financed by different donors. The mechanical–bureaucratic organizational structure of T&V; the uniformity and simplification of extension messages; the T&V focus on production-increasing strategies; and the condescending attitude of researchers vis à vis extension agents are other constraints to effective cooperation (Manig, 1992). As has been reported in Zimbabwe (Cousins, 1988), in many situations, the capability of extension agents to be efficient partners in the process also remains a problem to be solved. Furthermore, feedback from extension to FSR and from FSR to extension often remains inadequate (Howell, 1988).

The participation of extension may be yet more difficult when a conventional approach to extension is used: this approach is often based on a linear model, which portrays research and extension as having sequential roles: this suggests that few opportunities will be created for meaningful interaction. The most difficult situations, however, are apt to occur in systems using a commodity approach to extension, because extension may perceive the FSR team as a threat or an intruder. This problem arises from differences in the perceptions, approaches and goals of the two actors, since FSR leads to a broader perspective than extension. Cooperation from extension may be maintained only if the research priorities of the two groups are not in conflict. In some cases extension has attempted to control the FSR programme. The best that can be expected in this situation is conflict avoidance (Bennell, 1989). Nevertheless, while in such systems participation of extension in priority setting may be difficult in the early stages of the FSR programme, matters may improve over time: if communication is maintained, extension may come to see at least some components of the FSR programme as being in its own interest. That has been the case in southern Mali, for example, where both the cotton extension system and the FSR programme now see the mutual benefit of working on soil conservation (Chapters 11 and 13).

Thus, each of the commonly used approaches to extension can contribute to difficulties in participation. Further, in all approaches the introduction of new, participatory methods may be difficult simply due to resistance to change, whether from research, extension or both. As outlined in the following section, there are a number of constraints to overcome before genuine participation can be achieved.

Intergroup climate

As implied in the preceding discussion, the participation of technology transfer agents in priority setting is influenced by the relationships established between the two groups. In fact, establishing good personal and group relationships can overcome many of the difficulties, but it is best to be aware of the potential for tension. The generation and transfer of technology is a social process involving actors with different personal attributes, status, attitudes and behaviours, motivations, interests and goals. Individual actors occupy specific positions, both at work and in a profession. Organizations differ with respect to prestige, status and incentive systems, authority and resources. Individuals naturally identify with their own work groups and professions. Such differences in personal attributes, professional group and organizational characteristics have been identified as factors contributing to poor linkages between research and technology transfer, because they create tensions and conflicts among the actors of the system (Bennell, 1989; Seegers and Kaimowitz, 1989; Bennell and Zuidema, 1988; Wuyts-Fivawo, 1992).

In most systems, researchers have a higher status than technology transfer agents; extension workers may have had much less education and training. There is a sort of 'pecking order' of occupations, reinforced by a general perception that researchers are to some extent the 'white collar' workers of technology systems, capable of identifying, analyzing and solving farmers' problems. This suggests that technology transfer agents are 'blue collar' workers, in charge of rather mechanically delivering the research product to farmers. Researchers seem to enjoy this situation, but technology transfer agents resent it. Often researchers would like to maintain the status quo and are therefore critical of attempts by technology transfer agents to become involved in research. For example, in 1970 the Colombian Agricultural Institute (ICA) set up integrated rural development projects in which research and extension were expected to collaborate on adaptive research. Due to disagreements between the two groups, extension set up its own trials. Researchers protested, and forced extension to refer to these trials as 'technological adjustments' – not 'research' (Wuyts-Fivawo, 1992).

This situation can easily lead to conflicts regarding what must be done to understand farmers' views. Technology transfer agents may assert that they have already incorporated the farmers' viewpoint in their policies and strategies. An FSR team will generally prefer to make its own assessment. If the results do not agree with the pre-existing ideas of the technology transfer agency, the situation must be handled carefully, especially if their ideas mirror the views and options of policymakers. This illustrates the importance of involving the technology transfer agency, including its policymakers, in the diagnostic phase: their commitment to the results is needed.

Where tensions and conflicts are high, effective participation of technology transfer in priority setting is problematic. The factors outlined here indicate that, without special measures, researchers and technology transfer agents may see each other as competitors, rather than partners. Therefore, it is important to recognize these difficulties from the beginning of joint discussions with technology transfer, and to look for ways to overcome them.

Mechanisms

Working with technology transfer agents has many points in common with collaboration with other actors. Before deciding what mechanisms are to be used, a strategy for involving others should be considered. For each stage of priority setting, think which technology transfer personnel should be involved, and how: for example, who has information needed at this stage? who needs to be involved to ensure their commitment later? who has common interests that can be used to develop a relationship? Answering these questions leads directly to looking at mechanisms for involvement. For technology transfer these mechanisms should take into account the degree of participation to be requested, the structure of the organizations involved, their schedules, and the capabilities of personnel – in fact, all of the factors discussed earlier. Activities can be planned to build interest and understanding. Many of the techniques suggested in other chapters, and in particular those covered by Norman in Chapter 2, can be adapted for use with technology transfer. Clearly, if a team is committed to effective participation, there will be a well-rounded programme of on-going communication, taking many forms – informal as well as formal. In some cases, priority setting may be preceded by joint surveys and/or field visits, to identify constraints faced by farmers. The involvement of extension agents in monitoring and evaluation of earlier FSR activities can also feed into priority setting.

Meetings and committees are one important set of mechanisms for involving technology transfer. They are apt to be basic techniques for FSR teams (and NARS – national agricultural research systems – as well) in the planning and review of research, and for setting priorities. Therefore, they deserve special attention. These mechanisms are a common part of life today; we tend to forget that holding a good meeting or getting good results from a committee requires thought and preparation. Awareness of the factors discussed here can allow a team to design meetings and committee structures that match their objectives and their situation. Some of the most frequently encountered managerial issues are discussed below.

Meetings and committees

Participants. Here, too, the participants involved – specifically who represents the technology transfer agency, for example – make a big difference. Are they the extension agents in charge of supervising field work, or are they directors and heads of agencies? Often decision-making on technical matters is vested in bureaucrats who are not fully familiar with the real issues in the field. Sometimes setting up subcommittees, each dealing with specific planning issues, can be a solution (Kaimowitz, 1989). On the other hand, sometimes participation of staff from higher levels is needed, to assure the commitment of an agency as a whole (see below).

Other problems with respect to who takes part are related to high turnover among those involved, and to absences. If representatives of either research or technology transfer change frequently, it will be difficult to develop well-functioning mechanisms. Those who take part in the discussions are apt to be the ones who are most interested in the resulting programmes. If decisions are taken when some important actors are absent, they are less apt to be concerned. The number of participants in meetings is also very important: if it is too large, the interaction between research and technology transfer agents will not be effective. Often researchers dominate the meeting or talk among themselves, suppressing the interests and contributions of extension workers.

Authority. A committee or a meeting that is expected to reach decisions needs a clear mandate, and a clear statement of the extent of its authority. It is difficult for committees (and sometimes also meetings) to operate effectively if their mandate and responsibilities are not clearly specified. A committee often is not sure whether it is a decision making body or a consultative one. Some examples: in Colombia, a committee consisting of departmental directors of institutes collaborating in an integrated rural development programme determined priorities for crop and animal production in the Province of Nariño. However, this mechanism was not effective, because the committee's decisions could not be implemented without getting agreement from the superiors of all of the participating directors (Engel, 1989). On the other hand, the Committee for On-Farm Research and Extension in Zimbabwe (COFRE) has been successful as a priority setting body because of its decision making powers, which make it more than an advisory body (Shumba and Fenner, 1989). Thus, it is preferable to have the real decision makers present at meetings, and even better if they are committee members. When this does not occur, it is clearly problematical, since the recommendations made in the meeting may be implemented slowly or not at all. In fact, when decision makers get their information secondhand, they may not even understand what concerns led to the recommendations; and they certainly will not be able to explain their own rationale – if they refuse to accept these recommendations, meeting participants will not know why.

Objectives. Effective meetings and committees require clear objectives. There should be a good reason for calling a meeting or establishing a committee; and those who attend need to know what is expected of them. Clear objectives, shared by the group, are needed. FSR researchers may state the reason for the meeting and its mandate – a final decision, a recommendation, or simply an FSR presentation, followed by a chance to react; or the group may be asked to set its own objectives. But no matter who decides the objectives, or what they are, they need to be clearly stated, transparent, and understood and accepted by participants.

Agendas and operating rules. A subject strongly related to the objectives of the meeting is that of the agenda. Often the agenda is not well defined. As a result, too many topics are covered, so that discussion is superficial, and no explicit recommendations are produced. The construction of an agenda – not only the type and number of topics to be covered, but also the order in which they are discussed and the way discussion questions are framed – has a great deal to do with the success of a meeting. In a truly participative situation, representatives of the groups involved might share the task of constructing an agenda; or participants might start their meeting by considering a proposed agenda, in which they may make changes before beginning. It is also important to establish proper rules under which a meeting will operate. In systems that use meetings for planning, loosely defined operating rules are all too common. This may be due to simple disorder, but it may also serve to give opportunities – to actors within either research or technology transfer – to control the process in the service of their own interests.

Among situations to be avoided are instances in which researchers come to a meeting with proposals already written, and are unwilling to incorporate changes (Seegers, 1990; Palmieri, 1990). Then meetings serve merely as fora, in which research informs technology transfer of its plans.

(In some such cases, the same information could be exchanged simply by sending written proposals to technology transfer personnel.) Also, sometimes researchers seem to be open to suggestions only if technology transfer is willing to contribute financially to implementation. Meetings that consist of rapid presentations of research results and proposals by researchers are also a problem. Sometimes extension progress reports are presented by extension officers, if they are given the opportunity and the time. Problems with time have been reported in Sri Lanka (Seegers, 1990).

Preparation and format. Meetings and committees can be planned to increase the likelihood of participation of technology transfer agents. For example, a two-stage meeting: transfer agents first meet among themselves and prepare a list of issues to be discussed later with researchers. This gives them an opportunity to express their views and ideas, and may increase their effectiveness in later meetings. Next, either a higher level technology transfer officer reformulates and summarizes the issues listed, and discusses these effectively with researchers; or the agents themselves take part. In this latter case the preliminary meeting serves to achieve a better thought-out set of ideas, and to decrease shyness. Subject-matter specialists and research–extension liaison officers can play an important role in this process.

Costs involved. The organization of meetings, seminars and workshops and the functioning of committees require resources, both in time and money. Using a two-stage meeting approach or a different strategy level, for example, does increase the cost of the priority setting process. Nevertheless, the gain and improvement in participation seem worthwhile. It is important to recognize this and make sure that sufficient funds are allocated when the use of these mechanisms is proposed, and/or to make sure that plans can be realized with the available funds. Another difficulty is that such systems are often not sustainable when donor funds are no longer available (Chapter 7).

Measuring the effectiveness of participation

It is important to frequently evaluate the effectiveness of the mechanisms that are used, with the intention of increasing the participation of technology transfer in FSR priority setting (Merrill-Sands and Kaimowitz, 1990). Mechanisms lose their effectiveness (or may even become obsolete) if their users see them as simple routine. Further, technology systems evolve over time, national objectives and policies are redefined, working procedures and approaches are altered. The approach and mechanisms used to ensure effectiveness also need to evolve, as the orientation and scope of the FSR programme changes.

Most of the FSR&D programmes discussed in this book assume that participation is effective, even though the criteria for effectiveness are not made explicit. Scientists tend to think that participation of extension staff is effective if they accept the proposals made by researchers, or if they make suggestions that can be dealt with easily, without altering the programme significantly. Serious or critical analysis of the programme by extension staff may be perceived as questioning researchers' competence; such participation may be seen by researchers as 'ineffective'.

This suggests a need for the FSR team to agree on criteria for what will be counted as effective participation. We suggest two basic criteria: first, the enhancement of programme relevance; and second, an improvement in the environment of the FSR team. These criteria are obviously rather broadly phrased; more specific indicators need to be developed. In any case, assessment should include the experiences of the researchers and extension staff who are directly and indirectly involved in FSR&D programmes. To date, few FSR projects or programmes have done such an analysis.

Conclusions

This chapter makes clear that increasing the involvement of technology transfer in FSR priority setting is not an easy task. Performance will be highly related to the overall institutional setting in which FSR&D and technology transfer take place. Often tensions and conflicts occur between FSR and technology transfer agents, even though FSR researchers are more field- and farmer-oriented than their colleague researchers working on-station. There are no standard ways to deal with defining a role for technology transfer in FSR priority setting. Each FSR team that sees a benefit in greater involvement of technology transfer agents will have to define an approach that fits its own situation.

While constructing and maintaining intensive linkages means expenditure, in both time and money (with costs varying from case to case), the increased relevance of research and effectiveness of implementation are apt to make creating and maintaining linkages more efficient in the long run. The need to achieve cost effectiveness makes it even more important to assess periodically the approaches and mechanisms used to create and maintain research–extension linkages.

Note

1   The author would like to thank D. Merrill-Sands for comments on an early draft of this paper.

Bibliography

BENNELL P (1989) Intergroup relationships in agricultural technology systems. Linkages Theme Paper no. 2. The Hague: ISNAR

BENNELL P AND ZUIDEMA L (1988) Human resource management for agricultural research: overview and issues. Working Paper no. 15. The Hague: ISNAR

BYERLEE D (1988) Agricultural extension and the development of farmers management skills. In: Howell J, ed, Training and visit extension in practice. Agricultural Administration Unit Paper no. 8. London: Overseas Development Institute

COUSINS B (1988) Agricultural extension and the development of technical messages in Zimbabwe. In: Howell J, ed, Training and visit extension in practice. Agricultural Administration Unit Paper no. 8. London: Overseas Development Institute

ENGEL P (1989) The Narino Subsystem. Unpublished case study document. The Hague: ISNAR

EWELL P (1990) Links between on-farm research and extension in nine countries in making the links. In: Kaimowitz D, ed, Making the link: agricultural research and technology transfer in developing countries. Boulder: Westview Press

HOWELL J (1988) Making agricultural extension effective: lessons of recent experience. In: Howell J, ed, Training and visit extension in practice. Agricultural Administration Unit Paper no. 8. London: Overseas Development Institute

KAIMOWITZ D (1989) Linking research and technology transfer in the development of improved coffee technologies in Colombia. Staff Note no. 89-54. The Hague: ISNAR

KANTER R (1983) The change masters: innovation and entrepreneurship in the American corporation. New York: Simon and Schuster

MANIG W (1992) Development and transfer of appropriate technologies for peasant farmers in developing countries: analysis of linkages between FSR and T and V system organizations. Agricultural Systems no. 38

MERRILL-SANDS D AND KAIMOWITZ D (1990) The technology triangle. The Hague: ISNAR

PALMIERI V (1990) Efectos de los cambio estructurales en el Ministro de Agricultura i Ganaderia de Costa Rica. Linkages Discussion Paper no. 7. The Hague: ISNAR

QUISUMBING E (1984) New directions in research-extension linkages. In: Elz D, ed, The planning and management of agricultural resesarch: a World Bank and ISNAR symposium. Washington DC: World Bank

RUANO S AND FUMAGALLI A (1988) Organizacion y manejo de la Investigación en el Instituto de la Ciencia i Tecnologia Agricola, OFCOR Case Study no. 2. The Hague: ISNAR

RUSSELL J (1991) Developing farmer-extension research linkages to address the needs of resource poor farmers in rainfed environment. In: Prasad D and Das P, eds, Extension strategies for rainfed agriculture. New Delhi: Indian Society of Extension Science

SEEGERS S (1990) The training and visit system and links between rice research and extension in the Matara District of Sri Lanka. Linkages Discussion Paper no. 8. The Hague: ISNAR

SEEGERS S AND KAIMOWITZ D (1989) Relations between agricultural researchers and extension workers; the survey evidence. Linkages Discussion Paper no. 2. The Hague: ISNAR

SHUMBA E AND FENNER R (1989) Linking research and extension through on-farm research and demonstrations. The Zimbabwe experience. In: Merrill-Sands D and Kaimowitz D, eds, The technology triangle. The Hague: ISNAR

SOUDER W (1980) Promoting an effective R&D/marketing interface. Journal of Research Management 3(1)

WUYTS-FIVAWO A (1992) Management of intergroup linkages for agricultural technology systems. Linkages Discussion Paper no. 12. The Hague: ISNAR

6 Policymakers, planners and donors in FSR priority setting

R. James Bingen

Policymakers, planners and donors expect FSR&D to help get agriculture moving throughout much of Africa, Asia, Latin America, and the Middle East. As a result of such expectations, the FSR&D priority setting process commonly looks like a major balancing act – between, on the one hand, the interests of researchers, and, on the other, the diverse, shifting, and sometimes conflicting, interests of policymakers, planners, and donors. In this process, the success of FSR&D programmes frequently hinges on the ability of researchers to identify these various outside actors accurately, and deal with them effectively.

This chapter challenges FSR&D programmes to think more creatively about the involvement of policymakers, planners and donors during their priority setting processes. I argue that FSR&D programmes can be more creative if they begin to draw upon these actors as partners, not as adversaries, in priority setting. Further, it is argued that more creative approaches to priority setting depend upon the ability of FSR&D programmes to assess and appreciate the various reasons why these partners want to be involved.

The first part of the chapter suggests that FSR&D programmes may find it useful to distinguish between the strategic and non-strategic interests which lead policymakers, planners and donors to be involved in FSR&D priority setting. These interests differ along one critical dimension: strategic interests are considered to be crucial to the operation or life of an FSR&D programme.

The following section reviews several formal and informal mechanisms used by FSR&D programmes to manage the influence of outside actors in their priority setting processes, and to accommodate their various interests. The chapter concludes with some suggested guidelines for improving the management of linkages with policymakers, planners and donors during FSR&D priority setting.

Position and role of policymakers, planners and donors

Why do policymakers, planners and donors participate in FSR&D priority setting, and what roles do they play, or seek to play? Two major assumptions underlie this discussion. First, most FSR&D programmes are embedded within some type of larger government structure – a national research agency or institute and/or a government ministry. This situation creates conditions that have an important impact on FSR&D priority setting. It means that the priority setting process must conform to some set or sets of pre-determined government rules, regulations, and guidelines. These can involve several different types of government directives or rulings, ranging from policy preferences and priorities to standard operating and budgeting procedures and processes. For example, FSR&D programmes frequently must submit proposed budgets for the next fiscal year before they have been able to review the results of on-going research activities.

FSR&D programmes must appreciate that their governmental 'embeddedness' creates opportunities for various government policymakers and planners to get involved in FSR&D. Policymakers and planners commonly take advantage of (and sometimes create) these opportunities irrespective of any formal or mandated responsibility vis-à-vis an FSR&D programme. In other words, FSR&D must anticipate that a variety of government policymakers and planners may use their positions to express an interest in, or to justify the exercise of some type of influence over, FSR&D priority setting.

The second underlying assumption is that FSR&D programmes can and do seek some reciprocal influence over the policymakers and planners who may get involved, and over the timing of their involvement in priority setting. That is, FSR&D programmes confront choices and can make decisions concerning how they want to create or shape the involvement of other government actors. FSR&D programmes should not simply react to their environments. FSR&D priority setting can be a proactive process. The 'supply driven' mode adopted by some FSR&D programmes illustrates this type of choice, and the efforts of FSR&D to exert influence on the environment (Dixon, 1991; Baker, 1991).

Strategic partners: national policies and financial resources

Policymakers, planners and donors confront FSR&D programmes with strategic contingencies. These represent major uncertainties for FSR&D. They reflect interests that are crucial to the operation of FSR&D and that directly affect the ability of FSR&D to achieve its programme goals.

Government partners

Government policymakers typically want to assure that FSR&D priorities respond directly to their concerns. National or local policymakers may require some evidence of conformity between FSR&D priorities and agricultural development policies. This interest may arise from a direct and well-defined policy objective or a more broadly defined agricultural development policy (Stoop and Bingen, 1991). The initial focus of the Zambia ARPT on hybrid maize, even in marginal maize production areas, illustrates the influence that national and territorial policymakers can exercise over FSR&D programming (Vierstra and Ndiyoi, Chapter 10).

Alternatively, national policy may want to assure that FSR&D priorities reflect a measure of conformity to more general development policy objectives. Recent decisions in Mali and Senegal illustrate the significantly different and critical influence that this type of concern may have on an FSR&D programme. In response to the government's territorial decentralization policy in Mali, the agricultural research system will be restructured into regionally based research programmes. This restructuring will clearly affect the way FSR&D balances its national programme priorities with more regionally based interests (Bingen, 1991). In contrast, the national agricultural institute in Senegal (ISRA, Institut Sénégalais Recherches Agricoles) combined its successful and well-known FSR&D department with other research departments, to achieve the operational and programme savings required under the country's structural adjustment programme agreement. It is not clear if these cost-saving moves have permitted FSR&D researchers to protect and sustain their farming systems research priorities.

Finally, government extension agencies may get directly involved in FSR&D priority setting as a function of a contract research agreement with an FSR&D programme. FSR&D programmes usually see such contracts as attractive sources of financial and logistic support, however, they may have to sacrifice longer term research priorities to meet the shorter term contract obligations involved (Faye and Bingen, 1989).

Donor agency partners

The policies of donor agencies typically represent the second major type of strategic contingency in FSR&D priority setting. These policies directly affect the financial resources required to implement FSR&D programmes. The chilling effect of recent policy shifts by two significant donors, the US Agency for International Development (USAID) and the World Bank, on

FSR&D programmes throughout Sub-Saharan Africa illustrates the crucial importance of donors to FSR&D: USAID's preoccupation with quantification of the impact of agricultural research, and the World Bank's preference for investments in research management and programme monitoring, have clearly influenced the priorities of many FSR&D programmes.[1]

Donor agencies frequently use their own policy priorities to influence those of FSR&D programmes. Most such agencies exercise influence through periodic project evaluations. These evaluations can affect FSR&D priorities in several ways. Most commonly, evaluation teams recommend programme modifications. In Mali, evaluations initiated by the Dutch government were instrumental, among other things, in establishing a research component to address women's issues; and in negotiating a research protocol with the government extension agency, to address soil fertility and conservation issues (Zuidberg and Kortbeek, Chapter 12; van Campen, Chapter 13). Donor agencies, however, may also use these evaluations to 'shock' a significant reorientation into an FSR&D programme (Bingen et al., 1992a). Similarly, several international research agencies or programmes, like the US-based Collaborative Research Support Programmes (CRSPs), are crucial to the operation of FSR&D programmes. International research agencies commonly involve FSR&D in running varietal trials (Stoop and Bingen, 1991) or in providing critical technical and training support (Bingen and Poats, 1990; Bingen et al., 1992b).

Non-strategic partners

Several other policymakers and planners do not have a strategic impact on FSR&D priority setting. Their interests do not represent critical uncertainties for FSR&D; they do not jeopardize the operation of an FSR&D programme. Instead, these policymakers and planners may seek to influence FSR&D priorities, or can be brought into the priority setting process by an FSR&D programme, because of the relationship between the official responsibilities of their office or agency and the FSR&D programme.

National partners

The relationship of many of these 'associate partners' with FSR&D is based on a definition of the links between the two programmes as complementary or collaborative. This may be initiated by either side. Major partners are extension and other research institutes, including universities. Some associate partners may express only a general interest in assuring that an FSR&D

programme includes certain themes or topics. Responsibility for a country's multilocational testing programme encourages many extension agencies to follow FSR&D programmes (Bingen et al., 1992a). In the absence of a contract or research protocol, however, most extension agencies usually reflect little more than general curiosity about FSR&D programme priorities and activities (Stoop and Bingen, 1991; Faye and Bingen, 1989).

Other, non-FSR&D researchers, may exhibit a similarly casual approach to FSR&D priority setting, especially when financing for their own programmes is relatively secure. On the other hand, financial uncertainty in non-FSR&D programmes can stimulate considerable, and highly competitive, institutional jealousies among other researchers (Merrill-Sands et al., 1991; Collinson, 1988). In some cases, these jealousies may even threaten an FSR&D programme. In Senegal, for example, it is possible that a coalition of non-FSR&D researchers effectively used the issue of financial uncertainty as grounds to terminate the FSR&D programme.

University agricultural scientists may be among the most important, though largely silent, associate partners of FSR&D. In several countries, agricultural science programmes usually include some type of student field practicum, which could both build upon and complement FSR&D programmes. In addition, individual university faculty and FSR&D researchers commonly carry out collaborative research activities. As reported in Benin, however, an entirely different 'working rhythm and objectives' has made broader collaboration between the Agricultural Sciences Faculty at the National University and the FSR&D programme difficult (Chapter 11). Furthermore, even when externally funded projects have provided the funding for such collaboration, it has been difficult for FSR&D programmes to develop institutional collaborative relations with universities (Bingen et al., 1992a).

International partners

Donor agencies, and especially the international research centres, frequently become very important associate partners in FSR&D priority setting. The influence of several international centres, especially CIMMYT (International Wheat and Maize Improvement Centre), IITA and IRRI (International Rice Institute) on FSR&D field methodology directly affects programme priority setting (Chapter 11; Bingen et al., 1992b). In fact, the fundamental differences between 'anglophone' and 'francophone' approaches to FSR&D essentially reflect the relative influence of different international research agencies on national FSR&D programmes (Faye and Bingen, 1989).

Formal participation of policymakers, planners and donors

This section reviews various ways FSR&D programmes can try to organize the participation of policymakers, planners and donors, thereby exercising a measure of control over the influence of these actors on priority setting. Government rules and regulations define the most formal, and usually fixed, occasions for national policymakers and planners to influence FSR&D priority setting. Each occasion represents an opportunity for FSR&D programmes to defend their programme priorities.

Annual reviews

Most governments require some type of annual programme review of agricultural research. In Mali, specialized technical commissions annually review research results and prepare programme proposals for the coming year. Based on these reviews and recommendations, the national committee for agronomic research sets national research policy and priorities.[2] The Rwanda agricultural research institute (ISAR) conducts a similar annual review among its researchers (Stoop and Bingen, 1991). In Senegal, on the other hand, the national research institute (ISRA) uses the mandated, annual meetings of its interministerial management and international scientific and technical committees to determine research policy and priorities (Faye and Bingen, 1989).

Local or provincial level reviews serve a similar purpose for the expression of other sets of interests in FSR&D programmes. In Zambia and Tanzania, for example, FSR&D priorities must correspond to provincial and district priorities (Chapter 10; Enserink et al., Chapter 8).

The actual influence of these annual reviews on specific FSR&D priorities can vary significantly from country to country. In Senegal, ISRA's scientific and technical committee decided to disband the FSR&D department. In Mali, on the other hand, the annual research reviews appear to be primarily a formal, public mechanism to recognize and validate previously agreed-upon research priorities.[3] Each type of formal review, however, offers opportunities for FSR&D to play a more proactive role by seizing the initiative and managing the influence of both its strategic and associate partners in priority setting.

Project-related reviews

Regular reviews linked to the planning cycles of donor projects reveal the vulnerabilities in FSR&D programme control over the priority setting process. These reviews and periodic evaluations may follow a regular, known calendar, but their agendas may represent real 'wild cards' for FSR&D programming. Under these circumstances, FSR&D programmes have little room for manoeuvre.

Informal and operational links

In addition to the formal and mandated review and planning processes, FSR&D programmes employ several types of operational procedures and mechanisms to link policymakers, planners and donors in priority setting.

Delivery-level links

Most FSR&D programmes use a variety of both formal and informal approaches to establish linkages with various planning and policymaking units that may be directly involved with farmers in the identification, development and transfer of improved technology. For FSR&D, delivery-level links are 'where the action is'. Some programmes engage other technical and planning services at the local level in formal planning workshops designed around special techniques, such as the objective oriented project planning (OOPP) method. Such workshops have helped to build inter-agency ownership in FSR&D priorities in both Mali and Zambia (Kooijman et al., Chapter 9, Chapter 10). Most programmes organize regular, formal 'research-extension' meetings that do not rely on the use of a special planning methodology. In some cases, these meetings may be driven by the need to respond to the conditions of a research–extension contract or protocol.[4] In many other cases, FSR&D programmes effectively use such meetings to help keep channels of communication open among the various local-level development actors (Meindertsma et al., Chapter 7; van Sluys and Silva, Chapter 14).

Policy-level links

FSR&D programmes may also organize formal, open presentations of their research findings and results. These presentations can help to improve the impact of FSR&D on public policy (Dixon, 1991). Equally important, such meetings can help FSR&D programmes identify, and thereby improve, their ability to manage the influence of others on research priorities. FSR&D research results from household level can both help to inform policy formulation and assist in policy analysis. As Low suggests, FSR&D may not only influence research and extension policy, it can also raise new policy issues and assess policy impact (Low, 1991; also see Tripp et al., 1990; Baker, 1991).

The pursuit of policy links, however, runs two important risks. First, these may lead FSR&D teams to rush to questionable policy conclusions (Tripp, 1992). Second, they can raise the political profile of FSR&D, and thereby increase its vulnerability to changing political winds. Given the minimal impact of FSR&D on agricultural development policy in general, however, such risks might be worth taking (Byerlee and Tripp, 1988; Dixon, 1991).

The variety of mechanisms used by FSR&D programmes to set up links to policymakers, planners and donors demonstrates considerable room for exercising a measure of entrepreneurship. In other words, FSR&D programmes can try to manipulate the influence that others seek to wield over FSR&D priority setting. By adapting to the political and institutional rules of the game, FSR&D programmes can successfully organize, and directly benefit from, the constructive participation and contribution of policymakers, planners and donors. Even the most successful FSR&D entrepreneurs, however, confront significant hurdles as they seek to manipulate their environment.

Issues and options

Shifting donor policy priorities

Fewer than 10 years ago, many donor agencies looked to FSR&D as a revolutionary force in agricultural research. Farming systems programmes were seen as vehicles for revitalizing the process of technology development and transfer. Some observers even suggested that FSR&D might give a voice to resource-poor farmers regarding agricultural development (Norman, 1980). The glow of the movement has clearly waned, and donor investments in agricultural research throughout the developing world are increasingly (and more closely) scrutinized. Under these conditions, those committed to FSR&D must ensure that their programme priorities are linked in a clearly identifiable way to donor agency interests and policies. More than ever before, FSR&D is under pressure to show results. Donor agencies want to see the impact of FSR&D. They want (correctly) to know not only if the financial and technical resources given to provide a product have produced the expected product, but also whether the product has had an impact on development.[5]

Such demands have been recognized for some time as misdirected (Biggs, 1989; de Lattre, 1990; Marcotte and Swanson, 1987). Nevertheless, in response to such a strategic contingency, as discussed earlier, FSR&D programmes commonly seek credibility – and, hopefully, continued funding – by working in agroecological areas where problems are presumably easier to solve. There is little evidence that such an FSR&D survival strategy has sacrificed attention to more critical, apparent or pressing development issues.

On the other hand, there is some evidence that donor policy swings and shifts can seriously jeopardize the contribution of FSR&D to more effective policy design and implementation. For example, just as FSR&D researchers were beginning to identify the impact of structural adjustment policies on Gambian farmers, FSR&D funding was cut (McPherson and Posner, 1991).

No amount of entrepreneurship will protect FSR&D from pre-determined policy decisions. Nevertheless, not all decisions are predetermined: as part of a successful survival strategy, FSR&D must shed its 'conservative stance' for a more proactive posture in the policy process (Byerlee and Tripp, 1988).

The institutionalization of FSR&D

The demand for FSR&D usually originates with national governments and donor agencies. Local, grassroots decision makers rarely press for FSR&D as a means to address local problems and concerns. Moreover, most countries lack a national lobby for FSR&D – despite the evidence that such groups have played especially critical roles in building strong national research programmes, especially in some Sub-Saharan African countries (e.g. Senegal and Zimbabwe). The establishment or renewal of research lobbies could be one means through which FSR&D programmes might find an element of stability in their uncertain environments.

More immediately, FSR&D programmes can address several more specific issues that may directly improve their effectiveness and success. First, it is widely recognized that the lack of experience and narrow backgrounds of many FSR&D teams significantly weaken FSR&D credibility in both scientific and policy arenas (Bingen and Poats, 1990). Narrow disciplinary training reinforces a tendency among agricultural scientists to collect a lot of information on a lot of variables, to improve their ability to generalize only within well-defined margins. As a result, cartons of questionnaires and data sheets tend to pile up in many FSR&D offices. In many cases, the data will never be analyzed, because the original research objectives lacked clarity, specificity and direct relevance to the real-world problems of rural households. Clearly, research leadership can help to overcome data blockages that stand in the way of effectiveness.[6]

Second, very few countries have successfully resolved the fit between national FSR&D programmes and subnational (territorial) policymaking priorities. In Rwanda, the heads of new regional research centres are to be responsible for making sure that agricultural research programmes respond to regional development priorities. In Mali, on the other hand, new regional technical committees are intended to ensure that national research programmes respond to regional development needs. Both cases reflect governmental decisions to use public agricultural research as a way to distribute political goods, and to respond to local development concerns and issues. Clearly, research managers need to be aware of the implications of such decisions as they seek working compromises between local political and scientific programme interests.

Finally, few national FSR&D programmes have successfully overcome what appears to be their historically determined destiny to favour larger farmers over resource-poor farmers (Clark, 1985). In the Cameroon, for example, research performance contracts that encourage the development of easy-to-adapt technologies tend to disregard both marginal agro-ecological areas and resource-poor farmers (Baker, 1991).

This suggests that FSR&D might explore ways to build a measure of institutional pluralism into its programmes. In part, this means creating opportunities to incorporate local NGOs and farmer groups into FSR&D programming. The NGO link is not a panacea for FSR&D, but there is evidence of some NGO successes in technology development and transfer for low-income farmers in marginal environments (Farrington and Biggs, 1990).

Ultimately, FSR&D might improve its ability to influence policymakers, planners and donors through its grassroots links in the countryside. As democratic and popular movements slowly gain power throughout the developing world, FSR&D should be prepared to build upon new, popular initiatives. In this way, perhaps the early ambition of FSR&D to give a voice to farmers can finally be fulfilled.

Notes

1   In addition, a donor agency's budgeting cycle can directly affect the FSR&D priority setting process. Frequent uncertainty in the availability of operating funds seriously weakened the FSR&D programme in Senegal (Faye and Bingen, 1989).

2   Burkina Faso organizes a similar national review of agricultural research; see Bingen et al., 1992a.

3   The role of the annual ISRA reviews in Rwanda appears even more formalistic; see Stoop and Bingen, 1991.

4   The effectiveness of such meetings remains doubtful (Faye and Bingen, 1989). The training and visit system of extension, recently adopted in many Sub-Saharan countries, also calls for regular planning and information meetings between research and extension. The effectiveness of these meetings remains questionable (Bingen et al., 1993).

5   In a similar fashion, in their contracts with FSR&D programmes, extension agencies usually require technical information and results.

6   Employment of more experienced rural social scientists may also help to assure the relevance, and thereby the connection to policy, of FSR&D research (Byerlee and Tripp, 1988). As the experience with FSR&D in Senegal shows, however, rural sociologists do not necessarily bring a strong policy orientation to a team (Faye and Bingen, 1989).

Bibliography

BAKER D (1991) Puzzle resolution in Southern Cameroon: building FSR-development linkages. Paper presented at the 11th Annual Symposium of the Association for Farming Systems Research-Extension. Michigan State University, October 5-10, 1991

BAKER D (1992) Inability of farming systems research to deal with agricultural policy. Paper presented at the 12th Annual Symposium of the Association for Farming Systems Research-Extension, Michigan State University, September 13-18, 1992

BIGGS SD (1989) A multiple source of innovation model of agricultural research and technology promotion. ODI Network Paper 6. London: ODI

BINGEN RJ (1991) Institutional analysis for the Mali SPARC project. Annex in: Agency for international development, Mali, strengthening research planning and research on commodities (SPARC), Project Paper (688-0250), unclassified, March 31, 1992

BINGEN RJ AND POATS SV (1990) Staff management issues in on-farm client-oriented research. OFCOR Comparative Study no. 5. The Hague: ISNAR

BINGEN RJ, LICHTE J AND MCMILLAN D (1992a) Mid-term evaluation report. Agricultural research and training support project (ARTS). Consultancy report of project 686-0270, prepared for USAID/Ouagadougou

BINGEN RJ, ADUPA RL, MASAMBU H AND TRIPP R (1992b) CIMMYT II farming systems research project. Project 698-0435-03. Final evaluation report. Mexico: CIMMYT

BINGEN RJ, BERTHÉ A AND SIMPSON B (1993) Analysis of service delivery systems to farmers and village associations in the zone of the office de la Haute Vallée du Niger. Consultancy report of the project Haute Vallée Development Project, prepared for USAID/Bamako under a subcontract with Development Alternatives, Inc. (DAI), Bethesda, Maryland

BYERLEE D AND TRIPP RJ (1988) Strengthening linkages in agricultural research through a farming systems perspective: the role of social scientists. Experimental Agriculture 24: 137–151

CLARK N (1985) The political economy of science and technology. Oxford: Basil Blackwell

COLLINSON M (1988) The development of African farming systems: some personal views. Agricultural Administration & Extension 29: 7-22

DIXON J (1991) Review of applications of the farming systems approach in agricultural policy analysis. Paper presented at the 11th Annual Symposium of the Association for Farming Systems Research-Extension, Michigan State University, October 5-10, 1991

FARRINGTON J AND BIGGS SD (1990) NGOs, agricultural technology and the rural poor. Food Policy: 479–491

FAYE J AND BINGEN RJ (1989) Sénégal, organization et gestion de la recherche sur les systèmes de production. OFCOR Case Study no. 6. The Hague: ISNAR

FRIEDRICH K-H AND HALL M (1991) The institutionalization of the farmings systems approach – from concept to operations. Paper presented at the 11th Annual Symposium of the Association for Farming Systems Research-Extension, Michigan State University, October 5-10, 1991

HEINEMANN E AND BIGGS SD (1984) Farming systems research: an evolutionary approach to implementation. Journal of Agricultural Economics 36: 59-65

LATTRE DE M (1990) La gestion stratégique des rélations des instituts de recherche avec leur environnement. Les cas des instituts de recherche agricole du Cameroun et du Sénégal. (Thèse de doctorat nouveau régime, Paris X-Nanterre, U.E.R. de Sciences Economiques et Gestion/Ph.D thesis)

LOW A (1991) The utilization of farming systems data in agricultural policy analysis in eastern and southern Africa. (Draft Working Paper, Farm Management and Production Economics Service). Rome: FAO

LOW A AND WADDINGTON S (1991) Farming systems adaptive research achievements and prospects in southern Africa. Experimental Agriculture 27: 115-125

MARCOTTE P AND SWANSON LE (1987) The disarticulation of farming systems research with national agricultural systems: bringing FSR back in. Agricultural Administration & Extension 27: 75-91

MCPHERSON MF AND POSNER JL (1991) Structural adjustment and agriculture in Sub-Saharan Africa: lessons from the Gambia. Paper presented at the 11th Annual Symposium of the Association for Farming Systems Research-Extension, Michigan State University, October 5-10, 1991

MERRILL-SANDS D, BIGGS SD, BINGEN RJ, EWELL PT, MCALLISTER JL AND POATS SV (1991) Integrating on-farm research into national agricultural research systems: lessons for research policy, organization and management. In: Tripp R, ed, Planned change in farming systems: progress in on-farm research, pp 287–316. New York: John Wiley & Sons

NORMAN D (1980) The farming systems approach: relevancy for the small farmer. MSU Rural Development Paper no. 5. East Lansing, Michigan: Department of Agricultural Economics, Michigan State University

STOOP WA AND BINGEN RJ (1991) 'Systems research' or 'research with a systems perspective' in Africa. Some organizational and technical issues. Agricultural Systems 35: 235–249

TRIPP R (1992) Expectations and realities in on-farm research. Paper presented at the CIMMYT workshop 'Impacts of On-Farm Research', Harare, Zimbabwe, June 23-26, 1992

TRIPP R, ANANDAJAYASEKERAM P, BYERLEE D AND HARRINGTON L (1990) Farming systems research revisited. In: Eicher C and Staatz J, eds, Agricultural development in the third world. Second edition. Baltimore: The Johns Hopkins University Press, pp 384–399

II Project experiences

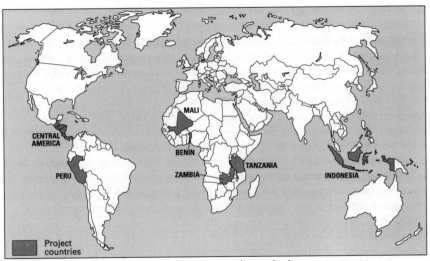

Shading denotes countries or areas where case studies took place

Project description: ATA-272, Indonesia

ATA-272 is a Dutch-funded project of the Indonesian Agency for Agricultural Research and Development (AARD). The project, based in Malang, East Java, started in 1982; its aim is to strengthen the research capability of MARIF, the Malang Research Institute for Food Crops. In Phase V of ATA-272, the name of the project was changed to 'Technology Development for Farmers' to express the new orientation towards adaptive research. FSR came to be an important component of the ATA-272 project, although research started in earlier phases continued, including pest control, post-harvest questions, virology, breeding, and a gene bank. MARIF and the ATA-272 project developed an FSR programme in pilot areas. The first FSR pilot programme started in Lombok, in October 1990.[1] It is a collaboration between MARIF; the extension service, the Agency for Food Crops in West Nusa Tenggara Province (DIPERTA-NTB); and the agricultural faculty of the University of Mataram (UNRAM).

The FSR programme focuses on Southeast Lombok. Southeast Lombok is known as a 'critical area', where there is still an imminent threat of food shortages in years with long dry spells during the rainy season. The agricultural year consists of three seasons: a rainy season, which lasts from November–March, a short dry season April–June, and a prolonged dry season July–November. Annual rainfall ranges from 800–1,400 mm. Only a small proportion of farmers in the area have access to water resources other than rainfall, such as small dams, man-made water reservoirs, and overflow water from irrigation schemes in the west. Lack of water is a major limiting factor for agricultural production in the area.

Lowlands occupy about 80–90% of the agricultural land. The remainder is made up of hilly uplands (tegal). The lowland is slightly undulating; the heavy clay soils (vertisols) complicate land preparation, due to swelling and shrinking. These rainfed lowlands are flooded during the rainy season and used for rice cultivation. Most of the lowlands are fully dependent on direct rainfall, which allows only two crops per year. The dominant cropping pattern in these areas is rice–soybean–fallow. Rice is the main staple food and is traditionally transplanted. Soybean cultivation is characterized by a very meagre technology and low production yields.

Only half of rural households own land. Half of the landowners have less than 0.5 ha, whereas at least one hectare is needed to satisfy the basic needs (food and cash) of an average household. Therefore, off-farm activities are an important source of additional household income.

7 From diagnosis to priority research themes: ATA-272, Indonesia

J. Douwe Meindertsma, H. Suyamto and Tri Wibowo

In 1990, the head of the Department of Food Crops of West Nusa Tenggara Province (DIPERTA-NTB) made a request to MARIF during a three-day seminar on 'Improvements in agricultural technology' to initiate an FSR programme in Lombok. Participants concluded that the results of research programmes presented at the workshop were fragmented, oriented to specific topics (some technical and some socioeconomic), and did not adequately take the place and role of the primary decision making unit, the farm household, into consideration.

This chapter focuses on the first two years of the resulting programme. It specifically addresses the diagnostic phase, a characteristic element of FSR aimed at identifying relevant problems and setting realistic research priorities. In the first year, programme formulation was done with minimal diagnosis of local conditions and farmers' problems. Second year planning incorporated the results of a rapid rural appraisal (RRA). Based on these experiences, the role of diagnosis – defined here as 'systematic efforts to assess farmers' conditions and problems' – in research priority setting is explored. We look at the way problems identified during the diagnostic phase are translated into research themes, with emphasis on the process rather than the outcome. As will be seen, researchers, extension workers, and farmers began with different perceptions of farmers' problems. The RRA was instrumental in achieving a common focus. Examples are given to illustrate shifts in research priorities.

Before going on to describe the process of programme formulation, the institutional structure, mandate, and research approach of the parent organization are reviewed. These factors indicate the boundaries for programme formulation and affect the priority setting process. The way an FSR programme is initiated and institutionally embedded determines its room for manoeuvre.

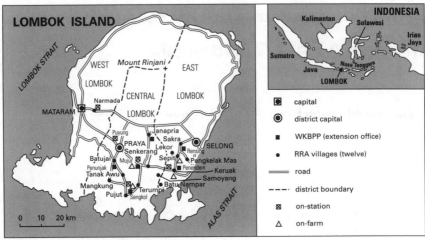

Indonesia, with an enlarged map of Lombok

Institutional setting

Beginning in the early eighties, MARIF conducted various types of on-farm, cropping systems and farming systems oriented research, supported by institutions such as CIMMYT *(Centro Internacional de Mejoramiento de Maiz y Trigo)*, IRRI (International Rice Research Institute), and several bilateral donors. Albeit following somewhat different approaches, these programmes were primarily commodity-oriented,[2] reflecting the commodity-based organizational structure of MARIF. Further, various commodity sections carried out their own on-farm research programmes (e.g. on maize, cassava, soybeans). Running parallel on-farm programmes had several shortcomings:

- analysis of the interaction of particular crops with other productive activities of the farmer (such as livestock, rice, and access to productive resources) was weak or lacking;
- lack of communication between on-farm researchers in the various commodity programmes led to duplication of efforts (e.g. the cassava section started cassava–maize intercropping trials and the maize section maize–cassava intercropping trials in the same area);
- the already poorly staffed socioeconomic section was unable to respond to requests from various commodity programmes to carry out diagnostic surveys, evaluate field trials, and so forth.

   In addition, MARIF changed the location of on-farm experiments frequently, sometimes after just one agricultural season. Therefore diagnosis was minimal, and relations with the extension service were superficial and of short duration. This situation called for more integration of on-farm research. Moreover, since its initiation, MARIFs' mandate had been to conduct research on non-rice food crops – *palawija* crops. But rice is a central crop in these farming systems, which cannot be ignored in conducting FSR. CRIFC, the Central Research Institute for Food Crops (and MARIF's mother institute), acknowledged that more flexibility was required, as 'the major FSR thrust is to improve farmers' incomes and productivity through suitable production technologies and crop diversification' (Manwan, 1989).

In 1990, MARIF was given a regional mandate, for the eastern part of Indonesia,[3] to commission research programmes covering all activities of farmers. This allowed a broadening of the scope of its research activities.

Because of the enlarged mandate, the opportunity to start an FSR programme in Lombok was very attractive to MARIF/ATA-272: it was in line with the Indonesian national development objective of increasing attention to the least developed part of the country; early involvement of the agricultural and extension services in planning and implementation of the FSR programme was virtually ensured; *palawija* crops, in particular soybean, were given relatively high importance; an FSR programme could build on existing MARIF commodity research and make use of a small number of MARIF staff already stationed in Lombok; the relatively small size of the province favoured both close collaboration, from provincial to village level, and the possibility of making a proportionately large impact on the agricultural development of Lombok. Therefore, by early October 1990, the project decided to initiate an FSR programme in Lombok.[4]

MARIF/ATA-272 agreed to adopt a pilot area approach; a pragmatic, comprehensive FSR programme would be developed allowing farmer-oriented, interdisciplinary research. No single methodology would be prescribed. Decisions and actions would be guided by the objective of producing quick and concrete results, of direct benefit to farmers. The programme would develop agricultural technologies for all food crops, including rice, which is the staple crop. In the diagnosis, all possible productive activities would be assessed. MARIF researchers would concentrate on food crops, while other research institutes would deal with farm activities such as tobacco farming, livestock keeping or vegetable growing. (Eventually, after the diagnosis, others' involvement was limited: priority was given first to achieving a major impact on food crops, in line with the interest of the majority of farmers in the drought-prone areas.) The agricultural services were to be involved in the FSR programme early on, not only in programme implementation but also in planning and evaluation. While these services primarily focused on rural extension, MARIF staff had to maintain a strong research orientation. Using this 'constructive tension' to really embark on development-oriented research was an on-going challenge for the FSR programme.

Organization and planning mechanisms

Within MARIF, no specific 'FSR group' was created. Researchers participating in the FSR programme continue to fulfil duties in their respective commodity programmes (grains, grain legumes, root and tuber crops) and/or disciplinary sections (crop protection, agronomy, breeding, socioeconomics). Depending on their workload and schedule, some researchers become more involved in the FSR programme than others. Their participation also varies from season to season. We consider this a favourable situation. MARIF researchers who are directly involved in FSR bring with them knowledge and experience of technological components and packages. They also help to maintain a smooth relationship with MARIF staff who are not involved. At critical moments in the research activities (monitoring trials, planning and evaluation meetings, diagnostic activities, and so forth) MARIF/ATA-272 researchers go to Lombok; in addition, collaborating parties from Lombok come to MARIF headquarters in Malang. The famous gap between FSR researchers – as a separate group – and other researchers is thus less likely to occur. On the other hand, extra care is required in the design of experiments. Some commodity researchers tend to simply shift their usual way of setting up trials from the station to farmers' fields. This has led to constructive discussions among agronomists and economists on trial type, design, lay-out, location, monitoring and data collection and, last but not least, farmer participation.

MARIF/ATA-272 has staff permanently stationed in Lombok: a site coordinator, an agronomist-extension specialist (expatriate), an agroeconomist, and a small staff of technicians. In addition to FSR research, these staff also conduct commodity research and work closely with extension staff. DIPERTA has assigned their FSR coordinator and four officers at provincial level (who are in charge of the agronomic research in the intervention zones) to work with the programme. The FSR coordinators from DIPERTA supervise DIPERTA field staff involved in trials; similar arrangements are used for MARIF/ATA-272 researchers. DIPERTA staff are also involved in socioeconomic research. University UNRAM staff are involved mainly in planning and evaluating activities, although they also render specific services if required, such as soil analysis. As their tasks are in essence not different from those of MARIF/ATA-272 researchers, their role has been difficult to define. Consequently, their involvement has decreased over time.

Before the start of each season (once every 3 to 4 months) a planning meeting is held, attended by the coordinators and heads of institutions. In these meetings, decisions are taken on new activities for the next season. All research activities are presented in a standard research protocol.[5] Yearly meetings are held to review the activities of the previous year and to plan for the next year. In addition, seminars or workshops are organized around specific events or themes. Examples are the seminar to present RRA results, and meetings to discuss seed supply, post-harvest problems, women's issues and so forth. Further, ad hoc meetings are organized for visitors from national research institutes or the donor to review the progress of the project.

During the season, the Lombok local team meets regularly, in peak periods weekly, to distribute work and discuss implementation issues. Apart from a small permanent team, the number and characteristics of the people participating in the programme are not constant. Adaptations can be made when and if needs arise. Therefore, flexible planning is required for effective researcher input. Specific arrangements have been created for the planning and review of activities. This is sometimes difficult, as both FSR and commodity research compete for researchers' time. It is also problematic that the more demanding tasks, such as the analysis, synthesis and writing up of RRA results must be done by a relatively small group. This work requires high quality and staff dedication. Staff participating for shorter periods (e.g. those on contract for specific activities) can make only a partial contribution to these essential activities.

Getting started: first programme year

At the start of the FSR programme in Lombok, the MARIF/ATA-272 FSR coordinators (a senior MARIF soil scientist and a Dutch agroeconomist, who were responsible for organizing the FSR programme, initiating FSR in pilot areas, and involving other MARIF/ATA-272 researchers) outlined a three-year programme, with agronomic and socioeconomic research as the primary foci (MARIF/ATA-272, 1990). This programme was discussed with the participating researchers and extension workers as well as the heads of collaborating institutions. It was agreed to concentrate first year research on activities of a diagnostic nature, with the following four components:

rapid rural appraisal; on-station trials; monitoring farm enterprises; and testing packages on farmers' fields.[6] Also, DIPERTA's proposal to concentrate activities in the rainfed, drought-prone areas in the southeastern part of Lombok was accepted: 80% of attention was to be devoted to this resource-poor area and 20% to the more favoured irrigated areas. It was further decided to focus on rainfed lowlands, as the uplands were already covered by another project.[7] Researchers and extension staff jointly selected specific research locations, such as substations and villages for trials and rapid rural appraisals.

Rapid rural appraisal as a major diagnostic tool

A rapid rural appraisal (RRA) was chosen as a major instrument for the diagnostic phase of the programme. Other instruments used were: a system of monitoring farmers' practices, for a selected group of farmers;[8] collection of secondary data; and an assessment of available production technology. Here we will focus on the RRA and, as RRAs are widely described in the literature, will simply highlight some essential features and experiences of this process in Lombok.

Scope and objectives. The objectives of the RRA were to:
• gain a better understanding of the farmer's environment (physical, climatological, institutional, socioeconomic and cultural);
• describe and analyze the agricultural production systems operated by farmers, taking into account farmer preferences, objectives and access to productive resources;
• identify major weak and strong points in farming systems and problems faced by farmers;
• based on the above, develop a research programme to improve the existing farming system.

The checklist, used for informal interviews, covered physical production conditions; the agricultural year as a whole, including cropping patterns and crops; household activities, including off-farm activities and access to resources; and institutional issues, such as credit, marketing and post-harvest. Therefore the RRA had a broad character, focusing on the farm household as well as village levels.

Participants and preparation. The team consisted of researchers and extension staff. In selecting the team, care was taken to include numerous disciplinary areas, such as soil science, agronomy, crop protection, economy, sociology and post-harvest/nutrition. FSR coordinators organized a short practical training for participants (two days) before starting the actual fieldwork. The training was set up because very few participants were familiar with this method. They needed to be introduced to the basics of conducting semi-structured interviews – intentionally, no pre-arranged checklist was provided; instead, these were prepared in subgroups.[9] An additional reason for training was to prepare for team interaction during fieldwork: this is crucial, and working together before going to the field favours later interaction. During preparation, intensive use was made of small working groups.

Implementation. The team of around 20 staff[10] was split into three multi-disciplinary groups; each covered two villages in two subdistricts.[11] During fieldwork the subgroups lived in the villages. First a meeting was held with the village chairman or secretary. Then group members went two by two (or individually) to selected hamlets. They made observations and held interviews with farmers, based on the prepared checklist. The sub-group coordinator ensured that the checklist was well covered by the group members. These interviews, held during the day (over two days), were complemented with village group meetings (one evening per village). In these meetings, the relative importance of issues and problems were assessed. Evening meetings were sometimes split up into smaller groups, in particular when local authorities dominated the discussion. Women's groups were also formed to encourage participation.

Daily interaction within the RRA subgroups centred around preparations for evening group meetings. During the fieldwork period, the three sub-groups interacted in two general feedback meetings, briefing each other and questioning each other's results. These sessions helped to clarify concepts and to focus more on major problem areas. Preliminary conclusions and hypotheses were also formulated. From start to finish, the whole exercise took 14 calendar days, consisting of preparation (2 days), fieldwork (7 days), 'feedback meetings' (3 days) and free days (2).

Major problems identified. A massive campaign to introduce the *gora* system took place in the agricultural year 1980–1981. This is a direct-seeded rice system. The basic idea of *gora* is to make better use of the short rainy season by having the land ready for planting (dibbling) immediately after the first rains. In this system the crop can be harvested about four weeks earlier than transplanted rice. The *gora* campaign was accompanied by introduction of an early maturing variety (IR 36), which increased the advantages of *gora*. After an initial success, however, many farmers ceased to use this system.

Table 1. Perceptions of the *gora* system

Farmers	(Based on information given by farmers during the RRA.)
Problem	We are obliged by the government to use the gora system, but this system does not fit all individual farming systems and/or is difficult to implement.
Cause	Gora implies land preparation in the dry season, on extremely hard soil (vertisols), using simple hand tools (crowbar, hoe); this work is arduous and expensive. Early planting of *gora* is not without risk (short dry spell after first rains); sometimes there are still crops in the fields, so land preparation has to be delayed: often the planting system leads to excessive weed growth, with high labour inputs. Some farmers have access to overflow water from neighbouring irrigation schemes, wells or small dams; they prefer to transplant, using their own or rented buffaloes. Production costs are much lower, and there is less risk of crop failure, both for the rice and for the following crop.
Extension agents	
Problem	Extension agents are convinced that gora gives higher yields and lower risk of crop failure than rice (can be harvested about 4 weeks earlier, also gives better results after rice, due to better use of rainfall pattern; in some cases it makes a second crop possible (otherwise rice is the only crop per agricultural year). Nevertheless, the area under direct-seeded rice (*gora*) and number of farmers using this system is declining from year to year. This is perceived as the major problem.
Cause	Reasons farmers apply gora less often, as stated by extension agents, include: farmers do not understand the benefits, or irresponsibly take high risks of crop failure (not all years are equally unfavourable); farmers do not like the hard work involved.
Researchers	
Problem	Yields don't match potential.
Cause	Researchers think that farmers use inappropriate cultural practices – low quality seed, poor use of fertilizer, etc.; poor access to inputs; late identification or failure to identify pests and diseases. New technical packages, improved support services and an increase in farmers' knowledge are needed.

While the RRA was being implemented, it became evident that the three stakeholders – extension workers, researchers and farmers – had different perceptions of this and other agricultural problems and their order of importance. Perceptions varied depending on how the actors understood cause–effect relationships, their specific interests and objectives, and the possibilities of a given group of actors providing solutions to problems. The problems identified also differ for different types of farmers and production systems. Extension workers, for example, formulated three major problems: reduced use of the *gora* system; reluctance of farmers to make use of government-subsidized credit; and failure to adopt fertilizer recommendations (or insufficient adoption) for elements other than nitrogen. Researchers (still new to this area) were primarily concerned with increasing yields, which they considered to be below the potential of the area. They looked at husbandry practices and questioned certain recommendations of extension. On the other hand, farmers did not find yield levels a problem, and questioned the feasibility of the *gora* system. They also had a different view of the main problems: insufficient availability of water; excessive cost of cultivating *gora*; and lack of working capital.

Table 1 presents a much-simplified view of problems related to the *gora* system. Not all problems are listed. Moreover, problems vary with conditions and for categories of farmers. The team further classified production systems based on the availability of water and related cropping patterns. In addition, various farmer categories were distinguished by the capacity of their farm enterprises to fulfil household needs.

Reporting findings and presenting results. Field team members prepared daily individual accounts of findings from observations and interviews. In addition, each subgroup prepared 'village reports', each containing a synthesis of major problems and constraints. These accounts, collected daily by coordinators, formed the basis for feedback meetings and finally the RRA report. A core group of the team (five staff members, from MARIF/ATA, DIPERTA and UNRAM) was in charge of elaborating the RRA report. This was presented during a one-day seminar in Lombok, about three months after the RRA.

In this seminar, the core group reported to the RRA team. Moreover, policymakers, other sectoral departments, local authorities from provincial to village level, and farmer representatives were invited to comment on RRA findings. The analysis of rice-growing systems, including direct seeding, made on the basis of RRA results was innovative in the sense that *gora* was discussed for the first time with respect to various production conditions and categories of farmers. Policymakers and planners from the provincial level were very active in this discussion, as it challenged their policies. The position held by the provincial government up to that time was that *gora* was the best system for all farmers and that 'the implementation of *gora* was the major aim'. After a hot debate, the conclusion reached was that 'the main aim is to ensure that farmers increase their productivity and incomes, and this may not be achieved by having all farmers adopt the *gora* system under all conditions'. This opened the door to changes in policy.

Of course, not all information collected and presented was 'new' to all participants; much had been said or written before. However, who conveys a message and how it is said are often more essential to its acceptance than the message itself. The way this RRA had been organized attracted much attention; therefore its results had considerable impact on the research programme.

Agronomic trial programme

Agronomic trials began during the first year, parallel to the RRA. The main reasons for beginning trials prior to the RRA results were to avoid the loss of an agricultural year; a belief that existing knowledge of researchers and extension workers was a sufficient basis for starter activities; and a desire to try out working procedures. In several working sessions, both research-ers and extension workers presented lists of trial ideas. There was a marked difference in their focus. Development/extension workers wanted to check on their recommendations (mainly fertilizer doses, timing and type). But they also brought in some aspects of local farming systems, notably the impact on yields of the type of land preparation used for direct-seeded rice. Researchers, on the other hand, suggested fertilizer and variety trials as well as crop protection (identification and control). These trials did not take into account specific local conditions, and were intended to serve mainly as a diagnostic tool. In the end, the programme for the first season consisted of 11 trials on rice-growing systems, covering aspects of fertilization, identification and control of pests, water manage-ment and cropping patterns. All experiments were intentionally carried out on substations, not in farmers' fields.[12]

Due to time pressures, clear criteria for priority setting were lacking, and thus the final list of experiments for the first season was a mixture of trials without a clear orientation. The process that led to the final list was not very clear either. An illustrative example: initially, extension staff sug-gested trials on weed control in *gora* rice and soybean, including the use of herbicides. However, these trials were not included in the research pro-gramme. It was not quite clear why this topic was dropped. The existence of a 'weed problem' was apparently denied. This is curious, because the RRA later identified this as a major problem of farmers. Environmental concerns and lack of experience of MARIF researchers in this type of trial may also have played a role. The final research programme may be charac-terized as the result of a kind of 'spontaneous consensus' and by the remark that 'nobody felt really bad about it'.

Research in the second season primarily built on the first season trials.

The same plots were used, and many of the trials aimed at assessing the residual effects of fertilizer used for rice on the following crops, as well as the impact of different rice-growing systems on the second crop (chiefly soybean). The other main effort consisted of cropping systems trials. In addition, three on-farm soybean trials were conducted: testing the MARIF technology package, the effect of an increased seeding rate, and the effect of drainage and method of planting.

Setting research priorities for the second year

Mechanisms and process

After the first year, a three-day planning and evaluation workshop was held in Lombok. This was attended by all researchers and extension workers involved in the programme, plus their department heads and directors. The workshop was immediately followed by a one-day seminar, attended by local authorities from provincial to village level, and by representatives of farmers. Here an opportunity was given to all parties involved to react and comment on the research results from the past year and the proposed research programme for the following year.

During the workshop, the research activities of the past year were evaluated. Results of the RRA, agronomic trials and farmer monitoring were discussed in-depth by intervention zone. This was rather unconventional, but forced researchers to reflect on both the relevance of their research activities to solving the identified problems and the interrelationship with other research. For each activity, the need for continuation and the form this should take were discussed. Some participants suggested new topics and themes for research. Participants argued for the inclusion or exclusion of themes in the research programme, indicating the importance they attached to each theme.

No definite programme was formulated during the plenary session. A small working group was given the task of making one consistent, manageable programme, which was presented to the plenary the next day. With some minor changes, it was accepted. The working group consisted of representatives of researchers and extension agents, the latter being in the minority. What the working group did, fundamentally, was to leave out all themes and topics on which no consensus had been reached during the first plenary; to recommend research that directly addressed identified major problems of farmers; to maintain a balance of activities throughout the agricultural year; to ensure a high priority for rainfed lowlands; and to focus on a shift from on-station to on-farm work.

Of course not only the workshop deliberations but also the knowledge and experience of the members of the working group were essential inputs into priority setting. The process of communication and interaction among those intensively involved in the programme played an important role. In this sense it can be argued that the real decision making moments lie outside formal structures or planned procedures.

MARIF researchers, in view of their many research activities elsewhere, considered the three-day duration of the workshop too long. From the viewpoint of the planners of the FSR programme, however, time was a constraint. There was insufficient time to conduct formal priority setting exercises, such as screening and scoring different research activities on predetermined criteria (ranking).

Outcome

The point of departure in formulating the research programme was clearly that the outcome should address farmers' problems. However, not all farmers' problems are researchable, and some problems should be addressed outside the agricultural research system. For instance, water – the major problem identified by farmers – could be addressed within the scope of FSR by researching the possibilities for better use of scarce water resources, such as alternative cropping patterns, drought resistant varieties, and improving soil properties. Other possibilities, like constructing new irrigation schemes or small-scale water reservoirs, lie outside the scope of FSR.

In the context of this paper, we will restrict ourselves to indicating the major research themes for the rainfall-dependent zone with no supplementary irrigation. This was the only zone for which *gora* was recommended as the appropriate system for growing rice. As a result, no trials were conducted using transplanted rice. All trials were conducted in farmers' fields. For *gora*, the major objective was to reduce production costs, while maintaining yield levels. For the first time in Lombok, research (agronomic and socioeconomic) was conducted on the mechanized preparation of land; weed control, including herbicides; and 'yellowing disease' of rice. Research on mechanization, out of the question one year earlier,[13] was accepted this time. Not only economic impact on returns to the owner of the crop, but also employment and income distribution aspects would be researched. As weeds in *gora* were now a recognized problem, the

Table 2. Research themes not implemented (NI) or rejected (R)

Theme or topic	Reasons
Interdisciplinary topic survey in irrigated areas, covering farmers' rationale for choice of cropping pattern (NI)	Pending, lack of time
Study of regional water distribution system and impact of changes in crops and cropping system (NI)	Need specific research team
Use of rice straw for cattle feed (R)	Involve other institute
Adaptation and promotion of rice–fish system (R)	Research content too low
Effect on growth of regular and foliar fertilizers in rice (R)	Not farmers' problem
Fertilizer trials for grain legumes (R)	No major impact on yields
Specific trials on rice pests and control (R)	Sufficient research done, improved extension needed
Employment or development of alternative land preparation instruments and tools (R)	Insufficient expertise in team, no capacity to tap available technology
Soil fertility studies, toposequence (R)	No follow-up on consultancy; lack of planning capacity

development of control measures was a logical consequence. 'Yellowing disease' is an example of a problem brought to the attention of researchers by farmers. This problem had never been researched before. Researchers could not identify the cause, so diagnostic trials were designed.

For crops sown after rice, increased emphasis was given to grain legumes, such as soybean and mung bean. Researchers acknowledged that their technological packages for grain legumes were only appropriate under conditions without water stress. Therefore a 'low-input' package was to be developed, with these main elements: use of good quality seed; proper timing and improved planting methods; and supervised control of pests. In areas with limited access to additional water, a relay crop would be tried, to be planted before grain legumes were harvested. The relay crop was expected to ease land preparation and increase the supply of cattle feed (extremely scarce at the end of the agricultural season).

A topic thought to be of interest the first year, but less so the second year, was the (political) need to change cropping patterns in semi-irrigated areas. The need to change the rice–rice–non-rice pattern into the recommended rice–non-rice–non-rice cropping pattern became less evident, as Indonesia had recently found it necessary to import rice after about five years of full self-sufficiency.

With respect to socioeconomic research, it was decided to continue the farmer monitoring, to assess yearly variations as well as to explain the wide variations in yields obtained by farmers. In addition, considerable differences were found in the management practices of large and small farmers. This was directly related to their access to resources and to the need for and possibility of income from off-farm activities. Therefore, research was to be initiated to assess the impact of off-farm activities (including seasonal migration) on the capability of farm households to intensify crops sown after rice.

To further illustrate the selection of research themes, those that were not included in the research programme (or not implemented), and the reason for these choices, are presented in Table 2.

Conclusions

Priority setting takes place at various levels. Government policies, institutional structures and the research mandate all strongly influence decisions about the area of work, research approach, and production systems to be covered. Therefore, the FSR team's ranking of potential research activities is restricted by decisions made higher up in the hierarchy. Nevertheless, projects and programmes generally have many choices to make. Priority setting is needed to make the best use of resources. In the case of the FSR programme in Lombok, two elements that considerably affected the priority setting process were the implementation of an RRA, and the systematic planning and evaluation of research.

Rapid rural appraisal. Without a good diagnosis, appropriate priorities are unlikely. The RRA proved to be an excellent instrument, providing an effective basis for priority setting based on farmers' problems. It allowed research to be focused on a reasonable number of major problems, and new horizons for research were opened up. Second, because researchers and extension workers all went through the same process, a common view and good working relations could be established. Third, interactions with other stakeholders, notably village and district authorities and policymakers, took place at an early stage. This chapter describes only the shifts in the research programme between the first and second years, which can primarily be attributed to the RRA. However, the implementation of the RRA does not complete the diagnosis. Priority setting is a continuous process. In successive rounds, more and more is understood about how farmers operate their farming systems, and where and how improvements can be made.

Planning and evaluation. The opportunities created by the FSR team for joint reflection and planning in meetings, seminars and workshops have been quite essential in enabling shifts in orientation, and the formulation of a clear focus for research. The institutional structures and mechanisms allowed the various actors to build up good working relations and confidence in each other, and in the end made it possible to guide priority setting for research.

The content of research programmes depends on the ways different stakeholders perceive problems, as well as their respective interests. Therefore, finding common objectives is a key element in a balanced priority setting process. Farmers could express their views and priorities, and comment on research feedback and the like during farmer meetings, field days and informal discussions. That is, farmers were given the opportunity to comment, but did not participate directly in the formulation of research programmes. This means that the extent to which the real constraints of farmers are translated into action still depends on others' sensitivity to their needs. Formal planning and evaluation meetings help to structure the priorities of participants, which begin to form during their many informal contacts with farmers, colleagues and other stakeholders. If differing views are expressed and opposing positions appear during planning meetings, a consensus is usually reached outside the formal meeting. Therefore, communication and interaction among those directly involved in the programme is of great importance. Formal priority setting methods can never substitute for good interpersonal relations.

Notes

1 Donor funds were withdrawn suddenly in March, 1992. Like all projects financed by bilateral Dutch aid, the ATA-272 project ended then, due to political problems between the governments of Indonesia and the Netherlands. Although MARIF continued the three- year FSR programme in Lombok, the use of the mechanisms that had been established slowed.

2 Cropping systems experiments were not a part of the orientation to commodities, but these were relatively small programmes, with few researchers involved.

3 The regional mandate of MARIF consists of East Java Province and the Provinces of Bali, West and East Nusa Tenggara (NTB and NTT) and East Timor. The mandate reflects the increased national interest in enhancing development in the eastern part of Indonesia.

4 The decision to locate the FSR programme in Lombok, NTB, was made without involvement of the donor, who had some preference for East Java. In fact, while MARIF/ATA-272 had in mind using a more or less structured procedure to select a location for FSR in an eastern provinces, the advantages of Lombok were such that no other provinces or

districts were considered.

5   These research protocols contain information on items such as staff involved and their tasks, research theme, background and justification, time, location, research design and a detailed budget.

6   In the second year, activities were to focus on adaptive research on farmers' fields; additional technology component research trials to support FSR; and socioeconomic farm planning and in-depth studies. In the third year, verification of OFR and pre-production technology development were to be the central elements.

7   The Nusa Tenggara Agricultural Support Project (NTASP), which also had a strong farming systems research orientation.

8   The farmer monitoring system was set up with three aims: to assess farmers' cultural practices in more detail; provide a basis for socioeconomic evaluation of farm activities; and assess farmers' capability and willingness to accept improved technology and intensify production. This monitoring could also be used to verify RRA findings on rice-growing systems. In addition, a subsample of the monitored farmers became the object of in-depth studies, such as the impact of off-farm activities on-farm activities.

9   If a well-designed formal method, for instance a questionnaire, is used, implementation can be delegated to a lower cadre (i.e., enumerators); the 'intellectual work' is done beforehand. The less formal the method, the higher the demands on the experience and quality of researchers.

10 Twenty is a very high number of staff and requires an explanation. DIPERTA and UNRAM in particular were very enthusiastic, and offered many staff members as participants. At the time the RRA was planned, it was still unclear how many MARIF staff could participate, due to many commitments. It was also difficult to decide who to leave out. Therefore, FSR coordinators decided to work with this large group. By splitting up into three groups of approximately six each, the basic working methodology of an RRA could be maintained. The coordinators visited all three groups and villages, to maintain a general overview and prepare feedback meetings. One advantage was the achievement of good coverage of the area. Further, staff who performed well could be identified and asked to continue to work in the programme.

11 Villages were selected by the RRA organizers prior to the implementation of the RRA. Detailing the selection criteria used is beyond the scope of this paper. Although theoretically it would be ideal to have villages selected by the RRA team during orientation visits to the area at the start of the fieldwork, this was not a feasible option for administrative reasons.

12 The design of these trials was complicated, as many variables were treated simultaneously. Interpretation of the trial data was difficult, and few conclusive results were obtained.

13 One benefit of *gora* was considered to be increased employment and redistribution of income (from land owners to landless/small farmers). Introduction of mechanization was politically sensitive.

Bibliography

ATA-272 (internal report, 1991) Project design. Technology development for farmers, ATA-272 Phase V. 1 March 1991 to 28 February 1994

MANWAN I (1989) Farming systems research in Indonesia: its evolution and future look. In: Proceedings of the international workshop, Developments in procedures for Farming Systems Research, pp 6–36. Jakarta: AARD

MARIF/ATA-272, FSR-Lombok, Work Plan 1990-1993 (1990) A collaboration between MARIF Malang/ATA-272, Kanwil/Bimas and Agricultural Agency on Food Crops Level I, NTB and Agricultural Faculty of Universitas Mataram (UNRAM), October 1990

MARIF/ATA-272 (1992) Risalah Seminar, Hasil Penelitian Sistem Usahatani di Nusa Tenggara Barat, dilaksanakan di Mataram, 22–26 Oktober, 1991 (Proceedings of the evaluation and planning workshop, FSR in West Tenggara Province, held in Mataram on October 22–26, 1991), MARIF

MEINDERTSMA JD AND HARTOJO K (1991) Rapid rural appraisal as a diagnostic tool in farming systems research, the case of Lombok, Indonesia. Paper presented at 'OFR-regional Course Training' organized by ESCAP-CGPRT Centre Bogor, Malang, May 13-25, 1991

MEINDERTSMA JD AND SUYAMTO H (1991) The gradual shaping of an FSR programme, the case of Southeast Lombok. In: Prosiding simposium nasional Penelitian dan pengembangan sistem usahatani lahan kering yang berkelanjutan (National Symposium Proceedings), August 1991, Malang, Brawijaya University

SUYAMTO H, HARTOJO K AND MEINDERTSMA JD (1991) Draf Terakhir Sistem Usahatani dengan Pola Dasar Padi Gogo Rancah di Lombok, NTB. Hasil Pemahaman Pedesaan dalam Waktu Singkat. (Final draft: Farming systems with Padi Gogo Rancah Pattern in Lombok; results of a rapid rural appraisal), MARIF

SUYAMTO H AND MEINDERTSMA JD (1991a) Farming systems research programme by MARIF, the Lombok pilot area. Paper presented at the OFR-regional Course Training organized by ESCAP-CGPRT Centre Bogor and MARIF, Malang, 13-25 May, 1991

SUYAMTO H AND MEINDERTSMA JD (internal report, 1991b) Agronomic experiments, FSR-Programme Lombok, first dry season 1991.

Project description: Lake Zone, Tanzania

The FSR Project Lake Zone is supported financially and technically by the Tanzanian and Netherlands governments. Headquarters are at Ukiriguru Zonal Research Centre in Mwanza; FSR field teams are stationed in two target areas: Bukoba District and Maswa/Meatu Districts (map). In all, FSR personnel include four agronomists, three socioeconomists, one livestock specialist and two extension workers. There is close day-to-day collaboration with local extension.[1]

The project started in 1988. Governmental agricultural policy objectives then changed and the research system was reorganized; agricultural research and FSR are now organized by agroecological zone. This facilitates coordination between commodity and adaptive research.[2] The long term objective of the project is to increase and ensure farm household incomes by improving the productivity and sustainability of smallholder farming systems. Institution building, formal and informal training, as well as improvement of physical infrastructure are among project responsibilities. Short term objectives are: to identify major short and long term constraints on farming systems in the two target areas; to test the suitability of current agricultural recommendations for the conditions of local smallholders, via on-farm experiments; and to help generate new recommendations, more relevant to the needs of local farmers. In addition, during the first phase, the FSR Project was asked to provide a detailed database for District Rural Development Programmes in the target areas (also sponsored by the Netherlands).

The two target areas have distinctly different farming systems. Bukoba District has one of the highest population densities on sandstone-derived soils in Africa: although the district average is about 49 persons per km^2, local densities may be as high as 500 persons per km^2. The district is characterized by a perennial crop system. Three land use types can be distinguished: *kibanja* fields around homesteads (on average, 10 to 15% of the holding; fertility accumulates due to mulching and applications of refuse and manure; bananas, coffee and beans are the main crops); less fertile *kikamba* fields (adjacent to tibanja; about 1–3% of the holding, used for annual food crops (maize, sweet potato and groundnut); and extensive *rweya* fields. (Often under communal ownership, these have very low soil fertility and support mainly grassland. Once every eight to ten years groundnut or bambara groundnut, followed by cassava, is grown.) Poor parent materials and the inherent problem of soil fertility, in combination with high annual rainfall (1,200–2,000 mm) and population density, are the main causes of the present problems: the land use system shows signs of overutilization and degradation.

In Maswa/Meatu Districts population density is 30–80 persons per km^2. In contrast to Bukoba, population is more evenly distributed, but is now increasing. Soils in these districts have distinct toposequential patterns. Rainfall is much lower (from 1,000 mm per annum in the northwest to less than 800 mm per annum in the southeast), with a distinct dry season (June–September) and mid-season droughts (January–February). Consequently, the districts are characterized by annual crops/fallow systems, with maize as the preferred cereal crop. In the relatively wetter areas of the north, rice cultivation, using trapped run-off water, is important. In the south drought-tolerant crops (such as sorghum and bulrush millet) and extensive livestock systems are important. In the past, cotton was the major cash crop. Nowadays, the importance of cotton depends largely on its price and on opportunities to grow other cash crops (e.g. rice). Migration, occupation of marginal areas and clashes between sedentary peasants and nomadic cattle owners are major issues. Land degradation is accelerating, due to soil mining and erosion.

8 From theme to on-farm experimentation: Lake Zone, Tanzania

Driek Enserink, Keija Bunyecha, Chris Bosch, Bert Meertens, Klaas Tamminga and Petra Penninkhoff

Getting from priority research themes to trials is often a bottleneck in the FSR process. Identifying possible solutions to systems constraints is not usually a serious problem. However, the subsequent translation of these solutions into the design of field activities is something else: teams must consider trial objectives and target groups, as well as available resources. The fact that priority themes are often stated in rather broad terms, with only an implicit identification of the target group, compounds the problem. In addition, the pressure on FSR teams to come up with adapted recommendations within a short time can lead to ad hoc trials that are difficult to match with the priority research themes identified in earlier stages.

This chapter describes how the FSR Project Lake Zone (see project description) in Tanzania tackled the translation process. An overview of diagnostic surveys and the experiment sequence is presented, followed by a discussion of key problems in the two target areas and an indication of research priorities and researchable issues. The process is illustrated by three contrasting cases: first, a diagnostic exploratory trial in cotton, using a few sites in farmer's fields to better focus research efforts in subsequent seasons; this case also gives an example of interaction with policymakers. The second case outlines a diagnostic rice on-farm trial (a few sites) followed by an on-farm verification test (many sites) plus a short topical survey, and culminating in a pre-extension campaign/on-farm test (two villages); the third covers on-farm activities used to study soil fertility in a perennial crop-based system. Each case starts with the identification of possible causes of core problems and formulation of possible solutions. Subsequently, trial design, implementation and results are outlined. Each case concludes with the translation of results into follow-up activities for the next season. The chapter ends with a discussion of the lessons learnt, including the impor-

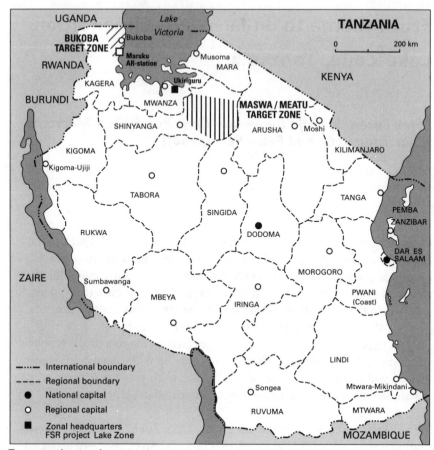

Tanzania, showing the project area

tance of collaboration both within the team and with others – farmers, extension workers, commodity researchers and policymakers.

The general process

In principle, all zonal FSR programmes in Tanzania follow the CIMMYT (*Centro Internacional de Mejoramiento de Maiz y Trigo*) methodology for farming systems research: progressively more refined research is carried out to develop technological alternatives suitable to actual farming conditions. Alternatives are developed for groups of farmers with similar farming systems – that is, target groups or 'recommendation domains'. In addition to agronomic considerations, the roles of social, economic and cultural variables at the household level are emphasized. Although the methodology is quite useful, it is rather crop oriented; practical examples of ways to deal with livestock issues or with perennial crops are less well documented. In planning and implementing activities, the CIMMYT approach includes several stages of activities, e.g. agroecological zoning, informal and formal surveys, on-farm trials, on-farm tests and dissemination of recommendations. In practice, the Lake Zone FSR programme team, like others, does not rigidly adhere to this linear sequence; some steps have been modified or are taken simultaneously. This is partly due to the additional task of providing baseline information for the district rural development programmes in Bukoba and Maswa/Meatu.

Figure 1 presents a schematic overview of the research process. After a study of secondary data sources, informal and formal diagnostic surveys were carried out. The main objective was to gain a better understanding of the local farming systems and identify key problems and constraints. Once key problems in the two target areas had been identified, they were picked apart to arrive at researchable issues. Some of these appeared to be suffi-ciently covered by other research programmes and not in need of FSR team attention. Issues not yet covered but outside the scope and/or expertise of the team were referred to the appropriate authorities. Research priorities to be addressed by the FSR team were described in more detail, gradually leading to the formulation of an initial experimental programme.[3] Results from the initial activities plus additional survey work formed the basis for

Figure 1. The FSR approach of FSR Project, Lake Zone, Tanzania

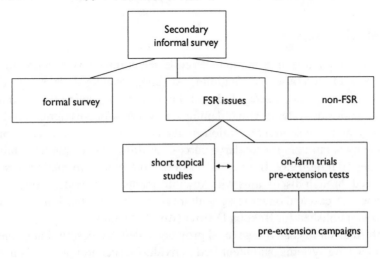

Figure 2. From broadly formulated key problems to research and extension programmes

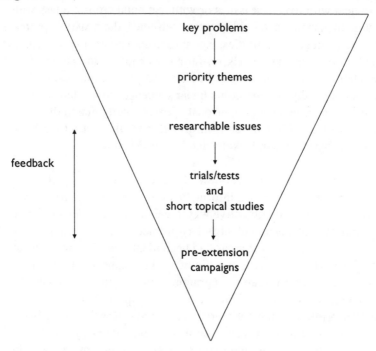

the subsequent experimental programmes (Enserink and Bunyecha, 1991). At all times, experimental plans were developed together with the extension service in annual work plan sessions. This process is illustrated in Figure 2.

Diagnostic surveys

For each target area, information was collected at three levels: subregional, village and farm/household–field/plot. At subregional level, data collection focused on acquiring a general idea of the study area; gaining insight into the dynamics of systems; and obtaining an overview of past agricultural research and extension interventions in the area. The team gathered information by scrutinizing secondary sources, resulting in two annotated bibliographies (Bantje, 1989; Bosch et al., 1989). Additional information was collected through discussions with key informants. A separate critical overview of past and ongoing agriculture research and extension activities has been published for Bukoba District (Bosch, 1990a).

Informal surveys at village level provided a detailed description of the local farming systems, and identified individual target groups and their constraints. During these surveys, resident FSR field teams were reinforced by the headquarters teams' agronomists and socioeconomists. Livestock officers of the respective district agricultural and livestock bureaus also participated, and a women and development consultant was commissioned to cover gender issues. Thus a broad-based group was involved in the production of the informal survey reports that were published for each of the target areas (FSR Team, 1989a, 1989b).

Informal surveys comprised two cycles of two weeks per target area, rather than the usual single two-week cycle. The reasons were twofold. First, most Tanzanian team members and cooperating extension staff were relatively inexperienced with FSR methodology and needed on-the-job training. Second, the extended period of field visits and the built-in two-week reflection time between the two cycles allowed collection of more detailed information.

Formal surveys were implemented to quantify the data collected during the informal survey further with respect to individual target groups. Formal surveys were coordinated and carried out by the team's socioeconomists. Enumerators who spoke the local languages were selected from staff of extension services, training and research institutes. Enumerators were trained and questionnaires pre-tested before surveys were implemented. In the Maswa/Meatu formal survey, women farmers were interviewed in parallel sessions by female enumerators using a separate questionnaire. Formal survey reports were published for each target area (FSR Team, 1990; Bantje, 1991).

A major objective of the formal surveys was to provide a detailed database for the rural development programmes operating in the target areas, as mentioned in the project description. This implied an increase from the usual samples of 60 households to 250 households. The team realized that analysis of these extensive formal surveys would require considerable time, which could delay the start of the experimental programme. However, the approach used in the informal surveys appeared to have generated an adequate understanding of the respective farming systems. Therefore, the team decided that beginning an initial on-farm experimental programme before completing formal surveys could be justified.

On-farm experimental activities

The Lake Zone FSR team distinguished four types of activities: 1) the diagnostic trial; 2) the verification test; 3) the pre-extension campaign (in which crop cuts are taken); and 4) the short topical survey focusing on specific issues. All on-farm experimental work was organized in 'clusters'. Each cluster is usually a part of a village. They are selected to represent certain rainfall zones, soil parent materials and cropping zones. If necessary, within these clusters farmers are selected to be representative of certain pre-defined target groups (e.g. ox plough owners and non ox plough owners; or female and male farmers).

Diagnostic trials address key issues identified during the informal surveys or derived from results of previous trials. Their aim is to gain further understanding of biological and other factors in the prevailing farming systems. Two types of trials are generally used: first, to determine which factors are most important ('yes–no' trials); and second, to evaluate what level of intervention is compatible with existing farming systems ('how much' trials). Diagnostic trials are always conducted in collaboration with relevant commodity research. Consequently, trial design and management are the result of compromises between FSR&D and commodity researchers. In diagnostic trials, clusters usually comprise 3–6 farmers, and two or three clusters are selected to represent a certain target zone. Treatments are replicated per farmer (at least twice) to test whether farmer fields really belong to the same recommendation domain. Plot sizes are usually small (8–20 m^2). Trials are always researcher-managed, although all management practices related to seedbed preparation are left to the farmer. Usually fields are selected on which the farmer intends to grow the crop addressed in the trial. If possible (e.g. fertilizer trials) treatments are superimposed on farmers' practices – that is, the treatment takes place in a field prepared according to the farmer's usual methods regarding, for example, time of sowing, choice of variety, and weeding. This allows for more farmer involvement. For Bukoba, where annual *kibanja* crops are usually under-sown in existing perennial banana stands, this meant that all bean trials were also undersown.

Compatibility with the existing farming system is the most important criterion. Clusters for on-farm verification tests usually comprise 20–30 farmers. Only one or two treatments are tested, in addition to farmers' practices. Contrary to diagnostic trials, treatments are not replicated per farmer. Tests are laid out in a part of the farmer's field, and large plot sizes are used (100–500 m^2). If possible, treatments are superimposed on the farmer's crop, in a long strip across the field. This allows for an easy comparison with the control (the farmer's own crop) and facilitates the use of a 'paired treatment' design, with crop cuts as experimental units. Consequently, sign or paired t-tests are the tools for subsequent statistical analysis. Village extension workers as well as collaborating farmers are intensely involved in organizing and implementing verification tests. Village field days are organized to stimulate discussion among farmers.

A pre-extension campaign is set up when a verification test shows promising results in the eyes of researchers, extension workers and farmers. The aim of such a campaign is to introduce the technology to a large number of farmers. Usually, 100–200 farmers in each of two or three villages, who are familiar with the previous season's test results, are involved. At this point the extension service is the leading partner, and research limits its activities to monitoring. Crop cuts are made on only about 30 fields, to evaluate the consistency of treatment effects under farm conditions. Preferably, pre-extension campaigns are also organized in such a way that the technology being introduced is applied to a broad strip in farmers' fields. This facilitates easy comparison and stimulates discussions among and with farmers. As far as possible, collaborating farmers buy their own inputs, although the project guarantees availability.

On-farm experimentation programmes address particular problems, but nevertheless are conducted so as to stimulate discussions with local households. In conjunction with verification tests and pre-extension campaigns, short topical surveys are carried out. Their objective is to quantify certain management aspects of specific crops and types of land use. Trial farmers as well as their neighbours are usually involved in these surveys, the number of households ranging from 30 to 60. Short questionnaires are used, and results are presented in separate field notes (e.g. Bosch et al., 1990, on beans in Bukoba; Jansen et al., 1991, on maize in Bukoba; 't Hart, 1991, on sweet potatoes in Maswa/Meatu; Meertens and Ndege, 1993, on rice in Maswa/Meatu).

Key problems and related research activities in Maswa/Meatu

FSR activities started with the collection of secondary data and discussions with key informants. The diagnostic phase indicated that general development issues in this target area are migration, occupation of marginal areas, land degradation due to soil mining and erosion, and clashes between sedentary farmers and nomadic cattle owners. Farmers must deal with four key problems: unreliable rainfall, low productivity in the livestock sector, decreases in cotton production, and labour constraints. Each of these key problems is briefly described below; some of these are researchable issues, and some are not.

The final decision on priorities with respect to researchable issues rested with the FSR team, but decisions were always preceded by discussion with district authorities and commodity researchers. This was greatly facilitated by the permanent assignment of two extension workers to the FSR team, and by the fact that the FSR project was carrying out a baseline survey for the district.

Unreliable rainfall. In the context of subsistence agriculture, rainfall is a parameter that cannot be dealt with directly: irrigation is either impossible or too expensive. Maswa/Meatu farmers therefore put strong emphasis on food security. They spread risks by crop diversification and by cultivating relatively large areas, using ox ploughs for land preparation. Because rainfall is a factor that cannot be influenced by FSR – and yet sets boundaries on farming – the Lake Zone team identified some issues related to rainfall and food security that have consequences for the design of an on-farm experimentation programme. These were based on the results of the formal and informal surveys.

Due to distinct differences in agroecological conditions, there is considerable regional specialization in cropping systems. These so-called 'cropping zones' were used as a basis for on-farm research planning and implementation. However, throughout Maswa/Meatu, sweet potato appeared to be the most important food security crop. Information about yields and management practices was limited, although it seemed that the labour demands of other crops influenced sweet potato planting dates. As sweet potato is mainly grown by women farmers, studying this crop provided an opportunity to initiate discussions with local women on their role in agriculture ('t Hart, 1991, 1992).

Ox ploughs are important to food security. A complete ox plough team was not owned by all households; the percentage varied between 20% and 60%, depending on the area. However, complex social arrangements allow many non-owners to have most of their fields ox ploughed. Others, especially in the more densely populated areas, prepare their fields with hand hoes. Therefore, access to oxen and ploughs was taken as a major characteristic to use in distinguishing target groups (that is, owners, borrowers, or hand hoe farmers).

Low livestock productivity. This problem is partly due to high (tick-borne) disease pressure in the area. Livestock services have deteriorated to a very low level. The lack of livestock services was referred to the appropriate district and regional authorities; the FSR team had no means and expertise available to involve itself directly in solving this problem. Moreover, based on past experience, the team anticipated that improved livestock services could quickly lead to overstocking and environmental degradation. Local Sukuma farmers have been reluctant to decrease herds. In their perspective, long-term risk aversion is more important than short-term cash availability. Cash earnings (for instance from cotton sales) are still used to buy livestock. In the current situation, these are the most productive long-term investments. The FSR team therefore decided to address the livestock production system indirectly, by improving crop–livestock interactions. This was expected to increase the value of individual animals and create opportunities for new productive investments (such as purchase of fertilizers). The rationale was that if the contribution of oxen to crop production could be increased, farmers would be better motivated to improve livestock management. The first steps in that direction were the introduction of ox weeders and oxen training (Ngendello, 1991). Key persons were sent to Mali to become familiar with the related concept. The two collaborating villages in Meatu selected two knowledgeable farmers to be trained in the use of ox weeders. Together with two livestock production researchers, they went to Mbeya, in the south of Tanzania, for a practical training course. Thereafter this group became responsible for local training and demonstration activities related to ox weeding in Masua and Meatu. Further details are presented in Case 1.

Decrease in cotton production. Cotton, the major local cash crop, had decreased over the years in acreage as well as productivity. Low cotton prices and serious delays in payments from buyers (cooperative unions) to farmers resulted in uncertainties and low benefits. Crop husbandry practices were deteriorating, and the use of inputs was declining; as a result, productivity was decreasing. The district authorities were attempting to enforce the use of a standard package of recommendations, but this was not working. The package had been developed for conditions in another area; also, the recommendations were too expensive for farmers to implement as a complete package. Thus farmers were not following the advice of the extension service. The package of recommendations needed modification. Case 1 gives details of the ensuing process.

Labour constraints. Because farmers cultivate relatively large areas, labour availability at peak periods is a major problem, particularly for weeding. Therefore, the FSR team initiated a series of short topical studies addressing labour availability. Households try to smooth out peak demands for labour by means of 'staggered planting' and crop diversification. Consequently, not all crops in all fields reach critical weeding stages at the same time.

Case 1. Yield gap determination leads to a focused research effort

The relative importance in the target area of fertilizer use, weed and pest control, and their possible interactions in cotton production were unknown. Diagnostic research was needed to provide new recommendations – ones farmers would use. Research and extension staff and district authorities agreed to implement a diagnostic programme. As a starting point, senior extension workers, commodity researchers and FSR staff were jointly involved in a training cycle. CIMMYT presented methodologies, and FSR presented case studies specific to the target area. Each step in the process was covered: survey development, priority setting and planning for experiments, on-farm research implementation, and analysis of research results. After training for each specific step, this step was implemented in the field; its results were used in training sessions for the next step. In 1989 a diagnostic survey was carried out, followed by an on-farm cotton trial to quantify the yield gaps and identify major contributing factors. The trial was repeated in 1990–1991; a short topical survey was conducted simultaneously. Initial survey results indicated that the 1989 and 1990 cotton prices had been far too low to make cotton cultivation attractive to farmers. The trial showed that weeding was by far the most important husbandry factor influencing local cotton yields. Insecticides had a minimal effect, and fertilizers were only beneficial in combination with improved weeding (Meertens et al., 1991, 1992a).

The general objective throughout the diagnostic process was to compile information that would be useful to policymakers in deciding which actions would be required to make cotton production more attractive from the farmers' point of view. It was also important to be able to make recommendations that would be valid for farmers who could not afford to implement the entire package. In presenting results to the relevant authorities, we wanted to increase the likelihood of influencing policy decisions. Therefore a role-playing session with senior district officials was included, in which they took the role of a farmer who, given a particular yield and price structure for crops and inputs, had to decide if the inputs were worth the price. Fortunately, 1991 producer price increases were such that farmers more than doubled cotton production.

Similar diagnostic research results were obtained with respect to husbandry practices for maize: weeding was by far the most important husbandry factor. As a result, the team decided to concentrate on the introduction of ox weeders to alleviate the labour constraint in the weeding of maize and cotton crops. It was realized that ox weeding presupposes row planting, while generally crops are broadcast or planted at random. If, however, farmers see possibilities for decreasing the labour required for weeding and increasing yield (due to timely and possibly more frequent weeding), the extra effort needed to plant in rows may be outweighed. This, in turn, may lead to an increased use of inorganic fertilizers: efficiency of fertilizer use can be greatly increased by applying evenly along the planting rows, instead of broadcast.

Introduction of ox weeding would also stimulate the application of farmyard manure. Although manure is low cost and readily available, it is a source of weed seeds. Farmers usually complain about the added weed competition and the extra labour required; ox weeding could alleviate this. However, it remains to be seen which is the main constraint to manure use: labour required for weeding or labour needed to transport and apply manure.

These aspects were taken into account during the evaluation of the first phase (1988–1992) of the FSR project in the Lake Zone. The re-formulation document for the second phase (1993–1998) recommended the recruitment of a livestock research specialist, experienced in ox management and ox traction. Moreover, the Maswa District Rural Development Programme started a similar programme, for which an expert was recruited. As collaborative ploughing efforts on fields of ox plough and non ox plough owners is common, it is anticipated that ox weeders will also be used on more farms.

This key constraint of labour availability was broken down into four researchable issues:
- identifying household strategies to cope with labour shortages, through crop budget and farm management studies;
- understanding, quantifying and removing weeding labour constraints;
- increasing farmers' flexibility with respect to time of planting;
- intensification of selected crop management practices.

Crop budgets and farm management studies became the focal point for the team's socioeconomists. Crop budget studies initially concentrated on rice and maize. The 1990 crop budgets showed that net returns as well as returns on family labour were much higher in rice than in maize production systems (Bunyecha, in press). Emphasis has now shifted towards farm management studies, investigating the relationships among crops within the same farm and understanding the dynamics of farmers' management decision making.

Studies to understand, quantify and remove weeding labour constraints focused on weed control in maize and cotton crops and on the prospects for the introduction of ox weeders. Details are presented in Case 1 and under 'Low livestock productivity'.

To ensure that farmers can stagger their plantings, recommended and released varieties of maize and sorghum should be adapted to a range of planting dates. Therefore, two on-farm diagnostic 'time of planting' trials were carried out in collaboration with the Ukiriguru maize and sorghum commodity research sections. Recommended varieties of both crops were tested in selected cropping zones. The end product should have been a flexible recommendation for farmers. Some medium-maturing maize varieties were promising, but farmers were most interested in the early maturing types. However, these varieties appeared very susceptible to blight (Enserink, 1990). All recommended sorghum varieties took too long to mature to be of interest to local farmers. These varieties had been selected under climatic conditions more favourable than those in the target zones. In the wetter cropping zones of Maswa/Meatu, farmers try first to establish maize or rice. If these crops fail, farmers may plant a late sorghum crop.

Thus, an early maturing variety is needed. In the drier cropping zones, where maize can only be grown at high risk and rice growing is impossible, sorghum is still grown on a large scale. However, the rainy seasons are short and unreliable. Recommended varieties should therefore be more carefully screened for early maturity, drought and *Striga* tolerance, plus improved grain quality.

The decision to investigate the possibility of intensifying some crop management practices was based on the assumption that higher yields may tempt farmers to cultivate smaller – but better managed – areas. In addition, smaller areas would require less weeding labour at peak periods. In this context, research focused on the use of manure and chemical fertilizers (nitrogen, N, and phosphorus, P) in maize and rice. Farmers in the rice and maize cropping zones had complained about decreasing yields. As the use of both inorganic and organic fertilizers had been limited, these decreases were thought to be due to a slow but steady decline in soil fertility. On-farm diagnostic maize and rice fertility trials to confirm this hypothesis were carried out. A detailed discussion of the rice trials is presented in Case 2.

Key problems and related research activities in Bukoba

The information collected during the literature review and informal survey gave the team an adequate idea of key problems in the Bukoba farming system; this was used to plan the subsequent programme of on-farm experiments and short topical studies. These on-farm studies greatly increased understanding of the farming system. At present, we believe the following three problems are of key importance: poor marketing infrastructure and low prices for cash crops; incidence of pests and diseases in bananas; and poor soil fertility.

Poor marketing infrastructure and low pricing. The marketing problem was addressed by the project economist in cooperation with a local consultant, using price monitoring and marketing studies. These studies led to the conclusion that producer prices for crops marketed through cooperative unions, such as coffee and beans, are too low to motivate farmers to increase their production. Local markets, where food crops other than beans are traded, are poorly developed and discourage production increases. This has consequences for technology development: to stimulate investments in external inputs (e.g. fertilizers to maintain soil fertility), their introduction would have to go hand in hand with improvements in possibilities for marketing.

Case 2. Fertilizer use in rice

Fertilizers can only be effective when sufficient water is available and general crop management, such as seed-bed preparation and weeding, is satisfactory. The rice production system in the wettest cropping zone of Maswa District was selected for study, because here conditions are optimal for efficient fertilizer use; conditions for other crops (such as sorghum, cotton and maize) are less satisfactory. Moreover, rice is the most important cash crop as well as a major food crop. This suggests that new technologies may be more readily adopted, increasing household income and thus reducing the need for cultivating other crops over large areas.

Rice cultivation was introduced some 40 to 50 years ago, but has only really taken off since the 1960s. Since then, farmers have been growing it almost continually, without fertilizers, relying on initial soil fertility and fallowing. Initially yields were adequate, but recently farmers have begun to complain of decreasing yields. Land and water management practices did not appear to constrain crop production, but mineral deficiencies were observed during the informal survey. This led to the hypothesis that the decrease in yields was caused by a slow but steady decrease in soil fertility.

A diagnostic on-farm trial was conducted in the 1989–1990 season. The objectives were to:
- record farmers' husbandry practices;
- test whether the use of manure and inorganic fertilizers could significantly increase rice yields;
- assess the economic feasibility of using manure or fertilizers;
- assess possible increases in weed infestation due to manure use.

A manure treatment was included because a slight majority of Maswa/Meatu households are cattle owners, with easy access to manure. Farmers felt fertilizers costs could be prohibitive. However, because of substantial rice producer prices, reflecting high demand, the team thought it worthwhile to test inorganic fertilizer effects as well. Urea and triple super phosphate were chosen. As the clayey soils contained adequate levels of potassium, this nutrient was excluded.

The trial was conducted in two villages. In each village a cluster of three representative farmers was selected, with representative fields along the toposequence. Three replications were used per farmer. Treatments were superimposed on farmers' practices. Trials were encouraging, with all sites belonging to the same fertilizer recommendation domain. Statistically, there were highly significant yield differences among treatments (Meertens et al., 1991b). Analysis indicated that the effect of the urea treatment (30 kg N/ha) was to increase the rate of return by a factor of 11. Farmers remarked on the clearly visible effects of urea. They also felt that manure (5 tonnes/ha) did produce better yields than their own practice, but they complained bitterly about the increased weed competition and weeding labour requirements. Assessments of triple super phosphate (20 kg P_2O_5/ha) use were variable. Unfortunately, farmers' access to urea was constrained. The team felt, however, that the high economic returns with urea use was a strong argument for policymakers to take further action to increase fertilizer supply.

Because of these results, the diagnostic trial was followed up with a urea on-farm verification test in the 1990–1991 season, in which 23 farmers cooperated. Objectives were to demonstrate the use and performance of urea (30 kg N/ha) to farmers in their own fields; to study the effect of urea in relation to toposequence; and to assess the economic feasibility of using urea in local rice production systems. A single treatment of 30 kg N/ha application was superimposed over the farmers' practice (a long strip across their fields). General production data, position on the toposequence and water level at time of fertilizer application were recorded. The upper fields with a lower natural soil fertility level showed the highest yield response. Urea use increased the overall marginal rate of return by a factor of 13 (Meertens et al., 1992b), confirming the results of the previous year. Consequently, a pre-extension campaign was planned in 1991–1992 (Kajiru, forthcoming).

Farmer interviews and meetings have made clear that declining soil fertility levels are of concern. Most farmers appeared to have been aware of the effects of fertilizer for some time, but had been frustrated in attempts to buy it due to irregular supplies in local cooperatives. When farmers realized the project could not guarantee urea availability, they became less interested. Field days were organized for policymakers and district representatives, to make them aware of the availability constraints. If no policy changes are made, these FSR experimentation efforts will be wasted.

Banana pests and diseases. Entomological and phytopathological aspects of banana pests and diseases appeared to be sufficiently covered by commodity research activities (implemented and sponsored by ICIPE and an EEC-funded banana project). Research results indicated, however, there may be strong interactions between pest incidence and soil fertility. As soil fertility aspects were not adequately addressed by commodity research, the FSR team focused on issues related to management of soil fertility.

Poor soil fertility. Soil fertility in fact proved to be the major general constraint, influencing banana crop yields not only directly but also indirectly. Soil fertility therefore became the focal point of the on-farm experimental programme in Bukoba District. Field observations showed that farmers who use farmyard manure have fewer pest problems and obtain considerably higher yields than those who do not. However, because only about 25% of farmers have access to manure, the team initiated studies to find alternative methods to sustain soil fertility. Inorganic fertilizers had been used in the past (e.g. on coffee), but earlier research results were inconsistent, and trials had often been conducted on non-representative sites.

Soil fertility problems vary across the district; they are related to land use types (*kibanja, kikamba* and *rweya* fields); parent material (soils developed on Bukoba sandstone or Karagwe-Ankolean (a granite complex); annual rainfall (from 1,200 to 2,000 mm, influencing leaching of nutrients); and farmers' management options (cattle versus non-cattle owners). One reason for the inconsistent results of previous research was that these variations in environmental conditions had never been properly defined and described. Therefore the FSR team wanted to be very specific regarding these factors. In collaboration with the National Soil Service (NSS) and Bukoba District authorities, two seminars were held on soil fertility aspects of the Bukoba farming system. It is now generally accepted that extensive field testing – taking into account the various land use types, parent materials and rainfall zones – is necessary. Further, not enough is yet known about the distribution of nutrient levels in relation to soil type. Consequently, further diagnostic work is required. Reliable soil analyses may become useful to farmers in future, but only if extensive field testing is done now, combined with soil and plant sampling to allow calibration of analytical results.

To create a baseline, an aerial photo interpretation study was carried out (Tolman, 1990). The three goals of this study were to map the various land uses and cover types for two different periods (1960s and 1990s); to measure the extent and types of changes in the relevant land use categories; and finally to analyse the relationships between the spatial distribution of these land use categories, the changes in land use, and the physical and social environment. Using the results of the aerial photo study, several activities were carried out.

The resulting studies of fertility management systems for different types of land use are rather complicated. Not only are we dealing with mixed cropping systems, including perennial and annual crops; there are also strong interactions between livestock and crop production systems. The FSR methodology developed by CIMMYT was not eminently well suited to dealing with these interrelated issues. The problem identified was of a different magnitude than that normally encountered in commodity-oriented programmes. However, the decision to focus on soil fertility issues brought with it the need to select test crops. Consequently, strong collaboration was established with the commodity sections. Together, we identified major test crops for each land use type and agroecological zone. The FSR programme became a kind of 'umbrella' for focused soil fertility research, under which several commodity programmes could carry out relevant research.

Initially, diagnostic studies and trials concentrated on *kibanja* soils, situated around the homestead. Some *kibanja* studies are described in Case 3. Later, the team started working with maize in the smaller *kikamba* fields (Bosch et al., 1991a). Research on the *rweya* fields has recently been initiated. In addition, nutrient cycle studies are being conducted in *kibanja* fields, carried out by and in cooperation with NSS (Tanga and Ukiriguru)

Case 3. Soil fertility studies in the *kibanja* land use system

Kibanja soils are far richer in organic matter and nutrients than *kikamba* and *rweya* soils; they are responsible for the bulk of agronomic production (banana, beans and coffee). Fertility has accumulated in these fields due to mulching and applications of refuse and manure. Within the *kibanja* fields, soil fertility varies considerably. It is influenced by, but also influences, management.

A decline in banana production, a result of both declining soil fertility and pest incidence, justified further investigation. However, a long-term investigation is needed for the measurement of results in perennial crops. Therefore, beans, the major annual crop undersown in banana stands in the district, were selected as the test crop. Another advantage of beans was the possibility of harvesting two crops per year, thereby obtaining more results in a shorter time.

Cooperation was established with the Maruku Research Station bean section, which was particularly interested in variety testing. Over a period of two years, covering two long and two short rainy seasons, on-farm bean variety trials were carried out. Bean yields were used as an indicator of soil fertility levels. Beans were harvested from more than 120 sites, providing sufficient reliable yield data to be analysed in combination with other field observations, including soil analysis (Bosch, 1990b; Bosch and Mukandala, 1991; Bosch et al., 1991b). Farmers exposed to the new bean varieties showed particular interest in one. A study to assess the adoption rate will be implemented.

In addition to field work, studies were initiated to investigate the effects of added nutrients on the performance of *kibanja* soils. Pot trials using some selected representative *kibanja* soil samples were carried out in collaboration with the soil section of the Zonal Research Centre in Mwanza. The main objective of these trials was to identify the major nutrient components of the soils and their possible interactions (Bosch and Gama, 1991). The results will assist in further planning of on-farm experiments.

and the Maruku Agricultural Research Institute. These studies include estimating nutrient exports by crops, losses due to leaching, and imports via e.g. mulching and manuring. Knowledge of nutrient cycles, combined with analysis of aerial photographs, is expected to contribute to quantification of potential nutrient supply lines (in the form of mulch materials and manure) going from *rweya* grasslands and valley bottom vegetation to *kibanja* fields.

Recently, a large intensive survey was carried out in *kibanja* fields to obtain more quantitative data on problems and constraints in this land use production system. In particular, the interrelationships between yields, pest and diseases, and soil fertility were investigated (Bosch, forthcoming). A francophone FSR method, developed by CIRAD for banana research, was used (Perrier and Delveaux, 1991).

Conclusions

As we have seen, once key problems had been identified, possible trial options were considered almost immediately. As usual, the process of translating key problems into priority research themes (which shapes the general outlines of the trials) resulted in a large range of possible studies and trials. Only a few could actually be implemented. The Lake Zone team tackled this selection by rapidly pre-screening the trial options.

Close collaboration with commodity research sections and local extension and policymaking organizations enhanced this process. Options that needed the attention of commodity research teams or required socioeconomic solutions could be referred to others. Those for which research costs would be too high, or which would be too complicated in terms of logistics, were broken down into more manageable components. This process led to the development of a well-balanced on-farm research programme. It is essential that such a process be well documented, to provide a frame of reference: this is useful both in readjusting the diagnosis and trial designs and in assisting new staff to become more rapidly acquainted with past research activities, thus helping to avoid duplication of earlier efforts.

To satisfy the need for more quantitative data, we conducted short topical surveys. These surveys were often carried out in combination with an on-farm trial. The team became very enthusiastic about their use. We had previously been working in a rather multidisciplinary way; in a short time, these surveys led to a more interdisciplinary approach. The formal surveys, however, were not very helpful in planning on-farm experimental programmes. The results came too late and did not add to or change the rank order of local key problems. We decided therefore that in future it would be more efficient to increase the time allocated to informal surveys, instead of implementing large-scale formal surveys.

On-farm trials have proved valuable in initiating discussions with farmers, as has the use of in-depth short topical studies to intensify the diagnosis. In the cotton and maize trials in Maswa/Meatu, this approach led to a refocusing, based on better insight into local conditions (introduction of ox weeders to alleviate the labour shortage during weeding). For rice production systems in Maswa, it led us to see that farmer priorities are based on their realization that fertilizer is difficult to obtain. The high potential benefits of urea use, however, should encourage the local cooperative union, its societies, and the district rural development programme to take proper action. Increased awareness that local nutrient cycles are very important is the main result of the Bukoba research programme. This increased understanding of nutrient cycles can be expected to assist in planning more appropriate intervention programmes in the future.

The FSR team is convinced that good collaboration with the commodity sections and extension service is essential. All three parties are vital to the process of developing an appropriate technological package. Each has a comparative advantage during certain stages of the process. Once the three parties had agreed on a collaborative effort, commodity sections took the primary responsibility for the implementation of on-farm diagnostic work. The FSR team took the lead in conducting on-farm verification tests and in-depth short topical studies. The extension service was the leading partner whenever pre-extension campaigns were implemented. This led to efficiencies of scale and avoided duplication of efforts. Nevertheless, realities (e.g. constraints in transport, budgets or personnel) often forced us to make compromises in this division of tasks. But once the concept of working with clusters of farmers had been accepted by all parties, efficiency in implementation greatly increased for all subprogrammes: the fact that all parties were working within the same process became more visible.

Notes

1   The Bukoba team – one agronomist, one economist and one extension officer – is based at Maruku Agricultural Research Institute. The extension officer is permanently assigned to the team. When required, two other extension officers participate in FSR activities. In Maswa/Meatu, there is no research centre; the team (one agronomist and one permanently assigned extension officer) operates from the Maswa District Agricultural and Livestock Office.

2   Initially, agricultural and livestock research fell under separate parastatals; these were abolished in 1989; a commissioner of research and training within the Ministry of Agriculture, Livestock Development and Cooperatives (MALDC) took over the related functions. At ministerial headquarters an assistant commissioner is responsible for farming systems research and extension activities. At zonal levels, FSR&D coordinators have been appointed. The FSR Project Lake Zone was one of the first with a zonal orientation.

3   CIMMYT terminology distinguishes two types of activities: surveys and experimental activities. Diagnostic trials and verification tests fall in the second category.

Bibliography

BANTJE H (1989) A review of literature on agriculture and landuse in Sukumaland, Tanzania. Working Paper no. 1. Lake Zone FSR Project

BANTJE H (1991) Diagnostic survey of Maswa and Meatu Districts (Part 2 – formal survey). Working Paper no. 7. Lake Zone FSR Project

BOSCH C (1990a) Agriculture research and extension in Bukoba District. Working Paper no 6. Lake Zone FSR Project

BOSCH C (1990b) Bean on-farm variety trial in Bukoba District – Short rains 1989. Field Note no. 5. Lake Zone FSR Project

BOSCH C, BANTJE H AND MAGANGA F (1989) Annotated bibliography of Kagera Region. Working Paper no. 2. Lake Zone FSR Project

BOSCH C AND GAMA BM (1991) Response of two consecutive crops, maize and bulrush millet, to applied nutrients in a pot trial with a sandy clay loam soil from Bukoba District. Field Note no. 25. Lake Zone FSR Project

BOSCH C AND MUKANDALA L (1991) Bean on-farm variety trial in the banana mixed-cropping system in Bukoba and Muleba Districts – long rains 1990. Field Note no. 12. Lake Zone FSR Project

BOSCH C, MKANDALA L AND NGAIZA P (1990) Bean husbandry in Bukoba District. Field Note no. 6. Lake Zone FSR Project

BOSCH C, ENSERINK HJ AND KARUGABA R (1991a) Maize fertilizer trial on kikamba fields in Bukoba District – short rains 1990/91. Field Note no. 14. Lake Zone FSR Project

BOSCH C, JANSEN T, MUKANDALA L AND ENSERINK HJ (1991b) Bean on-farm variety trial in the banana mixed-cropping system in Bukoba and Muleba Districts – short rains 1990. Field Note no. 17. Lake Zone FSR Project

BUNYECHA KF (1994) Comparative analysis of rice and maize based production systems in Maswa District. Field Note no. 16. Lake Zone FSR Project

ENSERINK HJ (1990) 1990 General results and detailed proposals for 1991 on-farm work. Workplan 1991 – Annex I. Lake Zone FSR Project

ENSERINK HJ AND BUNYECHA KF (1991) Past activities and proposed future orientation of the FSR Project, Lake Zone. Policy Paper. Lake Zone FSR Project

FSR TEAM (1989a) Diagnostic survey of Bukoba District (Part 1 – informal survey). Working Paper no. 3. Lake Zone FSR Project

FSR TEAM (1989b) Diagnostic survey of Maswa and Meatu Districts (Phase 1 – informal survey). Working Paper no. 4. Lake Zone FSR Project

FSR TEAM (1990) Diagnostic survey of Bukoba District (Part 2 – formal survey). Working Paper no. 5. Lake Zone FSR Project

HART D 'T (1991) Sweet potato production in Maswa and Meatu Districts – an on-farm study. Field Note no. 19. Lake Zone FSR Project

HART D 'T (1992) Wanawake watafikia malengo yao. An on-farm study about the gender issues in agricultural production in Maswa and Meatu Districts. Field Note no. 29. Lake Zone FSR Project

JANSEN T, KARUGABA R, NGAIZA P AND BOSCH C (1991) Maize in the banana mixed cropping system in Bukoba and Muleba Districts. Field Note no. 15. Lake Zone FSR Project

MEERTENS HCC AND NDEGE LJ (1993) The rice cropping system in Sengerema Division, Maswa District. Field Note no. 37. Lake Zone FSR Project

MEERTENS HCC, NDEGE LJ AND ENSERINK HJ (1991a) Results of the cotton yield gap analysis on-farm trial; Maswa/Meatu Districts 1989/90. Field Note no. 18. Lake Zone FSR Project

MEERTENS HCC, NDEGE LJ AND ENSERINK HJ (1991b) Results of the rice on-farm fertilizer trial using a farming systems perspective; Maswa District 1989/90. Field Note no. 13. Lake Zone FSR Project

MEERTENS HCC, NDEGE LJ AND ENSERINK HJ (1992a) Results of the cotton yield gap analysis on farm trial. Maswa District 1990/91. Field Note no. 27. Lake Zone FSR Project

MEERTENS HCC, NDEGE LJ AND ENSERINK HJ (1992b) Results of the urea test in farmers' rice fields; Maswa District 1990/91. Field Note no. 26. Lake Zone FSR Project

NGENDELLO A (1991) Ox management in Maswa and Meatu Districts – a preliminary study on the introduction of ox weeders. Field Note no. 9. Lake Zone FSR Project

PERRIER X AND DELVEAUX B (1991) Une méthodologie de détection et de hiérarchie des facteurs limitant la production à l'échelle régionale. Application à la culture bananière. Fruits 46, no. 3: 213–226

TOLMAN M (1990) Land use survey project, Bukoba. Final consultancy report. ITC Enschede.

Project description: DRSPR, Mali

Département de Recherche sur les Systèmes de Production Rurale – DRSPR – or the Department of Farming Systems Research falls within the structure of the Institute of Rural Economy (IER), under the Malian Ministry of Agriculture, Livestock and Environment. Established in 1979, DRSPR is the youngest IER department. IER's thematic research covers agronomy, livestock, forestry and hydro-biological research. Each of IER's six regional research centres has or will have its own farming systems research team. The DRSPR team presented in this chapter was the first to be set up, in Sikasso, southern Mali, in 1979. This project is financed by the Netherlands' Ministry of Development Cooperation.

The intervention area comprises three agroecological zones. The northern zone, around San has low, erratic rainfall (less than 500 mm/year). The main crops are cereals, such as millet and sorghum, with some groundnuts. The area is not quite self-sufficient in food. The second zone, around Sikasso and Koutiala, has a well-developed farming system. Most project activities are carried out in this zone. In the 1960s, shifting cultivation and manual agriculture with fallow periods of 15 to 20 years began changing into permanent cultivation systems. The major driving force has been cotton production, for which animal draught power has been essential. Crop rotation is changing from a triennial (cotton–cereal–cereal) to a bi-annual rotation (cotton–cereal). Cotton accounts for about 50% of the cultivated area. The area produces a marketable surplus of cereals in most years. The conservation measures taken are insufficient to guarantee sustainable use. Land use in the southern zone (Kadiolo) is still based on shifting cultivation, with long fallow periods. Cotton and maize are the main crops.

Family households are the agricultural production units. Agriculture, with some livestock production, is the main activity. Cotton production requires more draught oxen; profits are also invested in cattle. Thus, the livestock population has increased steadily over the years at an estimated rate of 5% per year, exceeding the carrying capacity of the land. The average farm household consists of 13 members, who cultivate about 10 ha. Pasture lands are open to community use, as is firewood, which is collected in the bush.

The project emphasizes the achievement of sustainable production systems. Erosion control methods and soil fertility maintenance are central themes. Current research is directed toward the development of community-based management systems for communal village lands. Intensification of crops and integration of crop–livestock systems have been chosen as the strategies for improving productivity and incomes of farm households. The role and economic activities of women are stressed. Further, farming systems research is not restricted merely to agricultural production; diversification of household income is considered as well.

Technical services in southern Mali include CMDT (*Compagnie Malienne pour le Développement des Textiles*) and regional offices for water, forestry and livestock services. CMDT, originally a cotton promotion board, is the principal development organization; it also still has a monopoly on purchase and marketing of cotton. CMDT also provides extension, particularly for agriculture, livestock production and erosion control. CMDT is the principal client of DRSPR/Sikasso, and therefore an intensive relationship is maintained. Support and extension programmes for villages are increasingly conducted through village associations (AVs). These pre-cooperative movements are key organizations in community development activities, including management of communal equipment, erosion control measures, and health.

9 Making research plans: DRSPR, Mali

Margo Kooijman, Amadou Diarra and Rita Joldersma

The experiences of the farming systems research project DRSPR/Sikasso (see project description) illustrate the process of annual planning and priority setting for specific research activities. Emphasis is given in this chapter to planning procedures and tools, rather than the actual content of the research programme. The project has a rich history, as it began in 1979; by mid-1989, three phases had been completed. The choice has been made to focus on phase IV, which started in May 1989. First, the strategic choices made before phase IV of the project are briefly indicated as a prelude to explaining why in phase IV it became necessary to develop more formal planning structures. The body of the chapter then describes the evolution of the planning procedures.

Strategic planning

The project began as a result of discussions at national level on the necessity for an FSR approach, to make research more demand-driven and to improve the transfer of innovations. In 1977, a small team of pioneers started socioeconomic studies in the centre of the cotton-producing area, southern Mali. In 1979, the FSR approach was formalized by establishing DRSPR as a department and beginning its first project, in Sikasso.
When this project began, the main points of its objectives and strategies had already been determined by national decision makers and the donor (the Netherlands Ministry of Development Cooperation). However, the recommendations of the pioneer team were followed regarding the choice of intervention zone (high potential areas) and mandate (rainfed agriculture). The project was approved for a period of four years. Because the results from these first years were promising, a combined Malian–Dutch evaluation mission then recommended its continuation.

Priorities for subsequent phases were determined on the basis of the results of previous phases, plus new strategic choices. DRSPR follows the

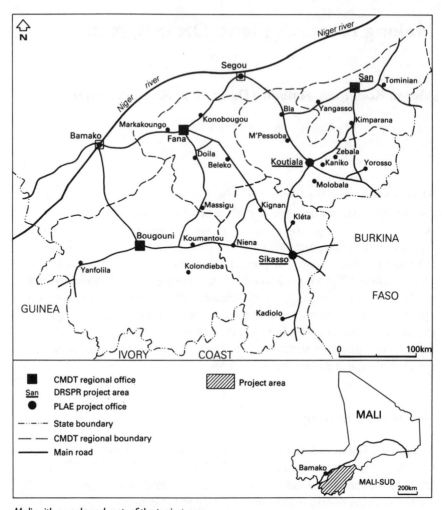

Mali, with an enlarged map of the project area

global research priorities and long term strategies of IER, as determined by the national committee for agronomic research (CNRA). Donor views are also incorporated at national level. Among the major policy orientations agreed between the donor and national institutions are paying attention to the poorest part of the rural population, and to women. In past years, reversing environmental degradation has become the central theme for DRSPR. Although this issue is now high on the agenda of national policy-makers and the donor, farmers themselves were the first to demand advice on their erosion problems (see also van Campen, Chapter 13). The project team did not determine the general orientation, objectives and strategies

Box 1. Project position when phase IV began

Objectives
- general: to identify and develop strategies, means and methods to allow the rural population to develop their production systems towards systems that are sustainable as well as profitable;
- specific: to identify technical, socioeconomic and institutional recommendations that promote development;
- to experiment with recommendations and determine the methodology to be used to transfer messages to specific target groups within the farm community;
- to train local project executives and the extension service.

Target groups
- agrarian sector (users of natural resources);
- small land users (without motorized equipment);
- rural women;
- rain-dependent farmers (no irrigation).

Strategies
- participatory research;
- strengthening linkages: farmers–researchers–extension workers;
- improving the institutional setting for environmental management at village level.

Research themes
- intensification of agricultural production;
- integration of crop and livestock production;
- improving soil fertility;
- seeking cost-effective erosion control measures, at village and farm levels;
- organizational structures at village level;
- extension methods.

Research
- completed: credit programme for purchase of oxen; methods and training for use with draft oxen; erosion control methods; methods for working with farmers on annual farm plans;
- ongoing: experiments on maintenance of soil fertility; integration of crops and livestock; diversification of crops; optimal means of collecting and use of rain water; herd monitoring; socioeconomic monitoring; participatory land use planning methods at village level.
- not yet started, but desired by:
  - DRSPR: greater focus on livestock research, agroforestry, marketing of alternative crops and livestock, and agricultural knowledge systems;
  - PROFED (see Zuidberg and Kortbeek, Chapter 12): development of strategies for improving the position of women; feasibility studies for income-generating women's projects;
  - PLAE (see Chapter 13): monitoring and evaluation of erosion control project;
  - evaluation mission: economic calculations with respect to intervention measures at micro level, impact of macroeconomic instruments, and quantitive impact of interventions on environmental durability (nutrient balances).

Composition of the core team at the beginning of phase IV
- sociologists, economists, livestock specialists, agronomists, and environmentalists.

for the project; nevertheless, they are rather autonomous in translating these into concrete research activities. Research and other activities are summarized in annual plans. Box 1 presents an overview of the objectives, target group and major strategic choices made before phase IV. Research topics are summarized in categories, including research that is completed, ongoing, and still to be started. This box summarizes the point of departure for phase IV.

Why better planning procedures were needed at the project level

Over time, the situation with respect to the formulation of annual plans has changed considerably. When the project began, the team was rather small. Communication channels between research, extension and policymakers were therefore transparent, informal and short. Formal planning procedures were not used. In the period 1986–1989 (phase III), a major change took place in the intervention area and staffing of the project. By the time phase IV began, there had been an expansion from one village to about 15, covering three agroecological zones spread over a distance of 300 km. From a small team of five, the staff had increased to about 60, including interviewers. Formal planning procedures then became necessary. DRSPR also became better known and demands for research increased (see Chapters 12 and 13).

In phase IV considerable efforts were therefore made to establish procedures for the formulation of coherent annual research plans. A more structured planning procedure – a strategic review followed by a medium term perspective plan, plus annual activity planning – was expected to encourage staff to be better informed about each others' research and to promote an interdisciplinary approach. It was also thought that better results would be obtained by intensifying contacts with thematic researchers and taking clients' needs systematically into account. Further, making procedures more transparent was seen as a way to help clients understand why some demands were not immediately included in the annual plan.

A large number of research topics had been suggested by DRSPR researchers in a draft plan of operations,[1] prior to the start of phase IV in March 1989. Improved management of natural resources and further intensification of agricultural production were taken as the two strategies for the project, following the decisions taken by national policymakers and the donor. But how could these strategies be translated into a logical set of research activities? Of course, an important prerequisite was for researchers to have a clear understanding of major problems and their causes, and the implications for the type of research required. There was also a need for the DRSPR research team and its partners (thematic research and extension services) to develop a common view of the problems and how to tackle them. But there were logistical aspects as well – most importantly, how to make sure that the research plan would be implementable, in the sense of matching the planned activities to the available resources. Financial constraints were not great, as the project had a generous budget. Human resources were obviously the scarcest resource.

A planning exercise

The project organized a planning workshop in November 1989. The researchers who were directly involved were invited, as were representatives from thematic research and the extension service. Over a two-week period, a total of 40 participants attended. The workshop had two objectives. The first was to achieve a common understanding among participants: what were the problems, their causes, and their effects? The second objective was to set priorities for problem-solving research activities, leading to a medium term, concrete and coherent research plan. The objective oriented project planning (OOPP) method was chosen to structure the workshop.[2]

At the workshop, two groups of approximately 20 participants each enthusiastically set to work. Problems related to natural resource management and intensification of agricultural production were identified. Each one was written on a card – 200 cards, in the end, and more could have been added! A great deal of time was then devoted to disentangling relationships, resulting in large 'problem trees' showing relationships between problems, causes and consequences. This exercise greatly improved the understanding of the participants. A number of key research areas were defined. Nevertheless, it was not possible to carry out systematic programming and priority setting for research activities. The number of problems stated was quite large, and the categories used in the problem trees were rather broad; this would have made priority setting a time-consuming exercise. The OOPP procedure does not suggest a way to deal with the question of getting from problem and solution trees to specific priorities. At the end of the workshop, there was no time to use the complementary tools or procedures that would have been needed to achieve the second objective. Further, at this time there was no official mandate to select priorities for research services other than DRSPR.

After the workshop – faced with a list of 200 problems – DRSPR researchers (split into two groups) had to set their own priorities. The OOPP process had not been enough. They used the workshop material as a background, but research topics that had arisen from formal and informal discussions with farmers were also rather haphazardly added, as were research topics proposed by extension projects including PROFED and PLAE (see Chapters 12 and 13). To a large extent, it was necessary to fall back on the original strategic plan: the project's formulation document was heavily used, but no structured comparison to the plan of operations or other criteria was made. The resulting plan for 1990–1991 was quite similar to the plan of operations made in March 1989; it did not include proper planning for manpower or time.

During implementation of the 1990–1991 plan, it became clear that the programme was overloaded. Time pressures brought several shortcomings to the fore. Insufficient time was available for four important activities: proper preparation, including literature studies, ex-ante analysis and evaluation of previous activities; feedback to farmers and extension services; reporting research results to extension, the IER head office, other researchers and so forth; and finally, transferring recommendations to extension services and then to farmers. Given this situation, the project could not escape the necessity of elaborating and carrying out proper procedures for priority setting and time planning. A process was needed that would lead to full clarity about the topics to be addressed and those to be left out or given a lower priority. This was important not only for the project team, but also for its clients, to avoid misunderstandings and disappointments.

More systematic annual planning

In preparing the 1991–1992 research plan,[3] systematic steps were taken to improve the planning process. In November 1990, the project team made an inventory of all ongoing research. The researchers responsible for each activity were requested to indicate what progress had been made. The results[4] of diagnostic studies and experiments were discussed with all of the interested farmers (women and men) in a village meeting. Not only the researcher who was directly involved but also a multidisciplinary research team, as well as extension service field staff, attended these meetings. Research results were discussed with farmers and extension staff, to see if they could verify the results from their experience; and the need for follow up or new activities was discussed. For each intervention zone (four in all), a researcher was assigned to prepare a working document containing preliminary research results and farmers' comments. These documents served as a basis for discussions with the zonal staff of the extension service. These meetings took place in January and February 1991; comprehensive minutes were produced by the researchers.

The next step was to combine information concerning ongoing and proposed research in the four zones. This was done in a general programming meeting, attended by all project research staff and management. Each activity was written down on a separate card and attached to the wall of the meeting room. The colour of the card indicated a phase in the research cycle: diagnostic, planning, experimentation, and transfer phases. Research activities were organized according to intervention zone and intervention level (village, farm, field/animal). A first screening identified activities that were clearly outside the mandate of the project. In this screening, the objectives and research capabilities of the project were used as selection criteria. The selection was approved by general consensus. The cards for the activities that had been rejected were put aside to be discussed with other research agencies at a later stage. From an original list of 70 activities, about 50 activities remained.

The remaining activities were then grouped into eight classes, which came out of group discussions: collection of general data; diversification and productivity of agricultural production; communal (village) management of natural resources; techniques for improving communal lands; farm management; intensification of crop production; land improvement techniques for individual fields; and intensification of livestock production.

At this point the meeting was suspended. The project management organized a second meeting, made up of DRSPR researchers and representatives from other research agencies active in the area. The approximately 40 participants discussed the possibility of implementing the research themes and topics that DRSPR saw as falling primarily under the mandate of other agencies. Again, the cards on the wall served as a starting point for the discussions. Cards with some new suggestions were added.

Now the real programming could begin. Each researcher indicated on a planning sheet the time they would actually have available for research during the coming season. Thus each researcher had to estimate the time required for other commitments and activities. This was done on a monthly basis. On the other side, the time requirements for research were assessed. On each card representing a research activity, the researcher responsible indicated the time required for implementation (both his or her own time, plus that of other researchers involved), again on a monthly basis.

An attempt at priority setting

The meeting proceeded to elaborate on the criteria to be used for priority setting. Previous investments of time and other resources were taken as an initial criterion. The meeting agreed that all relevant ongoing research would have to be finished before new activities could be considered. As a second criterion, the meeting concluded that the programme should be well balanced with respect to the various intervention zones and phases of the research cycle. A list of additional criteria was also made, covering eight points: research requested by a client (farmers or extension service); magnitude of the problem to be solved; size of the target group; economic feasibility of the solution to be tested; sociocultural acceptability of the solution to be tested; ease of introducing a proposed solution; impact on the environment; impact on the position of women. It proved difficult to apply each of these criteria to all research phases. It was also not clear how great a weight should be given to each one.

These problems would have made scoring quite difficult. However, no scoring exercise actually took place! With some slight modifications in the activities to be carried out by certain disciplines, the group decided the whole programme was implementable. The supply and demand of researcher time were also compared later by computer, confirming that all of the proposed research activities could be carried out. Of course, this was a surprising result – the expectation had been that the programme would be overloaded, as it had been in previous years. During the execution of the programme, however, it became clear that researchers had underestimated the time needed for research, and overestimated the time they would have available. Unfortunately, no time monitoring took place, because no proper procedures had yet been developed. In the 1992–1993 season, the lesson was learned: it became clear that a large number of activities in the previous year's programme could not be completed. Scarcely any new activity could be proposed, when the first criterion for priority setting was taken into account: ongoing activities had to be completed first. In addition, improvements were made over previous years, in that standard formats for research protocols were used, and guidelines were provided for literature research and editing of reports.

Conclusions

The many problems, clients and creative ideas at the start of phase IV resulted in an excess of activities. Much was started but, due to a lack of planning, programming and priority setting, many objectives were not reached. The OOPP process was useful in generating enthusiasm and inter-action among the participants; however, the difficulties experienced suggest that this process must be used with care. We learned that it is necessary to scale down the number of issues early on, and to provide proper managerial guidance of the process. When no preliminary criteria are established, the possibility that a very large number of problems will be stated by the group must be anticipated. Additional tools will then be needed to narrow down the number of problems before starting to work on causes and consequences, and it is important to have an experienced facili-tator in charge of the meeting. It is important to state what the expected out-put is at the beginning of the process (Eponou, Chapter 5). This increases satisfaction and helps to guide both facilitators and participants in planning the use of the time available.

Alternately, a different process, as used by DRSPR in 1991–1992, may be needed. Although priority setting was only partially achieved, the planning procedures used in phase IV had a number of positive effects. Researchers became more aware of the possibility and of the need for specified proce-dures. The process has also facilitated communication with DRSPR's various partners. Communication with the extension service and other develop-ment organizations, thematic researchers and farmers has intesified and become more structured. Research plans were made more coherent, consistent and complementary; this improved research efficiency. The process also created much more clarity for the outside world, concerning what the project is about and what can be expected from it: there are limits to what can be done, and procedures to follow in proposing new items. Even in phase IV the entire process was more participatory and transparent. Consequently the final result, the proposal for the annual work programme, was more satisfactory.

It is still too early, however, to draw conclusions on the effectiveness of the procedure used to elaborate the annual work plan. Procedures are not yet fully defined and tuned; experience is still lacking on how effective time planning and monitoring can be realized. Nevertheless, researchers are better aware of the need for planning and for realistic research plans. This suggests the process can be applied more successfully in future years. Continued work on improving tools and techniques (especially use of selection criteria and time monitoring) is needed.

Another important aspect is that the process of priority setting was well documented. If not written down, information regarding the arguments and reasons for past choices may be lost or difficult to retrieve. This process has begun to build up an institutional memory for DRSPR/Sikasso, which can help to avoid research efforts that re-invent the wheel. A process like the one begun at project level is also taking place on national level. It is hoped that in the future, transparent procedures involving all parties will lead to coherent, efficient and effective research programmes, both within the project and at regional and national levels.

Notes

1 The plan of operations contains objectives, activities, organization and a budget for a project or new phase of a project; it is comparable to a project document.
2 Objective oriented planning put to the test in Pakistan. MDF Journal, no. 9, 1990.
3 The annual agricultural year runs from April 1–March 31.
4 Where experiments had not yet been completed, partial results were discussed.

Bibliography

COLIBALY A AND KESSLER JJ (1990) L'agropastoralisme au Mali-Sud. Analyse des contraintes et propositions d'amélioration. Rapport de mission d'appui. Amsterdam: Royal Tropical Institute

COLLION MH AND KISSI A (1991a) An approach to long term program design including priority setting and human resource allocation. The Hague: ISNAR

COLLION MH AND KISSI A (1991b) Programmation à moyen terme. Elaboration des projets et leurs opérations. The Hague: ISNAR

DRSPR (1989) Programme de l'atelier sur la planification de recherche du 6 au 18 Novembre 1989. Sikasso: DRSPR

DRSPR (1991) Commission technique sur les systèmes de production rurale. Proposition de programmes pour la campagne 1991/92 DRSPR Volet Fonsébougou. Sikasso: DRSPR

JOLDERSMA R, KOOIJMAN M, KÉBÉ D AND KONÉ Y (1991) Approche recherche système. Note méthodologique no. 1. Sikasso: DRSPR

KLEENE P, SANOGO B AND VIERSTRA G (1989) A partir de Fonsébougou. Système de production rurale au Mali. Volume 1. Amsterdam, Bamako/Amsterdam: l'Institut d'Economie Rurale/Institut Royal des Tropiques

MINISTÈRE D'AGRICULTURE/L'INSTITUT D'ECONOMIE RURALE (1981) Les études et la recherche agronomique au service du développement rural. Bamako, Mali

MINISTÈRE D'AGRICULTURE/L'INSTITUT D'ECONOMIE RURALE (1991) Rapport Annuel 1989. Bamako, Mali

SANOGO ZJL (1991) Choix des villages de recherche. L'expérience du DRSPR/Sikasso. Sikasso: DRSPR

Project description: ARPT Western Province, Zambia

Adaptive Research Planning Teams (ARPTs) were established in 1981–1982 as a part of Zambia's national agricultural research programme. By 1990, eight of the nine provinces had an ARPT. Their specific objective is to generate recommendations to meet the felt needs of the small-scale farmer. Therefore, ARPTs adopt a farming systems approach, and develop location-specific recommendations. ARPTs are based at provincial research stations. This favours the development of intensive linkages with thematic and commodity researchers and the strengthening of research–extension linkages. The primary natural partners of ARPT are the agricultural extension branch of the Ministry of Agriculture and Forestry; Department of Veterinary and Tsetse Control Services, for livestock extension services; and the Cooperative Union (WPCU), for marketing, credit and farmer's associations. Most ARPTs are funded by foreign donors. ARPT Western Province (WP), began in 1981; it is co-financed by the Dutch government. The ARPT team consisted initially of two economists and one agronomist (1982–1987). During the second project phase (1987–1990) the number of researchers increased to seven (sociologists, livestock specialists and research–extension liaison officers were added). ARPT's technical field staff consists of extension agents, seconded to ARPT by the extension branch. In Western Province the ARPT team is now by far the largest research unit at the research station, with more staff than all four commodity research teams together.

Currently, Western Province is among the least developed provinces of Zambia. It can be characterized as having an agropastoral subsistence economy: 85%–90% of the people are farmers, 95% of whom produce mainly for their own consumption. Land is evenly distributed among individual families; average farm size is around 3 ha. The region is characterized by high out-migration, and about 30% of rural households are headed by women. Western Province as a whole is not self-sufficient in food. About 20,000 tonnes of maize, the staple food, is imported annually – equal to the maize production of the province. Presently maize accounts for more than half of total crop production. Kaoma district is the grain basket of the province, supplying other districts with maize through the Cooperative Union. Cattle play a crucial role in the economy. Cattle produce material goods (including manure, milk and meat) but are equally important in providing the social status and security of the owner. Although only 20% of households own cattle, many more have access to their products and labour.

The province has two major land systems: the uplands or dry lands (90% of the area), and the lowlands or wetlands (10%). There are distinct wet and dry seasons. The rainy season usually starts in November and ends in March/April. Average annual rainfall varies from 1,020 mm (north) to 730 mm (south). Erratic rainfall distribution (between and within years) is one of the major constraints to agricultural production. ARPT works in three zones:

- the commercial-crop-based agricultural system or 'surplus area' (Kaoma and Lukulu-East). Soils in the eastern part are fertile. Rainfall is 1,000 mm per annum. Kaoma District produces 90% of the maize marketed within the province.
- the traditional agricultural system or 'deficit area' (Senanga-West and Sesheke). Annual rainfall is 750 mm. It has poor sandy soils (*Kalahari*) and is a typical maize deficit area.
- the wetland based agricultural system (Zambezi flood plain, its tributaries and deflation pans). This area and its fertile soils makes up only 10% of the total area of the province, but 60% of the provincial cattle herd is held here.

10 Planning research in an interdisciplinary team: ARPT Western Province, Zambia

Gerben Vierstra and Mukelabai Ndiyoi

The Adaptive Research Planning Team (ARPT) in Western Province (WP), Zambia, works in three intervention zones (see project description). This chapter examines the development of research in only one – the commercial-crop-based farming system, in particular of the Kaoma District. The research programme evolved over time: ARPT1 paid a great deal of attention to this district for more than ten years, with the first activities beginning in the 1981–1982 agricultural season. The story of this evolution presents tools that, for ARPT, served as an impetus for strategic planning and change in a long-running programme that needed to re-assess its priorities.

The initial aim of ARPT was to improve the commercial-based (maize–cassava) farming systems of the Kaoma district; most research has been oriented toward developing recommendations for the production of one particular crop, notably maize, the staple food crop. Over time, the programme evolved from a narrow focus on production to a broader orientation including the sustainability of agricultural systems. Until the 1987–1988 season, research thinking within the project mainly followed a production-oriented approach: research efforts concentrated on testing and verification to better adapt technologies to farmer conditions. From 1987–1988 onwards, the evaluation of factors related to the transfer of technology became increasingly important. Research has been carried out with respect to the distribution of inputs and marketing, methodology and impact of extension services, credit, draught power and farmer organizations. There has been increasing emphasis on flexible recommendations and, since 1990, on sustainability. During the more than ten years of research, four periods can be roughly distinguished:
- an initial period of on-station tests, combined with on-farm data collection (1981–1985);
- verification of results at farmer level (1985–1987);

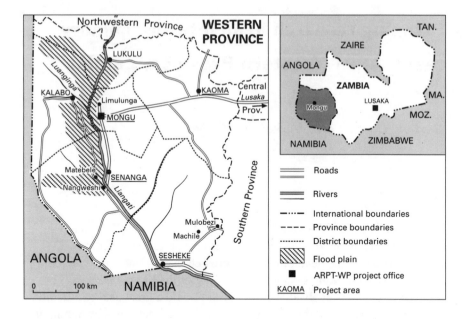

- formulation of flexible production recommendations for maize and transfer of technology (1987–1990);
- increased emphasis on sustainable production and crop diversification and production of a booklet with maize recommendations (after 1990).

This chapter begins with a description of the development of the research in Kaoma district in these four periods. We then turn to some of the factors related to this development. First, the role played by other actors is reviewed, since their strategies and policies can have an important impact on priorities. Next, some constraints and useful mechanisms – primarily related to the research team – are explored. Particular attention is paid to the development of interdisciplinarity within the team. State of the art papers are seen as extremely helpful, both in this context and from the standpoint of strategic planning.

The development of research in Kaoma district

Initial research (1981–1985). ARPT's first activity in Kaoma was an informal survey (Ndiyoi and Zimba, 1982). Three constraints on the commercial crop-based agricultural system were identified: labour shortages in the peak period, October–January; scarcity of draught power; and cash shortages. This has various effects – late planting, with increased risk of diseases (streak); restriction of the area cultivated; and suboptimal use of fertilizers, particularly inorganics. In response, the research team formulated three intervention strategies (Muwamba, 1990):

- increasing production of maize as a starch staple by testing improved and streak-resistant varieties; changes in application, optimum level, mix and timing of manure and fertilizers; reduction of weeding labour; intercropping (including the necessary spacing); and more favourable planting dates;
- increasing availability of draught power, through supplementary feeding, reduced calf mortality, and improving pastures;
- reducing post-harvest losses by improving grain storage.

Research focused primarily on the first strategy, increased maize production. The problem of draught power could only be addressed indirectly through data of planting experiments, as the team had no livestock specialist. The situation for post-harvest activities was similar. Experimental work concentrated on variety testing (mainly hybrids, early and late maturing), in relation to planting dates and fertilizer application. These trials also verified the national fertilizer recommendations (known as 'LIMA recommendations'), published in 1979. All varieties were tested on-station, starting in the second season (1982–1983), under simulated farmer conditions. Information about farmers' circumstances was collected by means of surveys, studies and field observations on specific topics, such as crop performance, actual fertilizer use, choice of varieties, and farm budgets.

By approximately the 1985–1986 season, planting dates were no longer regarded as a problem, as various varieties for late planting (MM 603, MM 502, MM 504) and early planting (MM 752) became available to the majority of small-scale farmers. Also, in response to ARPT work new hybrid varieties suitable for different planting dates were developed by commodity researchers.

Verification of on-station work (1985–1987). From 1985–1986 onwards, activities focused on field verification of the on-station results of previous years. There were two major results: a positive response of some varieties (MM 603 and MM 504) to fertilizer applied at a much lower rate than the LIMA recommendation; and the good performance of e.g. MMV 600 in poor environments (that is, with late planting dates and improper methods and rates of fertilizer application).

Technology release (1987–1990). The team reassessed all past research activities in the district during the 1987–1988 season. This took place against the background of the provincial agrarian policy, which stressed food self-sufficiency at provincial level. The strategy was to increase cereal (maize) production in surplus (or potential surplus) areas such as Kaoma, to compensate for areas with deficits. The transfer of already available production technologies was seen as the main vehicle for increasing production. There was, however, a major problem. As a result of the maize research, farmers had come to prefer one particular hybrid maize (MM 603). However, the Cooperative Union (the sole supplier of agrarian inputs in Western Province) had considerable problems in securing this seed. As the provision of fertilizer was directly tied to seed, the policy of the Cooperative Union was to sell whatever seed it could secure. Farmers had no choice but to use these varieties. Waiting for their preferred variety often led to planting too late. To make matters worse, neither farmers nor extension workers were familiar with the varieties that were available. Therefore a vast programme of on-farm demonstrations had to be set up, including the full range of available hybrids. Simultaneously, research on issues such as input supply; reach and impact of the extension service; and training of extension staff took priority. When for the first time a livestock section became available within ARPT, research addressing the problem of scarcity of draught power intensified. The exclusive preoccupation with maize finally ended. On the one hand, this research looked into the feasibility of alternative, cash-earning crops, which would perform well without adding fertilizer. On the other hand, traditional crops such as sorghum and bulrush millet received new emphasis, and on-farm trials of improved varieties gave promising results. ARPT developed flexible maize recommendations, to assist farmers in adapting to the uncertainties of limiting factors such as seed supply, draught power and cash reserves.

Economic and environmental sustainability of production (from 1990 on). Important changes took place at macro-level, reinforcing the need for sustainable low-cost production and diversification: the national government phased out all subsidies on agricultural inputs and on marketing and transportation of produce. This began in the 1989–1990 season and continues today; it altered the economics of commercial crop cultivation tremendously. Now farmers not only had to consider returns on cash investments, but also how to get the cash required.[2] Economic monitoring of farmers' reactions and efficient use of all inputs (seed, fertilizer and draught power) became important research topics. Finding new avenues for diversifying crops while maintaining soil fertility has become a major theme for research.

The implications of continuous use of fertilizer on maize plots had already been a point of concern in earlier years. ARPT on-station research data showed that maize yields in the fourth or fifth year after clearing the land may decrease to around 50% of the highest yield obtained in the first two years. Increased soil acidity as a result of applying nitrogen fertilizers to the soils in Kaoma, which are sandy and have a relatively low pH (below 5.5), is thought to be the main reason. In the near future, animal draught power will continue to be a major limiting factor for maize production, so the expansion of fields will be difficult. In addition, increasing population density will put greater and greater limitations on the possibility of shifting to other, still unused plots. In the long run maintenance of production will have to come primarily from a stabilized return per unit of land. Therefore questions of improving the organic matter content of the soil, crop rotation, and low rates of fertilizer application will figure on ARPT's research agenda in the years to come.

These issues are also linked to the concept of sustainability, which has become a central focus for agricultural projects worldwide. This development has meant a clear shift in emphasis, namely from problems raised by farmers, to problems farmers face but do not yet recognize. Such a change requires a well-balanced approach. For the average farmer in Kaoma, not yet troubled by acute problems of land scarcity, research on environmental sustainability appears rather uninteresting. Besides, research on this problem will not produce quick results. Thus to increase and maintain farmers' interest in their work, the ARPT team must combine its long-term soil fertility aspirations with work on topics that are of interest to farmers now, and promise results in the short term.[3] However, in Kaoma real short-term alternatives are not easily at hand. Therefore work related to increasing the availability of draught power and improving economic sustainability (that is, a search for alternative cash crops) must be used to maintain farmers' interest, even though both are medium-term solutions.

Other actors

Throughout the development of ARPT, other actors have influenced research priority setting in a variety of ways. On-station research, extension, supporting services, farmers and policymakers are considered, respectively.

On-station research. ARPT's research experiences in Kaoma underline the critical factor of availability of technologies developed by commodity and thematic research. When ARPT began in Kaoma, knowledge already 'on the shelf' and relevant to Western Province was minimal (only a few late maturing hybrid maize varieties were available).[4] This situation changed spectacularly around 1984–1985, when a series of new hybrid varieties developed for other situations also became available in Western Province and rapidly solved problems related to late planting.[5]

This illustrates the importance of coordination between the research priorities of FSR and on-station research. Yet in the course of the Kaoma programme, the practical responses of on-station researchers to requests from the ARPT team were rather modest. ARPT's endless requests for open pollinated maize varieties have never adequately been met. Collaboration with on-station research on food legumes (based in Eastern Province) was mainly limited to a supply of seed for testing. Questions to the soil fertility team remained unanswered. Some practical reasons might be mentioned, but more fundamental forces are at work, in particular, the prevailing focus of the commodity programmes on high-yield varieties and maize hybrids. At least as fundamental is that quite often ARPTs may feel they are seen by on-station researchers as 'service units' of commodity research, rather than as 'autonomous systems research teams'. In other words, although on-station researchers are positive about ARPT carrying out their trials in remote areas, they are not inclined to integrate ARPT-generated priorities in their research programmes. In such a situation, ARPT needs to avoid taking over the commodity research role, even though this is a great temptation. In the case covered here, the size of the ARPT on-station programme in the first two periods (1981–1987), in comparison with the on-farm programme, might indicate that ARPT became too preoccupied with on-station research.

Extension. A strong point of the maize programme was its relatively close collaboration with extension staff in the field. Extension workers participated in selecting and monitoring test farmers. At the start of on-farm research, they made specific proposals for research topics (for example, seed germination). This latter role became less significant once the programme was under way. However, in general, extension staff played a minor role in defining further research topics. Their main interest was in receiving clear recommendations they could give to farmers regarding maize production. Not surprisingly, extension was disappointed that it took so long before concrete recommendations became available.

Cooperative Union. ARPT was unable to find effective ways to initiate a constructive debate with the Cooperative Union. Institutional barriers appeared too strong. This was much regretted, as one might argue that improving the performance of the Union (e.g. timely fertilizer supply) would have more impact on production than ARPT research could. However, the officials of the Cooperative Union scarcely reacted to ARPT's research results, and did not play a role in setting priorities for future research.

Farmers. Farmers participate in the programme in many ways. They provide fields for tests, attend field days and meetings, provide information during surveys and so forth. However, thus far farmers have not been involved in strategic planning of research. They are also only indirectly involved in planning the annual research programme. Feedback of research results to farmers takes place shortly before a new season begins, during preparatory meetings with them. Here plans for new activities and tests are launched. Farmers' reactions and opinions are not entirely unknown – they state their ideas during farmer field days, earlier in the season. However, the project still lacks opportunities for farmers (and specifically for collaborating farmers) to participate directly and systematically in setting priorities for research activities. The research team acknowledges that more could be done in the search for methods to obtain more farmer participation. The recently introduced village research group approach (in which village groups become the working partners of ARPT, rather than individual trial farmers) may improve feedback to and from farmers.

Research coordination and policymaking. Three platforms offer opportunities for policymakers and other stakeholders to influence ARPT's research programme: the annual ARPT national meeting, the Region II meeting and the ARPT steering committee meeting (provincial level). In practice, most of these official meetings have had limited effects on the content of ARPT research programmes. Only highlights of the past season and a sketch of the next year's work programme are presented. Time for comments on the presentations is very restricted. However, the informal discussions are useful for covering topics of mutual interest, exchanging experiences and making agreements on collaboration.

For the annual ARPT steering committee meeting at provincial level, partners and potential users of ARPT research results are invited. This includes commodity and specialist researchers, livestock specialists, representatives of supporting institutions (the Cooperative Union, LIMA Bank), extension service and provincial planning officers. This is the meeting that should have the greatest impact on work programmes and orientation. The steering committee meeting could influence ARPT in some strategic choices, such as the extension of intervention zones and the addition of a livestock component, but not so much in choosing substantial research themes. Unfortunately, the supporting institutions are usually absent or represented only by staff lower in the hierarchy, who do not have the background knowledge (or, most likely, the right) to engage in meaningful discussions. Others, too, have little knowledge of what is presented (due to high staff turnover and failure to read documents); moreover, the number of participants is very high. Efforts to make this meeting more effective and supportive to ARPT have failed.

In their 1988 reassessment of their earlier research, ARPT took the initiative in attempting to involve other actors. ARPT staff members then had intensive contacts with representatives from other structures and organizations active in the field of provincial agricultural development, including the provincial planning unit, extension, the veterinary department and regional development projects. The general feeling (also supported by the Netherlands donor) was that ARPT should play an active role in integrating and supporting the scattered ongoing research efforts in the province. With this in mind, ARPT offered to provide 'service research' for other development teams, covering their priority themes and problems.[6] A hidden objective of this research was to improve ARPT's general image, which was rather low at the time. But one year after its initiation, service research died a gentle death. Although the modalities of collaboration were clearly defined beforehand, too often the result was that ARPT conducted the research entirely alone, without involvement of the partner. Further, the follow-up on the results of this research usually left much to be desired.

Constraints on priority setting

ARPT's emphasis has evolved from mainly technological attention to the maize production system to a holistic approach, and later to a search for a diversified sustainable cropping system in an adverse economic environment. Such an evolution is not unfamiliar in the implementation of FSR&D projects. In their first year, programmes frequently begin with agronomic tests, very often variety tests (either on-farm or on-station or both). Once communication has been established, there is no need to stick to this initial scope of work. But ARPT's preoccupation with external factors such as input supply only began six years after the start of the programme. Why did ARPT continue on such a limited basis for such a long time in Kaoma? Which factors determine the orientation and research strategies of a project like ARPT? We will look first at some general constraints on proper priority setting, and then at some of the mechanisms ARPT has used to try and overcome these constraints.

Planning and organization

ARPT has suffered over the years from over-ambitious annual work pro-grammes.[7] Researchers seem to strive for an 'ideal' programme, and they conceive this as one that is 'as complete as possible'. The dangers are understandable – when a work programme is first conceived, it is easy to overlook many practical factors: to make no real estimate of the time required for the necessary field work, to leave no room for setbacks, and above all to reserve little or no time for preparation – or, even more frequently, for report writing.

For a team like ARPT, the schedule within which annual work program-mes are drafted and implemented (Table 1) obviously depends primarily on the agricultural season. At the start of the season (the end of October), the team must to be ready to install tests and trials on-farm as well as on-station. Before that date, all thinking, analysis and synthesis, reporting, and preparation of field staff and farmers for the activities of the next season must be finished. As complete results of field tests only become available in July, the period July–November is usually hectic. Not only must the annual report be written, including the work programme for the next season; it must be approved at various levels. Thus the cycle of preparatory phases that would in theory assure a well-justified and planned set of research activities for the coming year is sometimes not observed.

Initial team discussions on the results of the past season and planning for the next season are usually scheduled for August. These discussions take place under relatively great time pressure: it is then necessary to finalize the annual report and to produce a provisional work plan for the next season. This is presented at the annual national ARPT meeting at the end of August. But in August it is impossible to hold detailed discussions, while keeping an open mind with respect to all possible alternatives. The work plan presented at the national ARPT meeting is therefore usually quite vague. Only on the eve of a new season is the researcher receptive to in-depth discussions. The real evaluation of the previous season only takes place shortly before the start of the new season, and in fact a final work programme will not be ready until the second round of team discussions, in mid-October. This could mean that the headings in the work programme (as presented in the annual report to ARPT's national meeting and steering committee meeting) no longer cover the activities that are actually to be undertaken.

The two-round planning procedure, with one session in August and the final in October, does have positive features. As the process goes on, the

Table 1. Drafting and implementing the annual research plan[a]

JUNE	• Results from on-station and on-farm tests come in from the field
JULY	• Analysis of results + reporting, either in separate synthesis papers or directly, in each section's draft contributions to the Annual Report
	• Economic analysis of test results
AUG.	• Rough drafts are made of plans for the next season, after discussions and feedback from colleagues within the team, commodity research and other relevant persons/organizations;
	• Three-day team discussion on contributions from all sections + proposed activities for the next year: this results in a final sketch of the work programme for the next season
	• Editing of final version of annual report
	• First drafts of research protocols for activities proposed for the next year
	• Presentation of report + provisional work programme to the national ARPT meeting
SEPT.	• Feedback from commodity research (notably on methodology), and from other relevant institutions and staff
	• Possible review and/or finalization of protocols for all activities planned for the next year
OCT.	• Presentation of report + provisional work programme to provincial ARPT steering committee
	• Second team discussion (3–4 days) on Annual Report, work programme, revised protocols and possible changes suggested by ARPT national meeting and ARPT steering committee; weighing of time, other resources, consequences and methodological alternatives
NOV.	• Discussion of final work programme with field staff (including feedback of results from the last season)
	• Preparation of field programme, such as selection of farmers, organization of inputs, instruction of field staff, etc.
NOV./DEC.	• Initiation of field programme
	• Meetings with all test farmers to explain tests and decide on location of test plots (+ distribution of seed, etc.)
JAN.	• Monitoring field tests
	• Main period for non-seasonal studies
	• Training (courses and informal) for extension staff
	• Feedback of results (in particular those from past years) to farmers
	• Analysis and elaboration of remaining material
	• Field days for farmers (while crops are still in the field)
	• Field staff make reports about the ongoing season, including writing field day reports
MAY	• From January until May, monthly monitoring meetings are held to review progress made in carrying out the research programme

[a] Obviously this timetable is too schematic. Some activities do not always follow precisely this chronological order, and shortcuts may be made. In addition, this schedule is more relevant for the agronomic and livestock sections than for economics and sociology sections.

programme becomes increasingly focused and takes on a definite form. Moreover, in the period between the first and the final draft of the work plan, researchers are able to look more objectively at their original ideas. This facilitates integration of colleagues' comments made during the final meeting in October. Obviously such a meeting only makes sense if the necessary preliminary work has been done. That is, if the meeting functions as a kind of culmination of all preceding efforts, both at disciplinary and team levels, allowing the project to arrive at a consistent, manageable, cost-conscious programme.

Monitoring. Within ARPT one team member was appointed to act as a permanent coordinator for each geographical intervention zone (1987–1988). This facilitated discussions within the team as a whole. However, monthly team meetings to monitor the progress of the work programme have been of limited value with respect to enhancing the scientific cohesion of the team. Too often these meetings are limited mainly to administrative problems. The introduction of regular technical meetings is no solution: generally staff members are already busy with many other meetings.

Research team composition and preferences

The composition and views of a team play a decisive role in priority setting. In its first six years, ARPT had to cope with an incomplete research team, with only one agronomist and two economists. There was no livestock specialist, sociologist, or extension specialist, and so forth. This restricted the scope to crops. But even more important to the overall orientation of research was the way the researchers interpreted their work. For instance, the economists limited themselves to economic analysis of agronomic tests; they did not pay attention to the conditions under which these tests were conducted. In fact, similar attitudes may explain the scant concern shown by ARPT before 1986 for traditional crops such as sorghum and bulrush millet, in comparison to maize. These crops should have received attention earlier: it should have been obvious that Zambia could not continue highly subsidized maize production and commercialization for long.

ARPT works in many geographical areas and on many research themes, and (at least until recently) individual team members operated rather independently, according to their seniority. Such factors seem to make a certain degree of separation inevitable.[8] The variety of disciplines and the usual mix of national and expatriate researchers also present difficulties. Professional respect and comradeship, loyalty and careful encouragement of interdisciplinarity can usually overcome these situations.

Personal research preferences of individual team members can be a potential threat to the internal consistency of a research programme. Many researchers have well-defined personal interests. These are often related to programme objectives, but do not directly contribute to their realization. For instance, sometimes researchers hope their participation will lead to a thesis. ARPT has a policy of examining each of these instances on a case by case basis. It is not wise to reject such research themes out of hand. The personal motivation and general effort of a researcher may increase considerably if personal scientific preferences are met. However, from the point of view of project management, the fear of too much attention to personal research preferences may have a basis in fact. ARPT has experienced both positive and negative effects of preferences.

Other human factors

Some textbooks on priority setting seem to begin from a number of implicit suppositions – including the idea that a team will be functioning smoothly, in an interdisciplinary manner. In practice, the situation is usually much less ideal. Sometimes a team will go through a conflict-ridden period. A striking example of such a time for ARPT-WP began at the end of the 1987–1988 agricultural season, and cut through the staff along lines of nationality. Difficulties, many originating in old sores from the time preceding Phase II, centred on team leadership. Questions about whether and when leadership should be transferred to Zambian staff were crucial. There was a kind of temporary team disintegration; as a result, proper working relationships were interrupted (and thus also the smooth flow of information). Obviously this bickering had an effect on the team, as well as on the programme. Peace returned only after March 1989, when the implementing agencies appointed a Zambian staff member as provincial coordinator.

The collaboration of national and expatriate researchers is a structural area of tension that often needs to be dealt with. The scope of these two groups usually differs with respect to their expectations of FSR&D. Whereas nationals are more programme oriented, expatriates are usually more project oriented. Within ARPT, Dutch researchers gave priority to the state of affairs in Western Province, and consequently to the potential of ARPT for improving conditions. Zambian researchers, in comparison, considered matters at national research level (ARPT National, Research Branch, etc.) at least as important as those in Western Province. It seemed that in their opinion bilateral funding should not be allowed to interfere with the long term process of national FSR&D development. (This difference in attitude and orientation had practical consequences, such as a suboptimal availability of Zambian team members at provincial level.) But also expatriates, who are usually temporarily assigned to both the project and the country, may be oriented to the short term. They aim at quick results within the project period, which is a rather artificial time horizon. To achieve a smoothly functioning team and thereby to have a positive impact on research priority setting, such differences must be reconciled. A first step is to discuss them explicitly during the formulation period of a project, and before each project phase begins.

National and expatriate staff also differed in their eagerness to collaborate with other provincial institutions and development projects, and in their assessment of the need to cut back on certain research themes in a timely manner and conduct action research on non-technical aspects.

Mechanisms facilitating priority setting

The success of teams like ARPT is greatly dependent on successful joint functioning of the disciplines involved. Thinking along with each other, even when this involves another discipline, is a condition for a well balanced and internally consistent final product. While personal relationships and many other psychological factors play a crucial (if not dominant) role with respect to the way the disciplines work together, management of human resources is an important aspect of FSR, which can help to create the conditions needed for successful priority setting. It can be helpful to have an active policy that stimulates interdisciplinary collaboration and the development of real interdisciplinarity, as discussed by Norman in Chapter 2. With this in mind, ARPT has developed several mechanisms, each of which has had some result.

The ARPT team consists of five disciplinary sections: agronomy, livestock, economics, sociology and research–extension liaison officers. Staff of these sections are given much responsibility with respect to defining their own future research activities. Little by little, they elaborate their plans for the next season. Analysis of seasonal research data, synthesis with former results, acquisition of additional information, feedback from others, conceiving and screening possible solutions, as well as determining new research questions and setting priorities for them – in the first instance this all happens at the section level. There are frequent consultations with relevant team members from other sections, so obviously a sort of osmosis occurs, allowing the ideas of one section to become somewhat known to others by the time the first official team meeting of the year is held. However, the interdisciplinary working plan takes shape only during the two official planning meetings. Based on 'state of the art' papers (see below) for each ARPT research area, major research themes are identified.[9] Similarly, primary target areas are taken into account. Each of ARPT's five disciplines indicate how much time they think will be devoted to a given research topic and research zone. This is made visible by using matrices. The five individual matrices are then combined into one general matrix, indicating the priority assigned in terms of total time the whole team will spend on each topic in each area. This result is subsequently confronted with ARPT's ideas about the relative priority of research themes and research zones.

One danger involved in elaborating ideas at section level before the final planning meetings should be noted. Flexibility – the possibility that the creators of ideas will do some objective re-thinking – may decrease. And yet re-thinking is necessary when an idea does not fit into the overall programme due to limited manpower, means, or even its own time perspective. In these cases project management must have the final say.

Realistic planning

By following a more or less fixed timetable, ARPT tries to respect the various phases of reflection and balancing of options necessary before establishing a definite new programme of activities (as suggested by Table 1). During planning sessions involving the several disciplines, ample care should be taken to establish a realistic work plan. Project management should not be afraid of timely adjustments to the work programme. It may be necessary to eliminate certain research issues, to prevent falling behind on the programme as a whole. A team is more apt to consent to such deletions if they take place in accord with a priority ranking of programme parts established beforehand, at the time the programme is defined. If research activities have to be scaled down or reduced in number, the atmosphere is critical – no discipline will be enthusiastic about cutting its own planned activities.

Tools for planning and evaluation

In setting priorities, the evaluation and planning tools used are an important aspect of the working methodology of the team. ARPT did not immediately take concrete, effective steps toward a thorough reassessment of its own cumulative experiences since the beginning of the project.[10] A tight schedule for year-to-year planning of the primarily agronomic trials – new trials had to be designed or even planted before the previous trials had even been analyzed – led to preoccupation with day-to-day business. There was no mechanism to react to or anticipate new trends and developments. Not that the need for reassessment was not seen: two internal evaluation missions had already insisted on the need for a synthesis of ARPT's cumulative results. Therefore, we must conclude that the team either underrated the importance of reassessment or lacked the tools to carry it out.

By mid-1988 the research team was at full strength. In the first half of 1990, a massive effort at synthesizing took place. This led to the production of 'state of the art' papers for each intervention zone, including Kaoma. These papers played a key role in redefining the issues. This process was highly interdisciplinary; relevant additional secondary data were collected, and scientific and work contacts with other researchers and institutions were revived. A positive public relations effect was an additional spin-off from these papers. Research protocols are a further tool that can stimulate discussion and help to make priority setting more transparent.

Research protocols. The elaboration of research protocols is a simple but effective tool in planning research. Protocols facilitate evaluation as well, by encouraging the statement of clear, agreed objectives. Also, they lead to interaction between team members of different disciplines, and finally to a coherent programme. ARPT makes research protocols for each activity, not only for agronomic trials, but for all types of research that are undertaken, including surveys, monitoring, and so forth. The protocol includes the 'why, what, how, where and when' of the activity, as well as the financial means and human resources required. In principle, all protocols must be ready at the time of the final team meeting on the work programme for the next year (around mid-October).

For the team as a whole, the advantage of writing protocols is clear. Too often researchers are inclined to start research activities more or less 'spontaneously'. A research protocol forces the initiator(s) of the activity to begin a process of reflection about implementation, both at an early phase and in a realistic way. In addition, it provides a good basis for discussion about the relationship of the activity to the programme as a whole. And above all, by indicating costs, it facilitates a correct weighting of all intended activities against available resources (manpower and funds) and other potential activities. If the proposed activity will require a disproportionate part of available resources, parts of the activity or even the whole may be dropped. Alternately, it is sometimes possible to modify an activity, so that it requires fewer resources.

Example 1. The wetlands programme

The wetlands programme became, in the opinion of the authors of this chapter, an example of ARPT at its best. After the clouds of within-team conflicts were past, a systematic approach in accord with FSR&D methodology was pursued. Based on an informal survey, in which all disciplines participated, four geographical research areas were identified. Crop and herd monitoring were initiated by the agronomy and livestock sections, respectively. In addition, a socioeconomic survey, specifically directed to cattle management questions, was conducted (in two of the four areas). In addition to a rich volume of 'cattle data' on ownership, grazing methods, management and so forth, this survey provided a basic understanding of the farming population itself. Access to factors of production, number and identity of marginal farmers, survival strategies, and so forth could be assessed and even quantified. Monthly work sessions of all researchers concerned with the wetlands had clear effects in terms of mutual complementarity and stimulation. At the end of the season, the team was able to present a rather complete picture of two of the four study areas, and a reasonable picture of the other two. The resulting research programme for the 1989–1990 season was thus well integrated. Although the research plan focused on the primary cash-earning activities (cattle and rice) and on food potential (cassava and maize) in the respective areas, it also paid ample attention to issues of equity, such as access to factors of production for marginal farmers. (Among these marginal farmers, female-headed households were the most important group to be monitored. These represent 30–35% of all farming households in the area.)

Interim best-bet solutions. One lesson we learned was that research topics, once defined, tend to stay on the agenda too long. Often researchers want a 100% answer. However, 100% is often irrelevant, especially since production conditions may change dramatically, so that another type of solution is needed. Recommendations need not be based on totally optimal solutions to lead to improvements in production systems – even suboptimal solutions may speed up development and be cost effective. That is, often it is more efficient to use 'interim best-bet recommendations', based on the best knowledge available at a given point in time. Such solutions should be used with the proviso that they can be modified in the light of later knowledge, but sometimes they are in fact the best solutions.

State of the art papers. State of the art papers are a way of synthesizing the results of research from previous years in one consolidated document. The ARPT team started producing a number of these papers during the 1989–1990 season. Under the responsibility of an editor (a staff member) for each of the three intervention zones, this work grew into a real interdisciplinary exercise. Not only were three highly acceptable documents produced; this also made it easier to formulate the work plan for the next project phase. Because all team members experienced the same process, an optimal team consensus was reached about what to concentrate on in the coming years. As it had been stated that these papers would give a real picture of the 'state of the art', the team made use of much old, unpublished (grey) literature produced by others. This stimulated discussions and led to new or revived scientific contacts and working relations with other persons and institutes related to the areas concerned.

The whole exercise took three to four months; the total number of person-months invested is estimated at 17 (20–25% of the total number of person-months available for that year). The state of the art papers were frequently used as reference material. They confirmed the importance of taking time for an overall analysis and evaluation of one's own activities (obviously against the background of what has been done by others). For ARPT, the positive experience of writing these papers initiated a whole series of synthesis reports during the next year (e.g. on sorghum and millet, manure and cassava).

Creating opportunities for interdisciplinary work. In addition to the mechanisms described above, on several occasions special research activities were organized, in which all team members were obliged to participate. Two instances of successful interdisciplinary work, the wetlands and livestock programmes, are given in Examples 1 and 2. Example 3 presents an attempt at interdisciplinary work that did not have satisfactory results: the functioning and role of the research–extension liaison officers (RELOs).

Example 2. Livestock programme

The livestock section was the last component to be added to the team (at the start of Phase II). This section began with an in-depth analysis of all existing research data on livestock. Then an OOPP exercise (objective oriented project planning) was conducted at team level. This resulted in an outline for ARPT's livestock programme for the next few years. Development of feeding strategies, appropriate management practices and crop–livestock interaction, as well as reduction of calf mortality and increase in calving percentage, were defined as the main lines of future research activity. For all research activities and themes elaborated from these lines, indications of the expected involvement of other sections were given. When these research ideas were screened with relevant other institutions concerned with livestock, some questionmarks regarding overlapping activities came up, notably from the Veterinary Department. In essence, however, the proposed research programme did not change.

Example 3. The position and role of RELO

The Research–Extension Liaison Officers' Section of ARPT is an example of attempted interdisciplinary work that failed. As a matter of fact, the RELO section joined the team too early – at the end of 1987 – at a moment when ARPT did not yet have any recommendations on hand. Therefore one of the essential tasks of RELO, transferring research results to extension staff, was left up in the air. In addition, the importance of concentrating on the reverse flow of information, namely the information flow from extension to research, was insufficiently recognized, certainly by the section but perhaps also by the team as a whole. Besides, as there was no general job description for a RELO at national level, the section did not have clear guidance. Interpretation of tasks depended entirely on the local situation. An improvised re-assessment of the section's tasks by the team, involving acquisition of more information about farmer dynamics with the help of extension staff, did not function well. The RELOs seemed to be primarily interested in conventional extension tasks. After the RELOs, for various reasons, left the team, they were not replaced. In practice, this meant the section was dissolved (1990). However, this was premature. Not long thereafter, the team completed a set of technical recommendations, ready for transfer to extension. In the last few years, having other ARPT staff members take over RELO tasks has proven to be a stopgap solution; the process of transferring new technology merits permanent special attention. In addition, notably during the dissemination phase, a RELO section can play an important role with respect to strengthening a team's interdisciplinarity by uniting the various team members in one joint pre-extension programme.[11]

Conclusions

The ARPT experience illustrates the danger of research with a limited scope, whether the limitations are due to political or practical considerations, or those of researchers themselves. ARPT research in Kaoma was guided primarily by short-term priorities (higher maize production) and practical considerations. For a long time, the research programme continued in this initial direction. At first, ARPT did not take either political trends (and their impact on the price system) or long-term sustainability trends in the agricultural system into account. As a result, when the economic viability of the maize production system was called into question, ARPT had very few alternatives to offer, even after about eight years of research.

Too often a research programme is a train that rolls relatively heedlessly along. New work programmes are often based on a hasty analysis of seasonal results, plus a lot of 'intuitive' knowledge. This process will never be entirely replaced by formal priority setting. However, this chapter suggests that time for thorough synthesis and reflection needs to be built in from the beginning, as part and parcel of a research programme. In planning FSR&D programmes time should be explicitly reserved for such pauses. In extreme situations, taking time for such necessary syntheses can be even more important than continuation of the field programme for another year!

When ARPT did take time for reflection, writing state of the art papers was a very positive experience. These papers clarified the strategies that had been adopted; they also led to a gradual concentration and prioritization of research, in terms of area, themes and researcher time. This effort also greatly enhanced the participation of intersectoral groups and increased multidisciplinary work within ARPT. As a side effect, state of the art papers increased recognition of ARPT's work and bettered its image in the eyes of critical outsiders. In later years, similar synthesizing reports were made; this continued to improve the quality of research priority setting. While we did not use them in this way, such papers would be good preparation for planning techniques such as OOPP.

Through trial and error, the FSR team made use of instruments that enabled a manageable, coherent, and cost-effective work programme with clear priorities. Facilitating interdisciplinary work has been a key element in this process. Interdisciplinarity within a team is not self-evident: it must be organized. It is necessary to create regular opportunities for interdisciplinary work: good examples are setting up a monitoring system, elaborating research proposals and writing state of the art papers. We would also urge more frequent use of 'interim best-bet' recommendations, as a way to get the most from the available researcher time. Exhaustive experimentation often leads to unacceptable delays, and is not always necessary to the development of useful information.

The success of the joint work of the ARPT team on the wetlands and livestock programmes (Examples 1 and 2) seems to indicate that establishing a real interdisciplinary atmosphere is particularly feasible when a new activity is just beginning – that is, in the diagnostic and planning phase. As soon as a programme develops within a particular field of research, it is important that the various disciplines contribute their specific skills and approaches. During that period contacts between disciplines can be less regular, without a negative effect on the final research process. Interdisciplinary activity intensifies at three points: preceding the annual research cycle; before a new project phase (project phases usually last two to three years); and in the start-up period before an important expansion of activities (geographic area or new research theme). At these moments disciplinary sections must bring forward both their standpoints and their results, as input for an integrated programme, reporting of results, or recommendations. Good interdisciplinarity can only be achieved on the basis of effective participation by each separate discipline involved.

Above all, even if one succeeds in elaborating a well-balanced programme with clear priorities, there is no guarantee of smooth implementation. Constant monitoring of progress by the project management is necessary. Moreover, a team must not be afraid to make interim adaptations when needed, even if these adaptations will most likely affect the original research priorities.

Notes

1   If not explicitly stated otherwise, ARPT refers to ARPT Western Province.
2   For instance, in the 1989/1990 season fertilizer prices increased by 346%, whereas producer prices rose on average by 125% (Muwamba, 1990, p.45). Cash requirements for hiring draught power rose 265% in one year (1989–1990); credit covered only 50% of purchased inputs (ibid., p.46).
3   The same strategy may be valid with respect to policymakers, other research structures and notably donors. Also they usually link credibility with results in the short term.
4   In the early years of ARPT's activity, the commodity research team for maize was only interested in research on hybrid maize varieties. It was not until 1987 that a team concentrating specifically on open pollinated varieties was established at Mount Makulu Research Station. Moreover, seen in a national context, the maize team considered Western Province a marginal maize-producing area, not justifying specific research activities 'on the spot'.
5   A similar situation occurred with the release of improved sorghum and millet varieties in Senanga West (another ARPT intervention area).
6   In addition to assistance with the on-farm trial work of some development teams, service research particularly concerned help with training and in planning and carrying out socioeconomic work. To prevent interference with ARPT's main programme, service research was usually planned for the period after planting time (i.e. from February onwards). Such research never took up more than 10% of the total available time of all sections concerned (agronomy, economics, sociology and RELO).
7   As such, ambitious programmes are not bad. To a some extent they may even have a stimulating effect. However, strict monitoring of progress then becomes extremely important. Falling too far behind the stipulated programme may lead to a situation in which members of the executing team become unconcerned with meeting any time limit at all. In addition, regularly failing to produce timely research results or reports will hurt the credibility of the team vis-à-vis the outside world.
8   ARPT-WP has no monopoly on problems of interdisciplinarity. At the 1991 ARPT half-yearly meeting (in Siavonga), mentioned earlier, all ARPT teams came forward with complaints about their interdisciplinary functioning.

9 Research themes are divided into three main groups: long-term sustainability issues, short-term production issues and issues related to equal access to information and resources.
10 An interim state of the art paper based on an analysis of all on-farm and on-station maize tests was not written until 1988. Feedback of test information to farmers was limited to inviting them to field days during the season; usually there were no meetings with farmers at which final yield results of all tests were discussed.
11 Naturally the opposite is also possible: the existence of a RELO section may be an alibi for other disciplines not to get involved in the process of dissemination.

Bibliography

ARPT NATIONAL (1991) ARPT in the 1990s. Report on the 1991 ARPT half-yearly meeting, Siavonga, 19–21 February 1991. Lusaka: Department of Agriculture, ARPT

ARPT-WP, Annual Reports 1987/88, 1988/89, 1989/90. Mongu: Department of Agriculture, Mongu Regional Research Station (MRRS)

ARPT-WP (1991) ARPT WP, 1981/82 to 1990/91. Presentation at ARPT Review, Siavonga, 19–21 February 1991. Mongu: Department of Agriculture, MRRS

BIGGS SD (1989) Resource-poor farmer participation in research: a synthesis of experiences from nine National Agricultural Research Systems. OFCOR, Comparative Paper no. 3. The Hague: ISNAR

DUTCH MINISTRY OF FOREIGN AFFAIRS (1988) Zambia Western Province 1979–1987. Evaluation report of the Dutch technical assistance programme in the Western Province. The Hague: Directorate General for International Cooperation, Operations Review Unit

MUWAMBA JM ed (1990) The commercial-crop based agricultural systems of Western Province (1980–1990 and beyond). State of the art paper no. 3. Mongu: Department of Agriculture, MRRS

NDIYOI MC AND ZIMBA B (1982) Results and prognosis from the informal survey in Kaoma District. Lusaka: Ministry of Agriculture, ARPT, Mount Makulu Central Research Station

VIERSTRA GA (1991) End of contract report of the expatriate sociologist. ARPT-WP, Mongu: Department of Agriculture, MRRS

Project description: RAMR, Benin

Recherche Appliquée en Milieu Réel (RAMR) began in 1986; it is financially supported by the Netherlands government, the Near East Foundation (until 1988) and the government of Benin. The Royal Tropical Institute (KIT) and the International Institute for Tropical Agriculture (IITA) provide technical support. The project operates within the Direction de la Recherche Agronomique (DRA), the Directorate – within the Ministry of Rural Development – in charge of agronomic research. Cooperation with agricultural extension agencies (CARDER), the agricultural faculty of the University of Benin, and NGOs is a high priority. The provincial branch, in Lokossa, develops and conducts FSR&D in Mono Province (map). The FSR&D team consists of an agronomist, an agroeconomist and a livestock specialist, supported by expatriate staff. The national branch in Cotonou coordinates and supports the dissemination of FSR&D results throughout Benin. In 1992 it was made up of six researchers (most part-time), and an expatriate co-director.

The project operates in three agroecological zones: 'barre soil plains' (Adja), vertisol valley (depression of Tchis) and forested savanna (Lonkly) (map). The climate is a sub-Guinea type with bimodal rainfall (900–1,200 mm per annum). Soil degradation and low soil fertility, due to continuous exploitation, pests and weed infestation, and frequent flooding are the main constraints to agriculture, on which about 90% of the population depends; often men and women have their own plots. Most adults are still illiterate. Well-developed private marketing channels allow farmers with money to obtain the products required. There are few opportunities for extra-agricultural activities. Agriculture in the Mono is mostly at subsistence level, with maize as a staple. Cotton and oil palm are major cash crops. Oil palm is cultivated mainly for *sodabi*, an alcoholic drink in high demand in the area. The average household consists of about eight people, who cultivate a farm of 1.2–3.5 ha. Typically they have three sheep or goats. The average annual household income is approximately US$ 450 (Ministry of Planning, 1983).

Initially, thematic and commodity-oriented researchers, as well as CARDER, saw RAMR as support for their programmes. However, the RAMR objective of developing a methodology for farming systems research incorporating farmers, usable as an example for other areas, was relatively new. (RAMR was one of the first FSR&D projects in Benin.) To establish the credibility of this type of research, the project started by testing simple technologies, providing quick results (e.g. testing varieties) that extension could transfer to farmers. At the same time, studies and tests aimed at long term results (e.g. baseline studies and alley-cropping trials) were initiated. Efforts were made to develop a methodology to strengthen participation of farmers in research. Further, the project introduces innovations tailored insofar as possible to specific target groups. Supporting the institutionalization of FSR&D in the national research structure of Benin is an additional objective.

RAMR has introduced innovations that are already being adopted by farmers, such as new maize and cowpea varieties and eradication of *Imperata* with *Mucuna utilus*. Other innovations promoted, such as alley-cropping, regeneration of exhausted soils and a methodology to increase vaccination of small ruminants, are part of a CARDER 'pre-extension test'. A quarterly project *Bulletin de la Recherche Agronomique* communicates results of agricultural research (including FSR&D) to potential users. The approach to FSR developed by the RAMR team has been well received by Beninese partners; the methodology and institutional framework have been chosen as a model for further FSR in Benin, to be financed by the World Bank. RAMR staff play a key role in training new teams.

11 Farmer participation in priority setting: RAMR, Benin

Valentin Koudokpon and Leendert Sprey

Even before the project *Recherche Appliquée en Milieu Réel* (RAMR) was initiated (see project description), both researchers and development workers had observed that most of the technology developed with farmers in mind was not being adopted by them. Apparently the technology offered did not respond to farmers' specific needs, about which little was known. The RAMR project was initiated to ensure that feedback takes place between farmer and researcher. From the beginning RAMR recognized that introducing innovations which adequately address the constraints of farmers would only be possible with strong participation by the target group. Such participation is especially important at certain stages: those involving the identification and understanding of these constraints; development of possible solutions; and appraisal of the solution being tested. However, the knowledge and experience of farmers can also make important contributions at other stages of the FSR&D process. The project therefore has been making efforts to gradually increase farmer participation in the research process.

Although the periods are not sharply divided, three phases can be distinguished in the development of the project from 1986 to 1993. These are:
- start-up: the project focused on tangible results, using on-farm research (OFR) methodology;
- project development: research activities became more geared towards the farming system as a whole; interdisciplinary research was initiated;
- project consolidation: project responsibilities were gradually transferred to counterpart staff.

The RAMR methodology will be described in this chapter, with particular emphasis on farmer participation, in accord with these three phases.

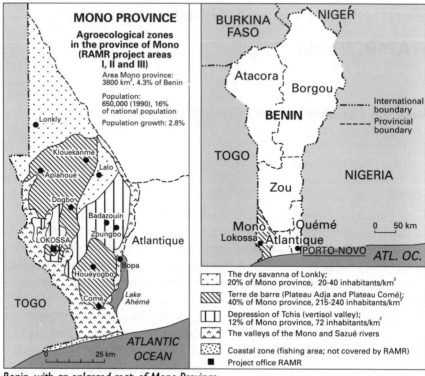

Benin, with an enlarged map of Mono Province

Conducting on-farm research and building linkages

When RAMR began, researchers and extension workers – although wel-
coming FSR&D concepts – doubted its effectiveness and long-term viability.
It was clear that the introduction of innovations adapted to farmers'
conditions could only be effective after changes in the mentality of these
two groups of actors. Priority was therefore given to conducting on-farm
research, to enable the project to gain credibility by quickly generating
tangible results.

Planning agronomic trials

Farmers' constraints recorded during previous studies, a rapid diagnostic
survey, and village meetings enabled researchers to select innovations that
would be relevant to existing problems. Decisions regarding the priority of
research themes and possible solutions were made by the agronomist. His
choice was based on his interpretation of the farmers' needs; the avail-

ability of related innovations that had been tested at the research station; and the potential for quick results. At this stage, the participation of agro-economists was limited to the analysis of results and in-depth diagnostic studies of households, making information available for the formulation of FSR&D themes at a later stage. The trials selected covered only one factor with respect to a particular crop, such as varieties, fertilizer or pesticide application, or cultural practices. Identical trials were executed in different agroecological zones, using a design similar to on-station trials. The field staff was responsible for recruiting volunteer farmers, and installing and monitoring trials. Field staff were trained primarily to collect data required in the analysis of the trial results; the RAMR team prepared a simple sheet for this purpose, to be filled in by field staff.

The trials selected by the researchers were discussed with farmers during a village meeting organized before the season began. Farmers expressed their views on the opportunity to test these innovations, and on the difficulties they might encounter. A slide show was included. These meetings were mostly informative, aimed at establishing good working relations. They were very well attended by farmers. At first, only a few women were involved (10–15%). After the project began to put more emphasis on their participation, the proportion of women increased to 30–40%. At first, the plan was to recruit 24 farmers for each trial, but in general only an average of 15 farmers participated; this appeared to be sufficient for the statistical analysis.

Implementation of trials

The inputs (fertilizer, seeds, etc.) required for the trials were distributed free of charge. Farmers managed the trials in accord with their usual practices, since researchers did not attach any further conditions to the implementation of the trial. This made it possible in the analysis to obtain a good picture of the technical performance of the innovation under current farming practices. There was little involvement of extension workers in the execution of these trials, but it was possible to reach more than 300 farmers with only six field agents (research assistants) and one researcher. The analysis was highly standardized, using pre-established formats. While the trials were being carried out, the FSR&D researcher visited the trial sites and talked with farmers about their impressions. Representatives of the agricultural extension staff and thematic researchers were invited to join in these visits.

At the end of the season, a village meeting was organized to discuss trial results with farmers. This meeting was organized by the field agent and conducted by the FSR&D researcher. Representatives of the extension organization and agricultural research were invited to attend. These meetings were enlivened by presentation of a slide show about the trials executed in their own village. These meetings were well attended by farmers; the maximum duration was 1.5 hours.

Evaluation. Agronomic trials proved to be an excellent forum for communication with farmers, extension agents and researchers, and for clarification of the constraint analysis. The results of the on-farm trials aroused the interest of farmers in project activities. Trial results provided a basis for fruitful discussions between FSR&D researchers, DRA researchers, extension workers and farmers in particular. These discussions revealed the inadequacies of the technologies that were available and being recommended. For instance, none of the maize varieties that had been tested was adopted by the majority of farmers. First, the increase in yields was too small (+30%) to compensate for some negative aspects, such as higher milling costs and storage losses and a lower organoleptic quality. Second, farmers were not very much interested in applying pesticides, because the products were unavailable and/or farmers could not afford them. Third, the fertilizer trials did not show conclusive increases in yields. Consequently, the limitations of this type of OFR became apparent, as detailed below. These three examples, however, did not mean that all of the trial results were unattractive to farmers. For instance, farmers readily used some outstanding varieties from the cowpea trials. This enabled the project to quickly begin a pre-extension programme, implemented jointly with the extension service.

Involvement of other actors

The pre-extension programme has proved an excellent means of actively involving the extension service in FSR&D. This programme allowed the performance of innovations to be tested on a larger scale. Similarly, the capacity of the extension service to implement such programmes could be assessed at an early stage. The OFR approach demonstrated to thematic researchers that scientifically viable results could be obtained through trials conducted under farm conditions. Thematic researchers and extension workers became increasingly familiar with research under farm conditions by visiting the trials, and discussing protocols and methods to analyse the results. Consequently, RAMR succeeded in gaining the desired credibility. This motivated extension staff and on-station researchers to attend the annual planning meetings organized by RAMR. There, project staff could further explain the results and discuss the methodology used, thus increasing the partners' understanding of FSR&D. However, these initial meetings still did not succeed in achieving their active participation in planning RAMR project activities.

Development of the project: transforming OFR into FSR

The process

On-farm research, as described in the previous section, initially had a narrow focus. It was based on technologies derived from on-station research; farmer participation was limited; the research had a monodisciplinary character; and it focused on improving productivity in the short term. In carrying out FSR&D, testing only technologies developed at research stations proved insufficient. For instance, researchers had to move from 'classic' fertilizer trials to developing alternative experiments aimed at alleviating decreases in soil fertility: use of legumes, agroforestry and fallow systems, alley-cropping and so forth. These technologies and practices had not been tested at the research stations; moreover, their development and design required a more profound understanding of the functioning of existing farming systems. Thus, to some extent, researchers were 'forced' to return to the farmers themselves, to make better use of farmers' knowledge and experience, and to have joint discussions with them about what could be done to improve the situation. OFR had to be transformed into FSR&D. The characteristics of this process of transformation may be summarized as follows:
- factorial trials covering complex problems;
- reinforcement of the role of agroeconomists;
- increasing participation of the extension service;
- development of FSR&D induced by farmers;
- priority setting in research themes with all actors taking part.

Factorial trials covering complex problems. The previous agronomic trial programme, centred on testing single factors separately, had progressively been complemented by adding trials geared towards the farming system, which took into consideration the long-term sustainability of the production system. The fact that the research process had become well established and a certain research capacity had been achieved made these changes possible. The acquired knowledge of the farming system, the analysis of trial results and the experience of the team in collaborating with farmers have facilitated the handling of more complex issues. The socioeconomic (land tenure system, marketing, credit) and cultural contexts have been increasingly taken into account.

Reinforcement of the agroeconomists' role. Taking the farming system as a whole into account implied involving agroeconomists. Knowledge acquired during the diagnostic phase allowed them to express a more critical view on the agronomic content of the project. They have introduced criteria covering farmers' appreciation of technologies, and have provided information on the socioeconomic differences among target groups. Moreover, they have stimulated discussions on the socioeconomic constraints that put pressure on the farmers' environment, and ways these constraints can be removed.

Increased participation of extension. Trial results were discussed by researchers and extension agents. Together, they established whether a follow-up with a pre-extension test was justified. This discussion enabled extension agents to exert more influence on FSR&D programmes by making observations and expressing criticisms. A pre-extension programme has been carried out each year, based on the results of the trials conducted. Examples are pest control in cowpea, new varieties of maize, and weed control. Supported by RAMR, the extension organization has evaluated the results of these programmes, and further actions have been defined jointly.

Farmer-induced development of FSR&D. Research activities carried out under farm conditions enabled the actors to conclude that the experience of farmers is essential in guiding agricultural development. Active participation of farmers makes it possible to conceive research activities based on their major constraints, and taking their knowledge and possibilities into account. Thus RAMR has established a framework in which farmers effectively influence the choice of future research and the development of research protocols.

The role of the farmer, as manager of a farm, goes beyond appreciation of the technologies featured in the first phase. The control of *Imperata cylindrica* is an example. Declining soil fertility is a primary constraint in the relatively densely populated Adja plateau. Researchers planted various legumes (woody and herbaceous species). Farmers detected that *Mucuna* was effective in driving out *Imperata cylindrica*. Some 20 farmers asked for seeds, and most were successful in controlling the weed. More farmers became interested, and RAMR encouraged the use of *Mucuna* by developing pre-extension campaigns.

Instead of working and having discussions with individual farmers, the RAMR team began a group approach. Meetings were organized with the objective of strengthening the participation of farmers in the entire process. Occasional informative meetings evolved into a succession of regular meetings, through which farmers directly influenced decision making. Several times throughout the agricultural season, these meetings were organized by field staff, with the assistance of collaborating farmers. They informed the population, inviting everybody who was interested in the topic to be discussed. To keep the discussion groups smaller, permitting a better exchange, the village was divided into two to three more or less coherent sections. Thus a group of around 20–30 farmers could discuss the topic with the project staff. For instance, in the savanna, groups were formed to discuss problems such as rats destroying crops, goat diseases, waterlogging and so forth. While the sections were consulted independently, meetings of the whole village were also held.

Field staff received training in involving and motivating the rural population. Before meetings, the process of communication to be used was discussed with field staff. Researchers conducted the first meeting, and the results were evaluated together with field staff. Farmers, extension workers and researchers detailed the problem (when, how, why, who), compared the efforts of different farmers and the effects in overcoming problems, and discussed alternative solutions. For example, the problem of rats was best attacked by mechanical means (rat traps) instead of using pesticides, because rats might be eaten and/or other animals might be affected. In general, these discussions lasted no more than one to one and a half hours.

As a consequence of this 'hamlet and village group approach', the research programme addressed local conditions; this led to diversification, to deal with situations in the various FSR&D villages. An example: in one area, farmers let their goats range freely, whereas in other villages they were tied up. In working to ensure an adequate fodder supply during the year, these different management practices called for different strategies. There were charges for inputs or these were distributed freely, depending on the type of trial being carried out. However, the basic design of the trials remained the same – they were entirely managed by the farmer.

Farmers became more active when they felt researchers were treating them as equal partners. Farmer participation has been considerable, both in numbers and in contributions. In the savanna, for instance, 30 meetings were held in just a few months. RAMR found that these discussions with farmer groups, covering their problems and formulating subsequent actions, always provided a solid base for farmers' commitment to the research and pre-extension activities that followed. Hearing farmers' points of view forced researchers to place the constraints identified by farmers in the context of the entire agricultural enterprise and socioeconomic environment. As a result, the need for interdisciplinary problem solving became clearer.

Similarly, the process of data collection has developed towards a more communicative approach. At first, technical issues were the main focus. Additional surveys on socioeconomic aspects were added, to complement this information. The research protocol was later revised to reflect both sources of data. The protocols also developed into basic documents on the trial in question, to be used for training and information purposes. We have also found that better trained field staff provide much more useful information, which is relevant to on-going and future research.

Involvement of others. The participation of other stakeholders was further increased by organizing a workshop once a year. At this workshop, project results and programme were discussed and amended. Although these workshops tended to be mainly an exchange of information, RAMR's objective was to encourage the real participation of these actors in decision making. Farmers themselves were not present during these workshops. More recently, an exercise using objective-oriented project planning (OOPP) was conducted to formulate a long-term plan for each of the agroecological zones. The result is a plan to which our partners, including farmers, have actively contributed.

Evaluation of the second phase

As the project developed, the participation of farmers and extension agents in the choice of technologies to be tested, and in their evaluation, increased. This was made possible by structuring discussions with farmers and establishing more functional links with the extension service. The development of farmer participation is one of the major achievements of the project. The learning by doing methodology corresponds with the capacities and resources of the FSR&D team, and permits a high degree of farmer participation.

Nevertheless, we would give a warning here: making farmer participation a goal in itself should be avoided. Although participation is extremely useful, it is not always necessary to have the same degree of involvement in all research activities. The more complex the problem and possible solutions, the more important strong, intensive farmer participation becomes.

But sometimes researchers may take the initiative. Alley-cropping is a good example. This was an innovation unknown to farmers in the area. Researchers took the initiative to establish demonstration plots, confronting farmers with the new practice. This can serve as a way to get them interested, and become a basis for discussion.

Although the project has successfully begun more complex trials, it was not easy to realize an interdisciplinary approach. Often the methods of the agroeconomists did not concur with those of the technicians. More than two years were required to achieve effective interdisciplinarity.

The project has succeeded in involving various partners in the FSR&D process. However, the sustainability of this collaboration has not yet been assured. Although the partners are aware of and agree with the participatory approach of RAMR, they still function within a top–down authoritarian structure, in which the farmer is told what to do. This implies that innovations, in particular more complex ones for which good communication with farmers is required, cannot be implemented without adjusting the overall system. Qualified personnel and adequate financing will be required to continue and follow-up RAMR project activities. The project has, with its partners, financed a number of activities that have improved relations in the short term, but further commitment from the side of the partners is still needed. The step from individual commitment to the institutionalization of FSR&D is not an easy one to realize.

Consolidation

The consolidation of the project started in 1991. During a national seminar held at the end of 1990, a consensus was reached regarding the organizational structure of FSR&D in the institutional framework of the country. This includes:
- application of results, once obtained;
- strengthening the national capacity for FSR&D;
- institutionalization of FSR&D;
- strengthening national coordination.

Application of results. From 1991 onwards emphasis has been put on the diffusion of methodological and technical results obtained by RAMR to other regions. At the same time, a programme was initiated to produce scientific publications. The project has also initiated an agricultural research bulletin to disseminate FSR&D results, as well as those of agronomic research. A secondary goal of this bulletin is to train researchers to write scientific articles. Dissemination of RAMR's results has started in the southern region of Benin; this involves collaboration with both other extension organizations in the region and non-governmental organizations.

Strengthening national capacity and institutionalization. Training in the FSR&D methodology at RAMR will be used to create new teams for other regions of Benin. RAMR will provide backstopping for current FSR&D programmes as they develop research protocols. Developing the methodology within RAMR continues to improve the participation of other actors in research. A full transfer of responsibilities to the Beninese staff is foreseen during this project phase.

The collaboration developed with technicians in other institutions is being formalized. A committee has been set up to enhance inter-institutional linkages. At a national seminar on FSR&D in 1990, an outline for a national framework was formulated. The various approaches adopted by FSR&D projects in Benin constituted the basis for this framework.

The implementation of more FSR&D units in Benin will require national monitoring and coordination. To that end, a national coordination unit (NCU) has been formed. Together with the partners, this unit will propose a strategic long-term development plan for FSR&D. Therefore, the NCU has an important role to play in ensuring the involvement of decision makers of agricultural research. NCU capacities will be strengthened to enable this unit to meet these new demands.

Conclusions

The general strategy adopted by the project was to start with simple activities, which gradually evolved towards more complex ones. First, research was conducted on cropping systems, following familiar monodisciplinary research methods. Agronomists conducted their trials independently of the economists, who needed more time to conduct diagnostic studies. Once the results of socioeconomic research became available, it was possible to develop interdisciplinary research. In RAMR's experience, it was only possible to accomplish a gradual transformation of OFR into research activities geared towards the farming system as a whole after the OFR model had been established and generally accepted. In other words, once the limitations of the old model for solving farmers' real problems became apparent, it became possible to introduce the FSR model and to increase farmers' involvement. Farmers oriented researchers to the need to take into account the entire farming system, including components such as livestock, soil conservation and agroforestry.

A second important feature of RAMR's approach was the involvement of many actors, beginning early on. First of all, cooperative linkages were created between farmers, extension workers and researchers. Initially, the initiative and the decisions were taken by the FSR&D team. Once these cooperative linkages became functional, other actors, in particular farmers and extension workers, progressively took initiative and decisions. Finally, when they were fully functional, formalization of these linkages within the national agricultural research structure of the DRA was begun.

The RAMR project demonstrates that farmers can be motivated to participate in FSR&D activities, when their priorities are addressed and when solutions take their needs and possibilities into account. Simple trial designs, well-explained to farmers, made a good starting point: they enhanced farmers' interest and participation. The trials encouraged an intensive interaction between farmers, researchers and extension workers. Researchers discovered that farmers could make valuable contributions to research programmes.

The RAMR project has also shown that it is possible to work with many farmers. This is important, to capture variations in farming practices and environmental conditions and to generate more alternative solutions. Working with many farmers can only be carried out successfully when a project has a well-organized, structured feedback mechanism in place. RAMR provided this by, first, organizing a sequence of relatively short meetings, each with a clear agenda and objectives; and second, by standardizing the planning of activities, using research protocols. Third, the analysis of agronomic research was standardized; this made trial results, which were needed for discussion with participating farmers, available more quickly.

Bibliography

CARDER-MONO (1985) Projet du développement rural de la province de Mono: Rapport général, BDPA, Coopération et Développement. Paris: Ministère des Rélations Extérieures

FSA (1984) Rapport du sondage diagnostic sur le plateau Adja. Abomey Calavi, Bénin: UNB/FSA

INSAE (1984) Recensement général de la population et de l'habitation (Mars 1979); La population du Mono – villages et quartiers de ville. Cotonou, Bénin: Ministère du Plan et de la Statistique, Institut National de la Statistique et d'Analyse Economique

KOUDOKPON V ed (1992) Pour une recherche participative, stratégie et développement d'une approche de recherche avec les paysans au Bénin. Amsterdam/Cotonou: Royal Tropical Institute/ Directions de la Recherche Agronomique

MUTSAERS HJW, FISHER NM, VOGEL WM AND PAALDA MC (1986) A field guide for on-farm research. Ibadan, Nigeria: IITA

QUENUM EK (1988) Role du palmier à huile dans l'economie des familles paysannes du plateau Adja. Abomey Calavi, Bénin: UNB/FSA

RAMR (1985) Projet de Recherche Appliquée en Milieu Réel, création d'une unité provinciale et support à l'unité nationale, dossier définitif. Cotonou, Benin: MDRAC/DRA/RAMR

RAMR (1987) Rapport d'activité de RAMR 1987. Cotonou, Bénin: MDRAC/DRA/RAMR

RAMR (1989) Sondage diagnostic: le village d'Eglimé. Cotonou, Bénin: MDR/DRA/RAMR

Project description: PROFED, Mali

The Women and Development Project in southern Mali (*Projet Femmes et Développement dans la zone Mali-Sud,* or PROFED) is a successor to PAAF (*Projet d'Appui à l'Animation Féminine*). Funded by the Dutch government, CMDT/PAAF/PROFED is a collaborative effort of KIT, the Royal Tropical Institute, and CMDT, the Malian Cotton Development Board *Compagnie Malienne pour le Développement des Textiles.* CMDT has accepted responsibility for the implementation of an integrated rural development programme in the southern part of Mali.

This chapter deals with the relationship of CMDT/PAAF/PROFED to the farming systems research project DRSPR/Sikasso – a part of the *Division de Recherche sur les Systèmes de Production Rurale.* (DRSPR is the farming systems research unit of the national Institut d'Economie Rurale, or IER, described in Chapter 9; the map of southern Mali given in Chapter 9 (P. 150) also covers PAAF/PROFED). PAAF/PROFED and DRSPR are funded by the same donor and receive technical assistance from the same institute. PAAF, a project to support the CMDT women's extension programme, was launched in 1987, about the same time that DRSPR added a women's component to its research programme (1986).

The aim of the project, started in 1987, is to strengthen CMDT policy, methods and means of integrating women in the rural development of southern Mali. The significance of this project is that within the framework of a policy of diversification of agricultural production, women are no longer ignored by the CMDT. Much emphasis is put on collaboration between male and female extension workers. Therefore, the project has helped to develop a policy on the recruitment of female extension workers and a training programme for both female and male CMDT extension workers at all levels. Objectives with respect to interventions on behalf of rural women are broad: generation of income, work alleviation and strengthening of decision making power.

The project is in its second phase. Although the objectives have not changed, the strategy has become clearer. The current strategy is twofold: to improve the identification of needs, so as to strengthen the impact of interventions, and continue the integration of the project's efforts in all CMDT activities. To date, the intervention domains have been limited to those productive and reproductive activities in which women manage and control resources and benefits. This means that the role of women as labourers on the family farm has not been a target for project interventions (though this has recently come under discussion). Whereas the project name PAAF referred only to extension for women, PROFED, the current title (adopted in 1990), is intended to indicate the use of a 'women and development' approach.

Halfway through its second phase, PROFED has become the Women and Development Division within the training department of the CMDT. The division is staffed by the expatriate project leader and a Malian assistant project leader; the latter is to be nominated as head of the Women and Development Division. In each of the five CMDT regions one women and development coordinator – who is also a member of the regional board – is responsible for the planning, implementation and monitoring of women and development activities in her region. In the field, women and development agents work in close collaboration with extension agents at the *secteur* level. Experiments with having women and development agents at *zone* level, representing a number of villages, are taking place in two CMDT regions. In these two test regions, research is being carried out by two expatriate associate experts of the project, to identify target groups and establish monitoring for the programme.

12 Research demands of an extension programme for women: PROFED, Mali

Lida Zuidberg and Simone Kortbeek

Relationships with farming systems research can be important to the success of an extension programme. Some of the issues involved – specifically the perceived need of extension to obtain research results – are illustrated in this chapter from the standpoint of extension. The focus is the relationship between the women's extension activities of CMDT/PAAF/PROFED (see project description) and the farming systems research project DRSPR, regarding research on the role of women in farming systems. This collaboration will be explored with respect to requests for pre-extension research submitted to DRSPR by the CMDT women's extension project.

In the four parts of this chapter, we will distinguish several stages in the development of increased collaboration. First, the development of a women and development component within the farming systems research project DRSPR will be described. This helps to explain DRSPR's response to PAAF/PROFED requests, as well as DRSPR's attitude towards collaboration. The next section covers the evolution of the CMDT women's extension project. Third, cooperation between the two projects will be discussed, illustrating that differences in team priorities and in perceptions of women – a target group for both projects – complicated collaboration. Finally, the solutions adopted by the two projects to advance their women and development programmes, and the implications for collaboration, are examined.

Attention to women in farming systems research

No diagnosis of female farmers'[1] constraints: DRSPR 1979–1986

Women became a topic of DRSPR research at the time the farming system and the components of the farming systems typology were defined (diagnostic phase, 1979–1983). DRSPR documents refer to two points. First, the distinction of various 'centres of decision making' regarding the organization of labour to be allocated to different types of fields; and second, the time allocated by women (married, unmarried) to agricultural tasks. With respect to type of fields, DRSPR focused on family fields, cultivated with staple foods or cash crops. The primary family field is controlled by the head of the patriarchal extended family; secondary family fields, which originate in the loosening of extended family ties, are controlled by married sons. In addition, older men and married women may cultivate their own plots. These differ from the family fields: they are small, dispersed, and characterized by shared cropping systems. Here women cultivate various food crops, for example groundnuts, *fonio*, rice, and *gombo* (Tangara and Vierstra, 1979). Because of the marginality attributed to these individual plots,[2] they were not taken into account in the constraint analysis and description of the farming system. This was despite several interesting village case studies undertaken by female student researchers in the early eighties, which pointed out two phenomena. Female rice cultivation may be an important means of preventing a food crisis during periods of shortage (Traoré, 1981). Secondly, time allocated to family fields by women seems to be inversely related to the size of the plots they cultivate as individuals (Bosch, 1980; Chaumont, 1985). Neither point was incorporated in the DRSPR constraint analysis.

There has been much discussion about the time women allocate to agricultural activities. In the farming systems typology produced by DRSPR, the number of 'labour units' was one of eight indicators of the availability of resources. Based on empirical observations, the *Sénoufo* women included were considered to be employed no more than half of the time as agricultural workers.[3] However, DRSPR's definition of agricultural activities excluded not only the time allocated to individual plots, but also activities such as gathering bush products, care of small livestock, processing and selling agricultural products, and preparing meals for agricultural workers.

The arguments for not taking the specific role of women in agriculture into consideration were diffuse. Vierstra (1985) attributes non-consideration to the great ethnic diversity, leading to great variation in women's roles. Postel-Coster (1986) refers to the invalid argument put forward by DRSPR that women produce only for consumption. In our view, the problem was not that women in particular were neglected in the diagnostic phase of the DRSPR research. It is that instead, in general DRSPR research was (and still is) not focused on target groups – that is, rather than looking at categories of individual farmers and their needs, they look at farming households as a whole, and the ways these fit into a typology designed by

researchers. Thus, neglect of women is related to the fact that they are sup-
posed to be represented by the male heads of households. In this respect
DRSPR suffers from the same problem as many farming systems research
projects, in that they consider farm households as homogeneous units (see
also Evans, 1989).

The evaluation missions of 1982 and 1985 had warned the DRSPR team
about using a definition of the farming enterprise that was too narrow. For
example, the 1982 mission (Luning et al., 1982), recommended taking
more account in future research of the role of the young and of women.
The 1985 mission (Zevenbergen et al., 1985) recommended increasing
attention to women by recruiting a female researcher. Further, the mission
recommended initiating a women's component based simply on existing
practices, with the immediate initiation of pre-extension activities. In other
words, no need was seen for a diagnosis, suggesting that women's constraints were already known! Therefore, we consider these recommendations to have been naive and erroneous.

DRSPR established a women's section, as noted, in 1986. However, a KIT
consultancy regarding DRSPR's orientation to this field also initially reinforced the idea of 'just beginning', without further diagnosis (Timmermans,
1985). This sequence of events also demonstrates that the subject of
women was always introduced by outsiders, notably by student researchers
and the donor.

From diagnosis of constraints to a village approach: DRSPR 1986–1989

With respect to the women's section, the text of the work plan for the third
DRSPR project phase was more precise than the preceding recommendations
of the evaluation mission. Four objectives appear (Nijssen, 1988): integration of 'women' in all of the DRSPR fields of research; continuation and
extension of specific experiments pertaining to the role of women in
production and processing, and to their need for work alleviation;[4] and
research on women's contribution to food subsistence and family income.
Further, research was to provide a typology of regions or villages, to
indicate potential domains for intervention.

This ambitious plan was to be supported by VENA, the Women and
Autonomy Centre of the University of Leiden (the Netherlands), which
carried out two consultancies for this purpose.[5] The first (Rookhuizen,
1987) assisted in the design of a method aimed at diagnosing women's constraints in a participatory way: the farming systems typology used by
DRSPR was not considered suitable for identifying domains of interest to
women. Second, it was expected that women's problems would often be

related to collective needs (such as water, health, or market infrastructures). The outcome of the consultancy was an approach oriented to women *(approche femme)*, rather than to farming systems.

The fieldwork that followed was carried out in four villages (two villages that had been part of the pre-extension programme of DRSPR and two new research villages). The results demonstrated a wide range of problems, but did not suggest possible solutions and did not refer to the context of the family farm. It is no wonder that the second consultancy (Bosch, 1988) recommended reintegrating the women's section in the project team; it had drifted away due to the village approach. There was an opportunity for re-integration for two reasons. DRSPR had started research in two other CMDT zones, Tominian (the *Bobo* ethnic group) and Kadiolo (*Sénoufo*), and had reshaped the ongoing collection of agroeconomic data in its research villages *(suivi-évaluation permanent)*. Further, the agroeconomic section was prepared to adapt the permanent survey, adding topics proposed by the women's section. Examples include the time allocation of all adult house-hold members; individual access to resources; agricultural production of family and private fields; and individual generation and use of income. These topics were spelled out during a third consultancy mission (also by Bosch,[6] in 1989). This led to a great deal of discussion, because of the mass of data the consultant's recommendations would have required adding to the agroeconomical survey. As a result, data collection was curtailed, and the individual time budget survey was carried out only for a subsample.

Integration of the women's section within DRSPR: 1989–1993

Two changes took place in the women's section during the fourth phase of DRSPR (1989–1993). First, the research team was reorganized into two main sections: socioeconomic and technical. Thus research on women was now fully integrated within the socioeconomic section. Second, the female agronomist was replaced by an associate expert, a female anthropologist.[7]

Although procedures for setting research priorities became more explicit during this phase, for DRSPR the general problem remained the lack of priorities in the past; this had left behind a huge amount of unanalysed data. The analysis and publication of these data now became the first priority. This included the basic research data on women's fields and women's labour (a part of the permanent agroeconomic survey), and topics pertain-ing to the case studies on individual time allocation, revenues, expenses, food consumption, and so forth. In the end, both types of analyses were delegated to the anthropologist; no effective integration took place between economists and women and development experts during analysis and publication of the results.

In 1992, the associate expert left DRSPR and was not replaced.[8] The results of the various research activities undertaken during these two subsequent project phases are available now (Perquin, 1993). Due to the isolation in which the analysis was done, however, the findings (though numerous and detailed) are considered fragmentary, and insufficient for a good understanding of women's contribution to the farming system. The members of the research team need to recognize that adding a few topics to the permanent survey and undertaking some case studies will not be a solution. At the 1991 KIT workshop on priority setting (see Preface), participants underlined the lack of a methodology for including gender variables in DRSPR research domains.

Women as a target group for CMDT

The CMDT women's extension programme begins: 1980–1986

By 1980, CMDT had named (female) regional women coordinators for four of the five CMDT regions. The recruitment of the first *animatrice régionale*, in the Koutiala region, can be seen as a coincidence.[9] The creation of the posts was however also in part due to 'foreign' influence, within the framework of the multilateral donor programme called *Projet Mali-Sud* (Belloncle, 1980). The Mali-Sud project financed the training programme and innovative new extension posts as well (such as those of c/DDR, c/ZAER, and animatrices).

During the first three years of regional women's programmes, activities for women were determined by choosing topics being covered by the CMDT extension programme, in which participation of women or coordination by women were considered favourable. Examples included supervision of traditional midwives (after their training), distribution of nivaquine to pregnant women and children, extension covering improved wood stoves, selling shea butter nuts to the CMDT, distribution and sale of cotton seed oil, and management of grain mills for the village association. These priorities were set by CMDT; they did not follow an analysis of extension needs felt by the women themselves. This goes against the idea that regional coordinators ought not to start extension activities before a village level inventory has been made of women's main activities, problems, and need for assistance.

After a first evaluation (Corrèze, 1983), the objectives were clarified for the first time, and formulated in three points: to improve and increase the productive activities of women, and their possibilities for income generation; to alleviate work burdens due to women's domestic, agricultural and processing activities; and to promote participation of women in village organizations, e.g. literacy programmes (Zuidberg, 1989). This gave priority to women's productive activities and income-generating capacity. However, the definition of 'women's productive activities' indicates the real priority (Corrèze, 1983): with respect to production, the women's extension programme should limit itself to the so-called 'autonomous' activities – those in which women use their own labour and from which they derive an individual income. Furthermore, a practical approach was recommended, taking into account the experience gained by the regional women and development coordinators since 1980 (Corrèze, 1983). These recommendations were accepted – implicitly[10] – in the project proposal submitted by CMDT to the Dutch government, containing a request for technical assistance and financial support for the women's programme (CMDT, 1986).

Development of a women and development project: PAAF/PROFED 1987–1993

In this period the new PAAF project started elaborating its approach, among other things defining intervention domains. The domains chosen were cultivation of rice, groundnut and vegetables; poultry raising; appropriate technologies to alleviate work burdens (grain mill, rice huller, shea butter press); making soap and other small items for local markets. Further, knowledge and field experiences were systematically exchanged among the regional coordinators.

PAAF was much in need of a justification of these choices among possible intervention domains, and for CMDT's decision to accept the evaluator's recommendation to restrict the women's programme to autonomous production activities for women. General data on women's economic activities (on-farm, off-farm) were needed to see the relative importance of autonomous activities (Bosch, 1988; Zuidberg, 1989). Further, PAAF saw a need for pre-extension research related to almost every aspect of its work: the content of technical messages, mode of intervention (collective, individual), criteria for access to credit, feasibility and profitability of new income-generating activities, the division of tasks between male and female extension workers, and the question of organizing women inside or outside village farmers' associations. Because CMDT had a policy of learning by doing, and disapproved of research being carried out by extension projects like PAAF and PLAE (described in Chapter 13), it was impossible for PAAF itself to conduct research prior to designing an extension method. The approach adopted had four parts:

- experimentation, on a trial-and-error basis, with the extension approach.[11] This had several elements: selection of villages (with the help of the *fiche d'étude du milieu*); diagnosis of problems (with the help of *sensibilization* and *animation* techniques); planning and implementation, together with regular field staff (*programmation et exécution*); monitoring (*fiche de suivi*) and evaluation (*bilan annuel*);
- requests for consultancies on specific problems (such as profitability of new activities, and integration of credit schemes in CMDT's organization);
- assistance to Malian students, allowing them to receive practical training alongside a CMDT extension worker (examples of topics are animal traction equipment for women; introduction of a collective grain mill; and integration of extension for women in CMDT programmes);
- whenever possible, looking for sources of needed technical inputs within other projects (whether within CMDT or outside, e.g. from DRSPR).

At the end of the first phase, there was an external evaluation of PAAF (Corrèze and Sissoko, 1990). Clarification within CMDT of objectives and extension programme strategy was recommended. Having observed a rapid and sometimes artificial multiplication of interventions, this mission insisted on concentrating extension activities by limiting the number of new villages; a better division of tasks among extension agents; and better monitoring and evaluation (CMDT, 1990).

With the initiation of PROFED in the second phase, the general objectives did not change fundamentally. Thanks to the project's efforts to encourage discussion about its activities whenever possible, women have become an accepted target group of CMDT. Increased credibility has given the project more room for experimentation and negotiation. Here experimentation refers to intervention methods, such as adapting CMDT messages and credit services for women; developing indicators for inclusion in CMDT monitoring and evaluation systems; making use of traditional women's associations; and so forth. Room for negotiation refers to the receptiveness of CMDT to discussion of changes needed to create the conditions[12] needed for successful implementation of the results of experimentation. A new strategy was developed, with 'action-research' as a major component. The renewed strategy and implications for the work programme of PAAF/PROFED cannot, however, be seen in isolation from relationships with DRSPR. Therefore PROFED strategy after 1990 will be further discussed below, in conjunction with an analysis of relations with DRSPR.

DRSPR–PAAF/PROFED collaboration: divergent interests

Collaboration between CMDT and DRSPR was formalized in 1983; this indicates that CMDT was interested in extension activities involving the messages being tried out by DRSPR. In 1986, CMDT addressed a request for assistance with its women's programme to the Dutch donor funding the two projects,[13] through the personnel assigned to DRSPR by KIT for technical assistance. DRSPR both assisted CMDT in formulating a project proposal and, at the same time, created its own women's section. DRSPR's interest is demonstrated by the initial proposition to locate the CMDT project in Sikasso, to ensure close cooperation with the DRSPR women's section (CMDT, 1986).[14] PAAF also had positive expectations regarding research that DRSPR could carry out for PAAF. Consultation between DRSPR and PAAF began with the two DRSPR female agronomists attending the monthly PAAF meeting for regional women and development coordinators. This occurred at their own request; they felt the need of more information derived from field experience.

Further movement towards mutual consultation was encouraged by the 1988 and 1989 consultancies of Bosch, in which PAAF participated actively. As noted, one result of these consultancies was a renewed focus on the role of women in the farming system. Pre-extension research, intended to serve the CMDT extension programme, became a second focus. Although these steps provided some potential for a complementary relationship, we believe there were five impediments to fruitful collaboration, despite the yearly consultations between the two projects that began after these consultancies.

First, CMDT began a women's programme in 1980, while the DRSPR women's section began only in 1986. No data were available in 1986, so there was still no basis for mutual consultation. Second, CMDT operated from the beginning in four regions, with four important ethnic groups (*Bambara, Bobo, Minyanka* and *Sénoufo*); DRSPR research was at that moment limited to the *Sénoufo* in the region of Sikasso. Third, DRSPR research covered only rainfed agriculture. This excluded not only wet rice cultivation, vegetable cultivation, small livestock, and gathering bush products, but also processing and trade in agricultural products. This variety of activities was explicitly included in CMDT's programme for women, which aimed at generating income from a diverse group of activities specific to women's possibilities. Fourth, the two projects differed with respect to female farmers as a target group. PAAF/PROFED has been oriented towards 'autonomous activities' – those in which women manage and control resources and benefits. For CMDT it was out of the question – until very recently – for the women's extension programme to deal with women's contributions to family cotton farming. Initially, DRSPR began along the same lines, doing pre-extension research relevant to women only for some so-called female crops (rice and *pois sucré*). Since 1989, DRSPR has taken the participation of women in family fields into account. Only recently did DRSPR begin to include research taking place on individual women's fields in the agroeconomic survey. Last but not least, both DRSPR and CMDT programmes were kept busy by the everyday demands of their own structures, rather than taking a wider view, including time to interact with each other. These circumstances led to an initially separate evolution of the two projects, even though they started at the same time, were financed by the same donor, and were carried out with technical assistance stemming from the same institute.[15]

Research demands from PAAF and DRSPR response

PAAF's research demands were initially derived from extension activities already being carried out by CMDT at an experimental level, but lacking a sufficient basis for a consistent extension approach. DRSPR paid attention only to research requests pertaining to technical agricultural questions. Advice on other technical topics was sought from other projects. Moreover, before 1989, requests for more pronounced gender differentiation in the agroeconomic survey were not accepted by the economists in charge of this activity. They opposed the collection of a larger volume of data.

From 1989 onwards, research requests to DRSPR have been discussed in yearly consultations between the two organizations. These yearly consultations have been fruitful with respect to pre-extension research, but this concerned only the women's section of DRSPR: this section was already conducting some pre-extension research on women's activities pertaining to the feasibility of some collective activities, such as cultivation and marketing of *pois sucré*, and the shea butter press.[16] However, the rest of the DRSPR team was not involved.

Consultations with DRSPR have resulted in the implementation of only a few research topics, primarily due to DRSPR's lack of expertise in areas proposed by PAAF; for example, traditional rice cultivation and the feasibility of a rice huller were new topics for the DRSPR women's section. Therefore some topics of great interest to PAAF have been offered to student researchers or contracted out to an NGO. The topics for pre-extension research proposed by PAAF for 1988–1989 are summarized here, with the

project or person carrying out the work given in parentheses (see also Bosch, 1989):
- constraints on traditional rice cultivation (DRSPR women's section);
- profitability of a collective rice huller, managed by women (DRSPR women's section);
- traditional cultivation and conservation of onions (student in home economics, Wageningen Agricultural University);
- the feasibility of vegetable cultivation for the market (CMDT/SNV – Dutch Development Organization – project on horticulture);
- technical improvements for keeping poultry (DRSPR zootechnical section);
- the role of women in erosion control measures at village or farm level (student trainees in the CMDT erosion control project, PLAE).

For 1989–1990, three additional topics were raised, of which one has been taken up by DRSPR (see Kanté et al., 1990):
- the impact of new technologies and commercialization of shea butter (*Gwa-Mina,* an NGO);
- the integration of women in the village farmer's association, the *association villageoise* (anthropology student from Montpellier, who has not been able to come);
- the expenditure of women's individual incomes (women's section DRSPR). Without going into details about the contents and results of these research needs of PAAF, we note that neither the approach nor the results were very satisfactory for PAAF. The CMDT women's programme expanded fast, causing a fragmentation of field activities; moreover, identification of the activities to be carried out was superficial, as was monitoring. The results of the research carried out by others was fragmentary as well, and unable to fill the need for clear technical, financial and organizational messages.

A division of research tasks between DRSPR and PROFED

The first phase PAAF evaluation showed on the one hand that CMDT extension activities lacked a basis for targeting and, on the other, that the quality of its intervention methods needed to be improved. Due to the changes discussed above – the acceptance by CMDT of women as a target group, plus receptiveness to negotiation – change was possible. In the second phase, when PROFED began, an 'action research' programme could be included in the work plan. This programme is intended to improve the contents and methods of extension activities. It includes all types of extension research, such as studies covering needs assessment and targeting, monitoring, and evaluation of impacts. The inclusion of the action research programme in the extension project was also in accord with a more distinct division of tasks between DRSPR and PROFED. Consultation between DRSPR and PROFED has led to a DRSPR commitment to study the impact for women, brought about by changes in the farming system survey; PROFED is to carry out research related to concrete extension activities.

To focus the experimental role of PROFED, four test zones have been chosen, in two regions.[17] To support the action research programme, two associate experts have been assigned to the project, each of whom collaborates with a regional coordinator. In short, the action research programme contains several elements. First, there are research and tests coordinated by the associate experts:
• one ongoing test related to the development of monitoring instruments, which are to be integrated in the CMDT system: a yearly evaluative progress report (*bilan annuel*), village files (*dossiers villageois*), and specific impact studies;
• improvement of the village inventory (*étude du milieu*) and a socioeconomic inventory of women reached by the programme for various extension activities (*fiche socio-économique*);
• better incorporation of existing women's organizations in extension activities.

Next, there is a training programme for young, unemployed graduates recruited on a temporary basis (12 months maximum) on the basis of a protocol defined for a given research topic.[18] For 1991, 17 themes (research protocols) were elaborated; six related studies have begun (for more details see CMDT, 1990; and CMDT, 1991):
• participation of women in cooperative saving schemes;
• profitability of goat raising;
• markets for *néré* and soja products;
• wet rice cultivation;
• participation of women in erosion control;
• inventory of teaching materials.

Finally, there is assistance to those student trainees at CMDT who wish to work on a subject related to the PROFED programme. The two themes for 1991 are:
• cultivation of fodder plants for cattle (together with PLAE);
• participation of women in village associations.

PROFED's experiences in 1991–1992 show that the trainees' programmes are far too ambitious; this demands much support from project staff, due to weakness in the research capabilities of the responsible regional coordinators. PROFED has limited the number of research fellows on the staff at any one time. In an attempt to solve the workload problem, a written guide is being developed for regional coordinators, and local consultants, hired by the project for this purpose, are being asked for assistance. The role of DRSPR in the action research programme is limited; sometimes DRSPR researchers are asked for assistance in checking the design of a PROFED research topic.

Given the broad scope of PROFED's research needs, it will be necessary to set priorities carefully and to better organize the way research activities are carried out. Setting priorities may involve limiting the number of research topics at one time, but also it suggests choosing among more and less urgent themes. In organizing the research, the intention is to seek coordination between CMDT services, research fellows and/or trainees and local consultants, and the research is to be done in such a way that experiences can be shared as far as possible with CMDT extension workers.

Conclusions

Collaboration between the women's component of the farming systems research project DRSPR and the women and development extension project PAAF/PROFED has been a continuous struggle. Many factors stand in the way. First, differences in priorities present a structural complication. For PAAF/PROFED, women's activities are clearly the overriding priority; but in addition the definition of both the desirable activities and the target group differ from those of DRSPR. For DRSPR, the idea of giving priority to research on women has always been brought into the project by outsiders. Female farmers, though considered relevant to some components of the farming system, were not clearly defined as being a target group in pre-extension research.

DRSPR's record on attention to female farmers reflects this lack of priority. In part this may be attributed to a lack of the methodological know-how that would be needed to incorporate a gender perspective in a farming systems approach. Although – in theory – the full integration of studies related to women into the socioeconomic section may seem a logical step, we fear that in practice the inclusion of gender methodology in the design of farming systems research will demand specific expertise in the field of FSR gender issues. But further, we wonder if the shift in research interests from farming systems to village land use systems may not (though this need not to be the case) tend to decrease attention to gender issues. Farming households and their members no longer seem to be a direct target group. Thus current research priorities do not favour an increase in attention to intra-household dynamics, such as gender relations within the farming system.

A second important constraint on real collaboration is the tension between the wish to implement activities together with female farmers as soon as possible, versus the need for applied background research. In this respect DRSPR and PAAF/PROFED were not very different during their early years of trial and error activities. The solution PROFED has found is to undertake its own action research programme. PROFED continues to look for assistance in safeguarding the quality of its research. Inside the CMDT structure, a linkage has been established with the monitoring and evaluation service: research on the role of women in agriculture has recently begun. Local consultants outside CMDT are contracted to cooperate closely with the research fellows and PROFED extension staff. Nevertheless priorities have to be set, limiting and choosing themes carefully and assuring solid coordination of research tasks.

As far as DRSPR is concerned, its research role in the field of women and development remains based in the permanent agroeconomic survey, which serves to measure changes in farming and land use systems. This survey is to be more selective in the future. This makes it even more important to seek ways to include the interests and constraints of both female and male farmers in the ongoing collection of data. Although the two projects have taken their own paths at the moment, it seems possible there will eventually be an exchange of knowledge on the role of women in farming systems, and the responses of women to the diverse extension activities on offer.

Notes

1   'Female farmers' is to be understood as referring to female members of the family farming system. In southern Mali, this means that women (like men) provide labour to various agricultural activities of the family farm. There is a distinct division of labour, and they may be assigned a small plot for individual cultivation. Assignment of land and decision making on the labour contributions of family members are controlled by the male head of the (often extended) family.

2   Although the exact figures are not known, the area covered by individual fields cultivated by women is small, varying from 0% (*Bobo* zone) and 3% in the *Minyanka* zone of Koutiala,

to 4% and 13%, respectively, in *Sénoufo* areas of Fonsébougou and Kadiolo (Perquin, 1993).

3 The typology based on the diagnosis was built on three sets of criteria: equipment, productivity and resources. Later this was simplified to one criterion – equipment (number of animal traction units) (Kleene et al., 1989). Unfortunately, the description of prevalent farming systems according to the three sets of criteria has never been published.

4 For example, the experimental shea butter press used by the women's association in the village of Yaban.

5 As women and development projects were a new experience for KIT, backstopping of DRSPR and PAAF in this area was initially delegated to VENA – Centre for Women and Autonomy (1987–1988).

6 This time as an independent consultant.

7 Once again there was much discussion about the need for a special women's researcher. For some colleagues, this was no longer necessary due to the integration of research on women into the socioeconomic section, and because this section already included two foreign women! The new associate expert was assigned to DRSPR thanks to the WID sector specialist at the Dutch Embassy. Since the associate expert was a part of the socioeconomic team, no real effort was made to recruit a Malian counterpart.

8 Priority has been given to filling the vacancy with an economist, who could finalize the analyses for the agroeconomic survey.

9 A female secretary married a CMDT agent assigned to the CMDT region of Koutiala, and moved from CMDT headquarters to the CMDT regional office in Koutiala. On her request, she was assigned an extension post, thus becoming the first female extension agent.

10 The project document is very vague and ambiguous about objectives, strategy and targeting. It lists proposed activities and financial means desired by the four regional training departments and the women and development coordinators with whom the project had to work.

11 With regard to community-based extension techniques, PAAF relied on CESAO (Centre d'Etudes Economiques et Sociales d'Afrique Occidentale) and GRAAP (Groupe de Recherche et d'Appuie pour l'Autopromotion Paysanne).

12 One such condition is availability of qualified personnel; for example, a Malian counterpart is now to lead the future women and development division of CMDT.

13 All the more interesting because CMDT had hitherto worked with French consultants from IRAM (Institut de Recherches et d'Application de Méthodes de Développement) in this field.

14 This was not acceptable to CMDT, though, because they had already started women's programmes in four CMDT regions.

15 For the associate expert assigned to the women's section of DRSPR, this was, however, not the case. The lack of funds in DRSPR's budget for a full-time expert indicates the low priority attached to the new section. This is related to resistance on the part of the Malian counterpart organization, which also disagreed on a socioeconomic profile for the female

researcher. The outcome (a junior female agronomist) was thus a compromise, as was the negotiation on recruitment of the Malian counterpart – also a female agronomist – who had to be paid from the project budget.

16 Research on the shea butter press was of much interest to the CMDT, which cooperated with GTZ (Deutsche Gesellschaft für Technische Zusammenarbeit) in the introduction of a manual press (designed by KIT) in the Koutiala region. After the departure of GTZ, PAAF/CMDT was responsible for motivating and training villagers concerning its proper use and maintenance. (This experiment failed, due to conflicts between women's groups in the village.)

17 In 1990, the CMDT women and development programme was in operation in all CMDT regions, the large region of Bougouni having been added. This made it even more necessary to focus interventions on well-defined target groups and activities.

18 This *programme de jeunes diplômés* also serves another goal: creating a reservoir of human capital for future recruitment of extension agents to work with women. Trainees are guided by the regional women and development coordinator, who designs research themes according to priorities perceived in her region.

Bibliography

BELLONCLE G (1980) Femmes et développement en Afrique sahélienne. L'expérience nigérienne d'animation féminine (1966–1976). Collection 'Développement et Civilisations'. Nouvelles éditions africaines/ Editions économie et humanisme/ Les éditions ouvrières. Dakar/Paris

BOSCH E (1980) La position économique de la femme dans un village sénoufo. Un examen de sa position dans quatre exploitations à Fonsébougou au Mali-Sud. Rapport d'une enquête sur le terrain dans le cadre du 'Programme de recherche socio-économique appliquée dans la zone cotonnière, région Sikasso (IER-IRRT)' du 15 mai au 15 septembre 1978. Sikasso: IER/IRRT

BOSCH E (1988) Rapport de la mission d'appui du 13 juin au 2 juillet 1988. Recherche action féminine DRSPR et Projet d'appui à l'animation féminine CMDT. Leiden: VENA

BOSCH E (1989) Rapport de la mission d'appui aux projets DRSPR et PAAF du 11 février au 8 mars 1989. Amsterdam: KIT

CHAUMONT E (1985) La contribution de la femme à l'économie de l'exploitation agricole en milieu sénoufo: aspects socio-économiques. Etudes de cas N'Golasso I. Mémoire ENITA Dijon Quetigny. Dijon

CMDT (1986) Proposition d'un projet d'appui à l'animation féminine dans la zone Mali-Sud (1986–1989). Bamako

CMDT (1990a) Plan d'Opération Projet Femmes et Développement dans la zone Mali-Sud, Deuxième phase 01-09-1990 au 31-08-1994. Koutiala: PROFED

CMDT (1990b) Plan d'Opération 1991 Projet d'appui Femmes et Dévelopement dans la zone Mali-Sud. Koutiala: PROFED

CMDT (1991) Plan d'Opération 1992. Projet d'appui Femmes et Développement dans la zone Mali-Sud. Koutiala: PROFED

CORRÈZE A (1983) L'animation féminine à la CMDT Rapport de la mission effectuée du 2 au 30 Juin 1983. Paris: IRAM

CORRÈZE A AND SISSOKO N (1990) Rapport d'évaluation du programme d'animation féminine à la CMDT. Paris/Bamako: IRAM/IER

EVANS A (1988) Gender relations and technological change: the need for an integrative framework of analysis. In: Poats SV, Schmink M and Spring A, eds, Gender issues in farming systems research and extension. Westview special studies in agricultural science and policy. Boulder/London: Westview Press

KANTÉ F, CISSÉ-KONÉ M, MAIGA-OUOLOGUEM F, COULIBALY-DJIRÉ T AND ZUIDBERG L (1990). Rapport bilan Projet d'Appui à l'Animation Féminine Campagne 1989–1990. Koutiala: CMDT/KIT

KLEENE P, SANOGO B AND VIERSTRA GA (1990) A partir de Fonsébougou. Présentation, objectifs et méthodologie du « Volet Fonsébougo » (1977–1987). Systèmes de production rurale au Mali, vol.1. Bamako/Amsterdam: Institut d'Economie Rurale et Institut Royal des Tropiques

LUNING HA, CORRÈZE A, KORTENHORST LF AND BUS GP (1981) Evaluation de la Mission d'évaluation PRSPR (Programme de Recherche sur les Systèmes de Production Rurale) de la DRSPR Volet Fonsébougou-Sikasso-Mali du 8 au 23 Septembre 1981. Sikasso/Den Haag: IER/DGIS

NIJSSEN O (1988) Inhoudelijke en methodische knelpunten in het onderzoek vrouwen inlandbouwbedrijfssystemen in Zuid-Mali. Paper presented at the workshop KIT 12-18 September 1988. Miméo KIT. Amsterdam: Royal Tropical Institute

PERQUIN B (1992) Les femmes et la gestion du terroir. Une approche pour intégrer les femmes dans le Programme Lutte Anti Erosive de la CMDT. Sikasso/Amsterdam: Ministère du Développment Rural et de l'Environnement/IER/DRSPR

PERQUIN B (1993) Les femmes dans les systèmes de production rurale au Mali-Sud. Rapport recherche. Sikasso: IER/DRSPR

POSTEL-COSTER E (1986) Boerinnen en boeren in de plattelandsontwikkeling. Een voorbeeld van systeembenadering in Zuid-Mali. Working Paper no.71. Institute of Cultural and Social Studies. Leiden: University of Leiden

ROOKHUIZEN M (1987) Les femmes comme groupe-cible de l'intervention de la Division de Recherche sur les Systèmes de Production Rurale, Volet Fonsébougou. Rapport d'une mission d'appui (provisoire). Sikasso: VENA

TANGARA M AND VIERSTRA GA (1979) L'exploitation agricole dans le contexte social du secteur de base de Fonsébougou. Rapport 2 du Programme de recherche socio-économique appliquée dans la zone de production cotonnière – région Sikasso. Bamako: IER/IRRT

TIMMERMANS M (1985) Tour d'horizon des problèmes de recherche-développement en matière d'action féminine en zone Mali-Sud. Compte-rendu de la mission au Mali du 28 mars au 30 avril 1985. IRRT. Amsterdam/Bamako: IRRT/Institut Royal des Tropiques

TRAORÉ K (1981) Contribution de la femme dans la production agricole: cas de Sakoro. Mémoire de fin d'étude IPR. Katibougou

VIERSTRA GA (1985) Onderzoeksprogramma over landbouwproduktiesystemen in Zuid Mali. DGIS Studiedag begeleiding plattelandsontwikkeling 26 juli 1985. Den Haag: DGIS

ZEVENBERGEN W ET AL. (1985) Mission d'évaluation et de programmation: 'Projet recherche sur les systèmes de production rurale' (IER/DRSPR), Volet Fonsébougou du 13/10/1985 au 2/11/1985. Résumé des observations et des recommandations. Sikasso: IER/DGIS

ZEVENBERGEN W ET AL. (1988) Programme de recherche sur les systèmes de production rurale (DRSPR-IRRT) Mali-Sud. Rapport de la mission d'évaluation et de formulation (7-28 novembre 1988). Eerbeek: IER/DGIS

ZUIDBERG ACL (1989) Vers une meilleure intégration de l'animation féminine dans l'approche de la diversification des sources de revenus. Réflexions sur le développement des actions féminines dans la zone CMDT. Document préparatoire pour la mission d'évaluation. Koutiala: PAAF/CMDT

Project description: PLAE, Mali

PLAE, an erosion control project in southern Mali (Projet de Lutte Anti-Erosive, 'Project for the battle against soil erosion') originated in the farming systems research project for southern Mali, DRSPR (see project description in Chapter 9). PLAE is primarily an implementation project carried out by the CMDT (Compagnie Malienne de Développement des Textiles), which, as described earlier, was originally a cotton development board: now in fact it is the primary regional development agency in the region. The map in Chapter 9 (P. 150) shows the PLAE and DRSPR intervention zones. Regular consultations take place between PLAE and DRSPR, to exchange experiences and give direction to the research to be carried out by DRSPR. Here DRSPR's activities in the field of environmental management are considered from the standpoint of PLAE, as a part of CMDT.[1]

The main objective of PLAE, which began in 1986, is to slow (and hopefully to halt) the degradation of the ecosystem in southern Mali, to create more favourable conditions for agricultural development. The project hopes to gradually increase erosion control by introducing conservation measures at village, farm and field levels that follow the priorities and capacities of farmers as closely as possible. For example, these measures might include buffer strips, terraces, hedges, incorporation of manure, contour farming, fodder production, re-afforestation, and improved woodstoves. Major project activities are:
- training of CMDT staff members and extension workers concerning causes of and possible solutions to erosion problems;
- motivation and training of farmers in the villages;
- implementation of soil conservation works by farmers, using local resources;
- improving the degree of self-sufficiency of villages with respect to wood and cattle fodder;
- introduction of conservation-oriented farming techniques.

The project has developed a methodology that is suitable for organizing erosion control at village level. This has been used as a model for environmental management in a CMDT proposal to the World Bank (Mali-Sud III) for the years to come. In 1989 the project entered a second four-year phase, in which the scope was expanded to all five regions in the CMDT area. The target is to have soil conservation measures in use in at least 400 villages. Training of staff and extension workers has become a key activity. In 1990, a massive training campaign began, together with other projects; a national training specialist was appointed.

The project also provides assistance to several other soil conservation and land use management programmes. Specific attention is being paid to the definition of a package of livestock control measures, combined with fodder production, for several zones in the region. In collaboration with DRSPR, the project is also experimenting with a new design for management of a village territory.

13 Reinforcing interaction between research and development: PLAE, Mali

Wim van Campen[1]

The cotton-producing area in the southern part of Mali is confronted with accelerating environmental degradation, which threatens future development. Farmers, rural development services, government and agricultural research institutions need to develop a common strategy for survival. Because of its current responsibilities for rural development, the CMDT is called upon to play a leading role in strengthening farmers' possibilities for the adoption of more sustainable agricultural practices. CMDT needs policy orientations, and in part these must be developed by Malian research institutions. The role of the Département des Recherches sur les Systèmes de Production Rurale (DRSPR), the farming systems research unit of the national Institut d'Economie Rurale (IER), in developing strategies for sound environmental management is described here. Further, collaboration between CMDT and DRSPR2 in the field of environmental management is described over time for their common intervention zone in southern Mali. Several phases are discussed, and some general conclusions are drawn. Table 1 provides a summary of phases and of changes in staffing over time. Both elements of the table demonstrate an increasing commitment to environmental management.

Diagnosis of main constraints

In the 1970s, little attention was paid to environmental problems in southern Mali. By 1977, IER, in collaboration with KIT, began to implement farming systems research; this programme provided the base for the present DRSPR. In an assessment, farmers mentioned soil erosion, and gully erosion in particular, among their main problems. In addition, soil fertility problems were a daily concern, mainly due to infestation of soils with *Striga*. The farmers' solution to the problem of maintaining production

Table 1. Primary environmental management activities of DRSPR and CMDT (1977–1991)

Phases		DRSPR	CMDT
I	1977-79	- diagnosis of constraints	- no particular attention
II	1979-84	- trials with diversion terraces - terracing in one catchment area; sounding the alarm	- first interest expressed - request to introduce diversion system in more villages
III	1984-86	- formulation of a proposal for a land management programme	- field assistance in testing proposals - request to finance the implementation project PLAE
IV	1986-88	- experiments with new soil conservation techniques - research on integration of agricultural and livestock production - research on carrying capacity	- introduction of land management programme starts in about twenty villages - training of extension workers and farmers begins - training to increase CMDT staff awareness

V	1988-90	- environmental problems at the centre of activities:
		  - conservation techniques
		  - studies on carrying capacity
		  - studies to quantify speed and advancement of degradation
			- introduction of PLAE in an increasing number of villages (40-100)
			- start of collaboration with forestry and livestock services
			- start of discussion including pasture management in the programme
			- regional adaptation of proposals in new intervention areas
			- training to increase awareness continues

IV	1990-91	- formal priority setting; tests of local management capacity	- further extension of PLAE (250 villages); tests of local management capacity
Personnel			
Prior to 1984		short-term consultancies on soil conservation	1 field assistant
1984		1 soil conservationist (expatriate), 6 month consultancies on land use planning; 2 field assistants	
1987		1 soil conservationist (expatriate)	1 junior agronomist; 2 field assistants
1989		1 soil conservationist (expatriate)	1 agronomist, 1 junior agronomist; 1 junior forester; 1 sociologist (expatriate, part-time); 1 senior sociologist (part-time); 2 field assistants; 3 village-based enumerators

levels sufficient to satisfy family needs was to clear new lands. Not only did this demand huge labour investments, but also land became a scarce resource. Farmers were less aware of problems related to overgrazing and over-exploitation of wood for fuel and construction.

DRSPR sounds the alarm

From 1980 onward, DRSPR informally expressed its concern regarding the alarming extent of environmental degradation to the CMDT. Some experimental soil conservation works were conducted in the field on a small scale. However, it took almost four years before the first public alarm was sounded (by Kleene, during a CMDT seminar in April 1984: Belloncle, 1985).

Discussions with farmers, plus field observations, showed that farmers who were winning the battle against weeds were losing the battle against erosion. Weeds were being eradicated, using modern technology such as ploughs, cultivators and herbicides. However, over-exploitation of natural resources was leading to increasingly high run-off, soil depletion, deforestation and overgrazing of pastures, and increased run-off was causing severe soil erosion.

In response to requests from farmers in the village of Fonsébougou, in April 1981 initial try-outs of anti-erosion works were proposed and implemented. By 1982, all fields within one single small catchment area had been protected. This intervention involved a system of graded terraces, constructed in individual farmer's fields. The recommended erosion control measures and subsequent working methods are a replication, based on experiences in Burkina Faso.[3]

Reactions to the work in Fonsébougou were positive: CMDT became interested. Based on the initial experience in Fonsébougou, further ideas were developed. CMDT submitted a request for funding for a follow-up programme in other villages near the 'capital of cotton', Koutiala. CMDT also selected 15 villages for experimental implementation of a soil conservation programme to be carried out by farmers and 'erosion brigades' (Anonymous, 1983).

DRSPR develops an approach to environmental management

From 1984 onwards, DRSPR employed a full-time soil conservationist. His first tasks were to start a programme in three test zones and to train brigades (about five people each) in four well-organized villages. Second, he had to develop a more complete soil conservation package. Supported by short-term consultancies, he developed a land management plan for a specific village (Kaniko) near Koutiala. Due to strong pressure from CMDT, farmers, and the donor agency, implementation began before the plan had been finalized.

The initial techniques for graded terraces were modified in accordance with the comments of farmers whose fields were involved, plus those of visiting farmers from the Koutiala region (van Campen and Hallam, 1985). Furthermore, the general approach was characterized by an effort to take into account the role of the different landscape units in the farming system (Roose, 1984). The main technical adjustment consisted of abandoning strict adherence to contour lines. In this rather flat area, contour lines were so irregular that following them was a source of great practical difficulty for farmers working with draught oxen, ploughs and sowing machines.[4] Further, impermeable ridges were replaced by permeable structures such as hedges and grass strips.

The main social adjustment consisted of a change from an individual approach to a village approach. Right from the start all discussions on erosion problems and possible solutions were held at village level. Villages were represented by village associations. When work was to be implemented, whether located on common lands or individual farmers' fields, its organization could be left to the responsibility of these associations. The main stimulus for the use of the village approach was the insight that in the near future village communities themselves will have to develop, implement and enforce management regulations for the area under their jurisdiction. Early involvement of the village association was a way to strengthen the organizational capacity of the village. The expectation was that the decision making process would improve as time went on (van Campen, 1991). At the request of the CMDT, the redesigned programme and modified erosion works were tested near Koutiala.

In 1985, DRSPR evaluated its experiences in halting soil erosion. A comparison was made to the Burkina Faso case. A proposal for tackling soil erosion on a large scale was then formulated (Bâ et al., 1985). CMDT was the obvious implementer; the Dutch government provided funds and technical assistance.[5] Generally speaking, the original scope of the programme to combat environmental degradation in southern Mali has been broadened, going from erosion control in individual fields towards a village land management scheme. The wider scope was not reflected in the choice of project title. On 1 May 1986, the *Projet Lutte Anti-Erosive dans la Zone Mali Sud* (PLAE) was launched (see project description).

DRSPR as a technical guide for PLAE

At the time PLAE started, a number of technical, socioeconomic and organizational questions were still unanswered. Nevertheless all parties concerned wanted to start implementation of a land management programme on a large scale. They believed the best way to strengthen CMDT's capability for implementation of such a programme was to 'learn by doing'. Moreover, it was thought that constraints could be better assessed when implementation was under way.

In PLAE's first plan of operations, the role of DRSPR was implicitly formulated in a single phrase: 'We foresee a close collaboration with DRSPR' (CMDT, 1986). PLAE was now in charge of the 'old' DRSPR soil conservation activities in three villages. DRSPR researchers could take up new research and simultaneously reinforce research efforts regarding environmental management. These activities consisted of continued testing of new soil conservation techniques; and research on both soil fertility problems and fodder-crop production. The carrying capacity of land for livestock production and extension to new ecological zones were newly identified research themes. Finally, ideas were to be developed on ways to introduce an environmental programme in marginal and less well-organized villages.

From 1985 onwards, DRSPR worked on technical feasibility and socioeconomic impact of grass strips, improved land clearance methods, trash lines, hedge species and soil tillage techniques. Sometimes only empirical experience was collected (such as land clearance methods), but field experiments were also conducted and reported upon (for example, see Hijkoop et al., 1987,[6] on hedges and grass strips; and Poel and Kaya, 1988, on tied ridging).

At this time PLAE was working mainly on the organizational aspects of project implementation, such as training extension workers and farmers, and developing criteria for village selection. PLAE was gaining experience in the technical aspects of the programme, via field observations and qualitative evaluations carried out together with farmers, but did no systematic quantitative research. The project team was still small: two expatriates and two Malian staff members.

After 15 months of PLAE, in October 1987, CMDT held an internal evaluation of PLAE's first campaign (in 10 villages). At this time, the PLAE team described collaboration with DRSPR as follows: 'A common programme has been developed for the "old" villages and during the year the project has been kept informed on the research progress by multiple informal contacts'. The team mentions stopping degradation of pastures and developing conservation techniques for agricultural production as research priorities they expected DRSPR to handle (CMDT, 1987).

Increasing research demands versus limits on capacity

In October 1988, the first phase of PLAE was evaluated. The evaluation mission endorsed the requests PLAE had made to DRSPR in a number of research fields. These were based on constraints encountered during implementation, but assistance was also requested in some new areas (CMDT, 1989). Included were requests to:
- carry out specific research in four areas: conservation techniques in agriculture, improved fallow, species for hedges and grass strips, and pasture improvement;
- research and develop new soil conservation techniques and methods for introducing them;
- collaborate with PLAE and government services in developing and implementing land management experiments to be carried out by farmers;
- indicate priority zones and villages for environmental programmes;
- spell out land management plans for the study villages;
- evaluate five points: effectiveness of the applied soil conservation measures; geographic spread of the programme; village participation; influence of the environmental management programme on the time schedules of male and female farmers; and the economic impact of the programme.

It is interesting to note that almost all of the above-mentioned points were included in the DRSPR/VF plan of operations for 1989–1993 (DRSPR, 1989). DRSPR proposed to develop and improve a number of technological 'packages', which they would first evaluate with respect to technical, social, economic and institutional feasibility.

The need to find methods that would quickly help in achieving sustainable agricultural development in the area was felt to be urgent. Therefore the main thrust of the technological packages was oriented towards combatting the accelerating environmental degradation. Six packages were to be developed: on land management; soil tillage; soil fertility and regeneration of soil cover; livestock management; extra-agricultural activities; and the village approach.

Environmental problems were now at the centre of DRSPR's efforts. This was the result of ongoing contacts between researchers, farmers and extension services; and of growing insight into the underlying mechanisms that lead to environmental degradation. Based on the alarming preliminary results of DRSPR research on the carrying capacity of land for livestock development,[7] concern about pastoral management increased. In October 1988, PLAE and DRSPR jointly organized a one-day workshop to inform the CMDT livestock department and the regional livestock service about the research findings. At the time, both institutions were still mainly oriented to animal health. Moreover, the regional livestock service was preparing a livestock development programme for southern Mali based on assumptions of food abundance, even in the face of water scarcity. The objective of this quite tumultuous meeting was clearly to once again sound the alarm, and to have an influence on the higher-level officials of these organizations.

It also became clear, however, that PLAE and DRSPR, as well as the other services, lacked hard evidence – quantitative data – on the severity of land degradation. The alarm raised was based on the field observations of farmers, extension workers and researchers: the problem was felt not only in the PLAE extension and training programme, but also among DRSPR researchers. Hard data were needed to convince CMDT staff and extension workers of the severity of the situation. Data were also expected to put extension workers in a better position in discussing long-term predictions with farmers (especially with respect to availability of fodder and fuel wood), and to help achieve better priority setting for research.

DRSPR responded by developing research related to environmental management, moving in three main directions. The first was oriented towards collecting basic data on environmental change and assessing farmer behaviour. Examples are studies on carrying capacity (Leloup and Traore, 1989, 1991), on increasing degradation in different ecological zones (Jansen and Diarra, 1990) and on farmers' reaction to the prices of fertilizer (Berckmoes et al., 1988). The second area of DRSPR research involved continued work on practical problems encountered by PLAE, e.g. regeneration of bare soils (Poel and Kaya, 1989). Finally, the effectiveness of PLAE's approach was assessed, for example in a study on adoption of soil conservation measures by farmers (Poel and Kaya, 1989).

The number of villages involved increased rapidly.[8] As a result of the adaptation of the original uniform programme to regional circumstances, PLAE had to diversify its programme. PLAE's strategy for training was to first assign each extension worker to a single village. After experience had been gained in supporting the village process and anti-erosion work, the extension worker was allowed to cover more villages. At the same time, the number of extension workers involved in the programme increased. Thus there was a regional spreading of 'PLAE villages', and consequently PLAE started to work in non-DRSPR zones. The growing number of experienced extension workers familiar with the original uniform, simplified programme made it possible to differentiate the recommendations in view of local (physical and social) circumstances. However, in this process, the number of practical problems and related research questions grew as well.

PLAE preferred not to change the original division of tasks, in which PLAE was not expected to carry out research. But as DRSPR continually tried to react to the practical problems forwarded by PLAE, a DRSPR capacity problem became evident. In implementing its environmental programme, PLAE brought up more questions than DRSPR could answer.

At the end of 1988, and again at the end of 1989, PLAE presented at least 30 research topics to DRSPR. It was not possible for DRSPR to satisfy these demands. Inside PLAE, dissatisfaction started to grow – older questions on the economic aspects of land management, development of an intervention approach for less organized marginal villages, and integration of women in land management programmes had still not been dealt with. PLAE held informal and formal discussions with DRSPR, and PLAE participated in DRSPR's 'objective oriented project planning' exercise (Kooijman et al., Chapter 9). Both parties agreed that PLAE would try to meet part of its research needs by incorporating students, and by giving temporary contracts to researchers (consultancies). PLAE and DRSPR planned to attempt a common negotiated priority setting for DRSPR research.[9]

Some may feel that at least part of the list of research requests made by PLAE to DRSPR could have been taken care of by PLAE itself. PLAE was reluctant to do this. There were three reasons to consider it logical for PLAE to restrict its activities to implementation of the soil conservation programme, and to a rapid increase in the number of villages involved. First, fieldwork and training activities already fully absorbed the limited PLAE staff and equipment. Second, Malian members of the staff were not trained researchers. Third, evaluation of messages to be transmitted to the extension service was considered an important phase in the farming systems research cycle (therefore it fell within the domain of DRSPR). Consequently, a division of work between research and implementation seemed more realistic, and training of farmers, extension workers and staff members remained the main task of PLAE.

Successfully negotiating priorities

Formal discussions took place between DRSPR and PLAE teams (about 25 people altogether) in February 1990. It was decided that DRSPR would focus its efforts on finding a basic solution – one that would change the circumstances that lead to the use of inappropriate farming systems, which then cause environmental degradation. This consensus was further developed in a proposal for research on environmental management, submitted to CMDT in December 1990 (PLAE/DRSPR, 1990). DRSPR and PLAE observed that environmental degradation was continuing. In spite of the project, farmers did not fundamentally change their attitude; extensive cultivation continued. The contradiction between the short-term interest of farmers and the longer-term interest of society – preservation of the natural environment – is thought to be the main reason for this slow progress. Only if these opposing interests are reconciled can a solution to environmental degradation be found.

The approach adopted by DRSPR and PLAE is to develop improvements in the system that produce short-term gains for the farmer, and at the same time lead to stabilization and even reduction of pressure on natural resources. Increased productivity of both land and labour is the objective: this would offer a better standard of living to a growing number of farmers, without the necessity of clearing new land. An additional condition was to find new technologies that would not increase farmers' risks in comparison with their current methods. Contributions not only from DRSPR, but also from commodity research were necessary to achieve this ambitious objective. In this process, the plan was that DRSPR would make better use of existing but often dispersed knowledge (on e.g. manure production, carrying capacity, fodder resources, fodder production, productivity of dams, soil fertility, and forestry).

PLAE was to continue the introduction of the soil conservation programme (which was becoming more diverse and regionalized), and of training for farmers and extension workers. This ongoing work of PLAE was considered a necessity for preparing both farmers and the extension service for the more basic solutions anticipated in the future. The organizational capacity of the farm communities is considered to be of critical importance, if major changes in farming systems are to be introduced. In addition to this work, a farmer-based land management programme was to be developed jointly with DRSPR sociologists.

One could also ask why almost six years elapsed before a clear definition of the problem emerged, with a formulation of possible limitations on proposed solutions. Could this period have been shorter? Or, in other words, could priorities have been set earlier? Our considerations suggest that the process described in Mali could not have been significantly shortened. Four factors are influential:

- the sequence of work followed the composition of the team, and team composition is generally an expression of the donor's view of the problem. Before 1984, the research team was composed of socioeconomists and more or less traditional agronomists. No soil scientist, soil conservationist, soil fertility expert, or forester was a part of the early team. Not surprisingly, few actions were undertaken in the sphere of soil conservation. It was farmers' observations of their physical environment that initially brought environmental degradation into view for the researchers, who in turn were able to convince the donor agency. Only much later did the availability of a more complete team, including sociologists, make it possible to conduct a testing programme, seeking the best options with respect to village regulations and village organization for the management of village lands;
- over a considerable period, DRSPR invested in building a team capable of implementing a farming systems research approach. This was needed because project staff had traditional educational backgrounds. They had not been trained to really listen to farmers;
- the team tried as far as possible to follow farmers' priorities. However, even when farmers indicated a problem with soil erosion, this did not mean they considered soil erosion their most important problem. Farmers tended to speak in terms of food security, yields and cash income. For this reason, even though some aspects of the early work are related to environmental management (e.g. manure production in kraals), they were not named as such;
- in the early eighties in southern Mali, the discussion of environmental issues had hardly begun (the problem was thought to be only a temporary shortage of rainfall). Research efforts on topics like carrying capacity were still in the stage of developing methodology.

Conclusions

DRSPR's role was not limited to typical research activities, such as the diagnosis of constraints, formulation of the necessary research, and conducting experiments. It also played an interactive role with extension and policymakers – sounding the alarm for policymakers, developing strategies, responding to demands of the extension agency, coping with a (temporary) loss of initiative, reorienting research questions to more basic issues, evaluating ongoing programmes, and formulating policy alternatives. Over time, emphasis shifted from one aspect to another, but some aspects were given continuous attention. A particular aspect of DRSPR's supporting role might increase in importance, given a particular issue and moment.

As this chapter shows, it takes time to provide sufficient information and practical, convincing examples to farmers, extension workers and higher-level administrators. This must be a carefully executed, step-by-step-process, to assure positive commitments at all levels. In this case, a gradual development took place, from informal contacts between KIT staff within the two projects (DRSPR and PLAE) to more formal meetings among developing Malian institutions. KIT was able to play a role as a facilitator, reinforcing interaction between Malian institutes.

A more profound discussion on priorities took place only at the moment manifest problems clearly outnumbered the capacity for researching solutions. In retrospect, we believe even a development-oriented extension service should anticipate a need for a certain amount of research capacity. This can avoid overburdening research institutions and allow a more flexible response to constraints on programme implementation. At the least, proper monitoring and evaluation capacity must be included, to help in identifying research priorities.

DRSPR made the right choice in helping to establish the implementation project PLAE and focusing research on basic issues, including the severity of environmental degradation in the CMDT region. Basic data (DRSPR) and quick results (PLAE) are both necessary components in convincing farmers, extension workers and policymakers of the need to act, and in supplying information on the actions needed. Together, PLAE and DRSPR have succeeded in bringing about a change of attitude within the extension services and in a growing number of village communities. This will surely increase the initiatives to overcome the present environmental crisis in southern Mali. In general, this experience in Mali makes clear that any farming systems research programme must take environmental aspects into account.

Notes

1 'DRSPR' refers to DRSPR/Sikasso. The author worked first with DRSPR and then with PLAE; he is thus well aware of the different cultures within the two institutions, and the images they have of each other.

2 In the following text 'DRSPR' refers to DRSPR/Sikasso (or DRSPR-Volet Fonsébougou). DRSPR/Sikasso is actually only one of three regional units of DRSPR-Mali. DRSPR/Sikasso is the origin of DRSPR-Mali; it was developed in collaboration between IER and KIT, and has been extensively described by Kleene et al. (1989).

3 This occurred after the complete failure of a large-scale project, in which bulldozers were used to move land; more successful erosion control projects were then developed, with farmer participation as a major feature (Reij, 1983).

4 The same problems were present for more mechanized farmers: when a group of farmers who possessed tractors and had major erosion problems were contacted about the possibility of implementing such a system in their fields, they showed little interest.

5 Technical assistance was contracted out to the Royal Tropical Institute (KIT).

6 This report was in fact a joint production of PLAE and DRSPR. PLAE had gained experience by introducing preliminary proposals.

7 Carrying capacity is sufficient on average, but is greatly exceeded in drier areas and in the old cotton basin.

8 Number of villages: 1987 – 10; 1988 – 20; 1989 – 120; 1991 – about 250.

9 The fortunate point here is that PLAE staff realized they could not just present a long list of research topics to DRSPR; they also had a responsibility to think in terms of priorities.

Bibliography

ANONYMOUS (1983) Notitie bij functieinhoud erosiebestrijdingsdeskundige/landinrichter. Amsterdam: Royal Tropical Institute

BÂ L, CAMPEN W VAN, HALLAM G AND VIERSTRA G (1985) La lutte anti-érosive et la conservation des sols, activités de la DRSPR. Sikasso: IER/DRSPR

BELLONCLE G (1985) Paysanneries Sahelliennnes en Péril. Carnets de route. Vol. 2 (1982–1984). Paris: L'Harmattan

BERCKMOES W, JAGER EJ AND KONÉ Y (1988) L'intensification agricole au Mali-Sud. Souhait ou réalité? Bulletins of the Royal Tropical Institute, no. 318. Amsterdam: Royal Tropical Institute/Sikasso: DRSPR-Volet Fonsébougou

CAMPEN W VAN (1991) The long road to sound land management in southern Mali. In: Savenije H and A Huijsman, eds, Making haste slowly. Amsterdam: Royal Tropical Institute

CAMPEN W VAN AND HALLAM G (1985) Réactions aux plaintes des paysans concernant l'érosion du sol dans les zones d'activités agricoles intensives au mali-Sud: des réponses fixes aux propositions flexibles. Fonsébougou/Sikasso: DRSPR-Volet

CMDT (1986) Plan d'Opération du Projet Lutte anti-érosive dans la zone Mali-Sud. 1986–1989. Koutiala: CMDT/PLAE

CMDT (1987) Rapport Bilan 1 campagne. Koutiala: CMDT/PLAE

CMDT (1989) Plan d'Operation Projet Lutte Anti-Erosive dans la zone Mali-Sud. 2 phase: 1-5-1989 au 30-4-1993. Koutiala: CMDT

DRSPR (1989) Plan d'Opération 1989–1993. Sikasso: DRSPR

HIJKOOP J, POEL P VAN DER AND KAYA D (1987) Compartimentation de la zone en culture avec haies-vives et bandes enherbées comme mesure anti-érosive. Une expérience au Mali-Sud. Koutiala: PLAE/DRSPR

JANSEN L AND DIARRA S (1990) Le Mali-Sud vu superficiellement. Quantification des superficies agricoles et la dégradation pour quatre terroirs villageois entre 1952 et 1987. Wageningen/Amsterdam: DRSPR/Landbouw Universiteit Wageningen/KIT

KLEENE P, SANOGO B AND VIERSTRA G (1989) A partir de Fonsébougou. Présentation, objectifs et méthodologie du 'Volet Fonsébougou' 1977–1987. Bamako/Amsterdam: l'Institut Economie Rurale/Royal Tropical Institute

LELOUP S AND TRAORÉ M (1989) La situation fourragère au sud-est du Mali. Tome 1. Région CMDT de Sikasso et de Koutiala. Sikasso: DRSPR/VF

LELOUP S AND TRAORÉ M (1991) La situation fourragère au sud-est du Mali. Tome 2. Region CMDT de San. Sikasso: DRSPR/VF

PLAE/DRSPR (1990) Note pour la réunion de concertation 'Etudes Gestion des Terroirs' 18 et 19 Décembre à Sikasso.

POEL P VAN DER AND KAYA B (1988) Résultats des tests sur le buttage à sillons cloisonnés et le grattage croisé à sec. Sikasso: DRSPR/VF

POEL P VAN DER AND KAYA B (1989) Comparaison des méthodes de régénération des endroits dégradés. La berge du marigot à Kaniko. Sikasso: DRSPR/VF

POEL P VAN DER AND KAYA B (1989) Adoption des mesures de lutte anti-érosive par des paysans de villages non-encadrés autour de Kaniko et Try en zone Mali-Sud. Sikasso: DRSPR/VF

REIJ C (1983) L'évolution de la lutte anti-érosive en Haute-Volta depuis l'indépendence. Vers une plus grande participation de la population. Amsterdam: Vrije Universiteit

ROOSE E (1985) Rapport de mission auprès de la DRSPR dans la région sud Mali, 3-17 décembre 1984. Sikasso: DRSPR/IRRT

Project description: PRIAG, Central America

PRIAG, the Regional Programme for the Strengthening of Agronomic Research on Basic Grains in Central America (Programa regional de reforzamiento a la investigación agronómica sobre los granos en centroamericá), works with six countries: Costa Rica, El Salvador, Guatemala, Honduras, Nicaragua and Panama. It provides technical assistance to CORECA, the Regional Council for Agricultural Cooperation. This programme is financed by the European Union and implemented by the consortium CIRAD/KIT (International Center of Agricultural Research, Montpellier, France, and the Royal Tropical Institute, Amsterdam). The regional management unit is made up of two Central American and two European experts, based in Costa Rica at IICA (International Institute of Agricultural Cooperation), which also provides logistical support.

PRIAG started in 1990 and is still in its first phase, which is to last four years. The overall objective is to reinforce initiatives to increase food security and equitable socioeconomic development in the Central American region. This is to be based on the production of grains and other food (including alternative nutritional crops) that is sustainable from both physical-biological and socioeconomic points of view.

The specific objectives of PRIAG are a) to strengthen national systems related to generating and transferring agricultural technology; b) to promote adoption of appropriate technologies by small producers of basic grains; and c) to promote and facilitate the integration of research and extension in the six countries in the region. PRIAG has three subprogrammes: thematic research, farming systems research and research–extension linkages. The manifold activities of PRIAG include agronomic research, both at experimental stations (thematic research, TR) and in farmers' fields (FSR&D zones), as well as supporting activities. Examples of the latter are specific studies (such as the impact of agricultural policies on farmers' production), and specific projects (e.g. establishing a regional system of information exchange). Linking thematic research, conducted on national experiment stations, with on-farm and farming systems research is a major challenge for PRIAG. A few zones have been selected in each country for the formation of FSR teams. The project aims to stimulate participation of these FSR teams in decision making and priority setting for agricultural research, including thematic research.

Today, agricultural research in Central America is conducted by a wide range of institutions: official government institutions, universities, non-government organizations and the private sector. Implementation of the PRIAG strategy – integration and coordination of agricultural research in the region – is therefore complex, as it requires dealing with a variety of levels (local, national, regional) and sectors (government, NGOs and the private sector). This increases the number of actors involved in the process of setting priorities for research. Since its initiation, the official sector has been heavily represented in the institutional bodies and committees created by PRIAG within the structure of the national agricultural research systems. However, increased involvement of other actors is a PRIAG aim.

14 Setting priorities for regional research: PRIAG, Central America

Fred van Sluys and Antonio Silva

Other chapters in this book describe experiences of projects in specific countries. Here we address another level of organization, in which several countries are working together. Regionalization of research and extension is of particular importance in Central America (and potentially in other areas as well), due to the relatively small size of these countries' economies, plus the diversity of their agricultural environments. A given agroecological zone may be more comparable to zones in neighbouring countries than to those in the same country. Thus in the long term, organizing at a regional level can increase both efficiency and sustainability. By working together, a group of small countries can assemble a 'critical mass' of resources to be used for agricultural research.

Regional organization has, however, a number of implications for FSR&D. While FSR&D must, by its location-specific nature, continue to be organized below the national level, collaboration can be supportive: it can not only provide opportunities for exchanging ideas, but also stimulate the development of FSR&D, by showing results in similar situations. Further, it can increase the availability of relevant research results – an FSR&D team could work with thematic researchers in more than one country, depending on the topic in question. This means, however, that regionalization requires specific attention to linkages between thematic research (organized at regional level) and FSR&D (organized per country), if the potential benefits are to be realized. This chapter illustrates both the potential for collaboration and the difficulties inherent in experimenting with new organizational modes.

PRIAG, the Regional Programme for the Strengthening of Agronomic Research on Basic Grains in Central America, represents a unique opportunity and example of priority setting in Central America for a programme of regionalized, integrated research (see project description). The desired

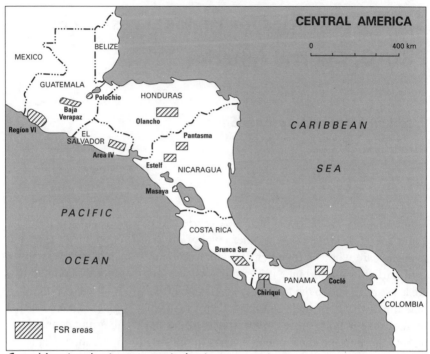

Central America, showing FSR areas in the six PRIAG countries

regional research agenda and strengthening of agronomic research for the six countries of the region is specifically oriented towards basic-grain-based farming systems operated by farmers with medium-sized holdings.

A short overview of the development of agricultural research in the six Central American countries participating in this programme, with a particular focus on farming systems research, begins the chapter. This helps to explain the variety of institutional responses that the NARS (national agricultural research systems) within member countries made to PRIAG interventions. Further, it helps to understand the role and mission of PRIAG, and the challenges it faces. In the following sections, the process of planning and priority setting is covered: first, the general process adopted by PRIAG – strategic planning, annual planning, and specific projects – and then specific issues related to thematic research (TR) and FSR. In the last sections, instruments created by the programme for use in planning and priority setting, the role of various actors, and the relation between agronomic research in thematic and farming systems research are discussed. The perspective for FSR in the process of integrating agronomic research within the Central American region will be highlighted.

An overview: background of the project

In the 1960s and 1970s, the governments of Central America promoted economic development via agricultural development. The agricultural sector was considered the most important with respect to population, employment, production of goods for both national and international markets, and generating gross national product. In this period, the agricultural sector – through agricultural research and extension services – promoted agricultural development by distributing improved crop varieties. To satisfy the demand, most research (about 70% of the total) was devoted to plant breeding; the rest concerned agronomy.

In these years, a gradual institutional evolution of agricultural research and extension organizations often took place within the NARS, geared towards improving performance and impact of their work. However, in establishing the objectives, priorities and strategies to be used in developing new technologies, the real needs of farmers were insufficiently taken into account, and the possibility of their active participation was not considered.

FSR approaches

During the 1970s, the ICTA (Institute of Technological and Agricultural Science) was established in Guatemala, with a farming systems research philosophy. The establishment of IDIAP, the national agricultural research institute of Panama, was the result of a similar restructuring of the research process. Two factors contributed to the creation of these institutes: first, the relatively high importance of the agricultural sector in the national economy of these countries; and second, the priority given to agricultural research. But this development of agricultural research and extension also came about because the impact of traditional programmes on agricultural production at farm level was too low; and further, farmers were increasingly demanding new technologies. Farmer demand was stimulated by integrated rural development programmes, being implemented at that time with heavy support from international donors, which stressed farmer participation.

During the second part of the 1970s and the first half of the 1980s, most Central American countries established FSR as their strategy for agricultural research. In implementing the new strategy, some countries included only minimal institutional modifications in their NARS – for example, El Salvador (CENTA – Center for Agricultural Research) and Honduras (PNIA – National Programme for Agricultural Research). The agricultural ministries of Nicaragua and Costa Rica also tried to implement FSR, without any restructuring of their NARS.

Variations in the extent to which Central American countries introduced institutional changes reflect the political support for agronomic research, especially with respect to availability of funding, and for FSR in particular. In Guatemala and Panama, intensive training programmes were conducted, and FSR teams were formed. In Guatemala, FSR was institutionalized as a research and extension modality at local level, in addition to thematic and commodity research. In the other countries, this occurred to a lesser extent. In all countries, FSR remained a rather isolated type of agricultural research, implemented by specific projects at various levels. As a result, there are now groups of convinced believers in FSR (mostly practitioners), but also some sceptics (who are mostly not directly involved) regarding its usefulness and impact. FSR teams developed a capacity to reach producers, but were unable to use the information generated by their research to influence the policies that affect producers' actions. Thus NARS usually ignore the work done by these teams, sometimes simply because they do not understand its relevance.

Declining importance of the agricultural sector

During the 1980s industrial activity and service sectors grew rapidly, and the relative importance of the agricultural sector in the national economies of Central America decreased. At the end of the 1980s structural adjustment programmes (SAPs) were implemented, due to the fiscal crisis caused by a heavy external debt load. This also implied a reduction in resources for agricultural research: in some cases, policymakers tended to consider agricultural research as a cost, not an investment. Budget and personnel reductions were made, and modifications were introduced in the research systems, limiting the operational capacity of FSR teams, or even causing them to disband. One contributing factor was that the NARS are themselves poorly linked to institutes in other national sectors; their position with respect to national resource allocation and policymaking is weak. This lack of technical and political linkages further reduces the possibilities of FSR programmes to influence policymaking.

In brief, this is the current situation in the member countries: in Guatemala, a close, centralized relationship between ICTA, the national research institute, and DIGESA, the extension service, makes the involvement of NGOs, universities and so forth more difficult. Moreover, it leaves little room for manoeuvre for local FSR teams. Nicaragua is going through a process of privatization of agricultural services, but at the moment little or no real support is being given to this transition. The situation in El Salvador is even more problematic, because CENTA is almost completely inoperative following adoption of a yet to be implemented law on restructuring. IDIAP, in Panama, is however displaying a strong commitment to FSR at local team level, even to the point of filling the gap left by the extension service. Honduras is showing strong commitment to the PRIAG mission, and is capitalizing on its experience by contracting out research to universities or private agronomic schools. And finally, Costa Rica is initiating a new strategy for its NARS, called INVEX (an acronym for research–extension), which is completely compatible with PRIAG's mission. INVEX is being well received at local level, but is meeting resistance at national level from those supporting the interests of thematic researchers.

New institutional configurations

The official agricultural institutions in charge of research and extension, whose capability to satisfy producer demands has been drastically reduced, have changed as a result of the situation. On the other hand, the lower priority given to the agricultural sector by government and the resulting contraction of agricultural research have stimulated non-governmental organizations to become active in generating and transferring agricultural technology, in particular for non-export crops. (Thus far the impact has not been significant.) The private sector has taken over research and extension for non-traditional export crops, such as horticultural crops, flowers and fruits. This suggests a new role for the NARS, in which they coordinate with other actors involved in research and extension.

Such a role may require new institutional configurations. In El Salvador, Nicaragua, Costa Rica and Honduras, the creation of such new configurations involving the NARS is now under way. This should make it easier for PRIAG, given its philosophy, to incorporate and consolidate experience and methodologies. Nevertheless, at present the situation of agricultural research and extension is still best described as lacking clear coordination and integration of the actors involved.

Role and mission of PRIAG

One aim of PRIAG is to revitalize dormant capacities within the region for carrying out FSR. This is to be accomplished by providing technical assistance, training and financial support. However, the wide variation from country to country, not only in capacity to conduct FSR but also in level of political and financial support to farming systems oriented research, is obviously a complicating factor.

In working to strengthen and regionalize agricultural research (and FSR in particular), PRIAG tries to involve not only the NARS, but also other institutions and actors. PRIAG's mission implies that existing relationships between research, extension and other actors must be changed; this may be perceived as a threat to parts of the research and extension community 'establishment'. On the other hand, a regional approach may create opportunities for NARS: by working within such an approach, they may in effect be able to maintain a 'critical mass' of researchers, scientists and institutions. That is, the regional programme provides work and vital contacts with others working in similar areas, identifying common interests and helping to keep a more substantial community in place. In fact, most of the NARS with weaker capabilities at national level could recuperate relatively easily, if conditions and interests were to change. Moreover, on-going political processes, with the gradual installation of democratic governments in the Central American countries, are a positive factor for PRIAG intervention. In recent years, a strong will and striving for collaboration between the six countries have developed at both economic and political levels. The PRIAG experience can be used as a reference and possible model for the realization of regional integration.

Regional management of agronomic research, as initiated by PRIAG, must cope with two additional (but not unrelated) major challenges. In its first phase, PRIAG must complete agricultural research that achieves at least some technical and socioeconomic impact. Second, PRIAG must mobilize and guarantee commitment, so that research will be followed up (whether within PRIAG or in a new form) and with or without external donor support. In many respects, the first phase of PRIAG should provide improved conditions for work to come, through:
- improved databases and information management;
- more real participation of farmers, providing, among other things, better assessment of farmer needs;
- increased skills, as a result of in-service training for scientists and technicians;
- improved capabilities of scientific institutions in the region;
- better networking among scientific institutions in Central America as well as between these organizations and extra-regional bodies;
- improved research management at all levels.

The regional management unit (RMU) of PRIAG has established a number of procedures to operationalize the mission and objectives of the programme. The complexity of the situation, including the fact that PRIAG is an intergovernmental initiative, makes agreement on priorities and ways to translate these into activities particularly important. Thus a process for setting priorities for agronomic research is an essential part of PRIAG. A description of this process, including the actors involved, follows.

Setting global priorities and defining strategic issues

After long and intensive interaction between Central American public institutions involved in agricultural development and the European Union,[1] the donor backing PRIAG, a general agreement (ALA 88/23) was signed in 1988. The importance of this basic agreement between the main political actors involved in the regional initiative was that it defined the programme mission and the global priorities for research: a focus on agronomic problems facing farmers who work within small and medium-sized grain-based farming systems.

In the process that followed, this broad goal was gradually translated into more specific objectives. Once the regional management unit (RMU) had been established (September 1990), its first task was to elaborate a strategic four-year plan (1991–1994). This plan involves primarily the national directors of research and extension institutes. Thus it simultaneously establishes frameworks for both institutional decision making and programming. Figure 1 presents a schematic overview of the various bodies and committees set up by PRIAG to operationalize the programme.

The strategic plan was elaborated by the RMU, in interaction with the scientific council (SC) and the regional research and extension linkage committee (RRELC), via a series of national workshops and regional encounters. Finally, the strategic plan was approved by the directorate, made up of vice-ministers of agriculture from the countries concerned, plus a representative of the EU as donor. The output from this global priority setting stage was a specific definition of the target group and actors to be involved in the programme; delineation of the geographical areas within which FSR would occur; and assessment of the institutional research and extension activities taking place at that time in the region. Another important outcome was the achievement of consensus on the priority strategic technological issues for agronomic research in the region: soil fertility; agronomic interaction (soil–plants–climate–management); and integrated pest management and weed control.

Figure 1. Overview of PRIAG components

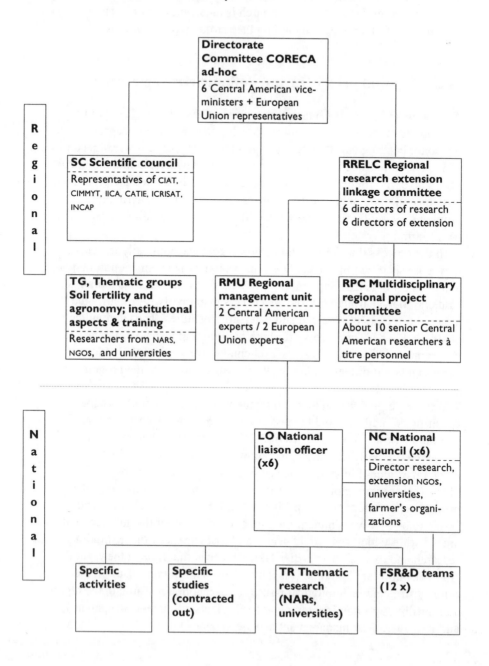

Adaptation of strategic plan priorities

In 1992, one year after PRIAG had become operational, the RMU was confronted with a call for modification of the strategic plan. This was due to an
accelerated process of liberalization and privatization of Central American
economies, in conjunction with attempts at regional integration. When the
directorate met in a special session, some vice-ministers of agriculture
strongly questioned the activities and basic concepts of the programme. In
response to these concerns, the directorate proposed a reorientation.
Changes were suggested in the interpretation of food security, PRIAG's
point of departure. The directorate passed a resolution presenting the RMU
with a challenge to mobilize major actors, apply the necessary mechanisms,
and elaborate a proposal to modify the strategic plan. This was to be done
in addition to activities already planned for 1992.

An intensive process of consultation among Central American technical
and political sectors and the European Union was then organized by the
RMU. Agreement on the 'Modification Addendum' to the strategic plan
resulted. This process also led to some resetting of priorities; in particular
the concept of food security has been redefined: research will involve not
only production aspects of basic grains, but will also include productive
activities to provide farmers with cash to buy food. This, in turn, made it
possible to define some new themes for agronomic research. These have to
do with diversification of agricultural production, in line with existing
farmer strategies for incorporating new or non-traditional crops in grain-
based farming systems. Moreover, the need for sustainable agricultural
production was stressed. The Addendum also resulted in a new level of
accountability to regional political levels within the programme, while
maintaining accountability to both the donor and farmers. It has increased
expectations regarding the potential future impact of agricultural research
in general, and also of PRIAG in particular.

Annual operational planning and priority setting

Once the global priorities or strategic issues have been established in the
strategic plan, a yearly planning process is implemented in two steps. First,
regional annual plans are elaborated (done in accord with annual administrative cycles), and second, concrete project proposals are formulated for
both thematic research and farming systems research (in accord with the
agricultural cycle in Central America).

Annual operational plan

Each calendar year the RMU, in collaboration with the RRELC, prepares an annual operational plan. This plan allocates resources for TR and FSR, and specifies activities related to development of both human resources and databases, as well as specific studies. After the plan has passed the RRELC, final approval must come from the directorate. In detailing specific activities, PRIAG uses three major instruments: regional thematic groups, specific studies and short-term European expertise. The thematic group on fertility and agronomy outlined priorities before starting to finance research topics on particular themes. Another regional thematic group deals with training, institutional development and agricultural knowledge and information systems. European expertise was called in primarily to work with these regional groups and to provide some aspects of training in FSR methodology and research management. Specific studies were conducted, covering for example the role of NGOs and the impact of structural adjustment on the development of production systems. These groups are also expected to play an important role in the internal monitoring and feedback systems.

Programming and carrying out research projects

The following step in the planning process, programming and carrying out TR and FSR projects, is based upon the strategy and priorities set within the regional operational plan. In each of the countries involved, planning begins at national level, and facilitates an interactive process in which project proposals are elaborated by national researchers and local FSR teams. PRIAG also receives research proposals from NARS and some universities. The national councils (NCs) responsible for linking research and extension play an important role in the planning process. These councils are headed by the directors of national research and extension institutes, who invite universities, NGOs and farmer organizations to participate. The council serves as a mechanism that links research and extension, and provides coordination among actors. Further, these councils are given the task of overseeing and monitoring all programme activities in their respective countries; assuring national and local relevance; finding ways to make regional, national, and local priorities for TR and FSR compatible; and mobilizing technical support at national level. The link of the NC to the regional level (RRELC) is made by the research and extension directors. This feedback function of NCs is especially important: it emphasizes farmer demand for technology, and creates possibilities for adapting priorities or establishing new ones, to be incorporated into regional year plans.

Obviously NCs are assigned highly responsible tasks. In practice, the capacity of these councils to carry out their tasks is often still insufficient. A national council is often biased towards thematic research, at the expense of FSR; and towards the NARS, limiting the involvement of other actors such as NGOs. A central figure in PRIAG's organization is the national liaison officer. In each country this officer is secretary to the NC, and is in permanent contact with the RMU. The RMU's potential for strengthening the capacity of national councils is heavily dependent on the vocation and attitude of these key persons. Creating such capacity and taking care that the interests of all actors are well balanced in priority setting is a continuous challenge to the RMU. Discrepancies or conflicts between regional and national interests are primarily expressed and discussed at the level of the NCs, which would like to lay claim to more of the autonomy and decision making power regarding allocation of resources that is now vested in the regional committees and the RMU. In accord with PRIAG's strategy, the NCs can be given more decision making powers once they succeed in representing farmer demands. During the first three years of PRIAG's operation, this situation led to some modification in the yearly programming process, which will be briefly discussed below.

Thematic research planning

In the first programme year, 1991, researchers sent their proposals to the NCs, which submitted them to the subcommittee on thematic crop research, made up of 24 members (4 crops x 6 countries). As the NC did not make any improvements in the proposals, this simply increased the red tape. Thus in the second year, proposals were directly sent to the subcommittee. The process was still complicated, as a large number of projects were presented, covering many aspects and increasing the difficulty of achieving a regional focus. Consequently, the subcommittee was replaced in 1993 by a multidisciplinary regional project committee (RPC). This committee is made up of approximately ten senior Central American agricultural scientists, appointed by the RRELC *à titre personnel.* This change allows PRIAG to achieve better integration and regionalization of thematic research.

Local FSR programming

As mentioned in earlier chapters, implementing FSR can benefit an agricultural research agenda by facilitating farmer participation; providing feedback on socioeconomic impact and extent of programme adoption; and demonstrating the necessity of particular thematic research. Therefore

PRIAG stimulates and facilitates FSR in selected geographical areas in member countries. Local FSR teams have been established in eleven zones, with a significant involvement of extension. These local teams, supported by the NCs and RMU, formulate research proposals that are expected to respond to local problems and to farmer demands. The RMU has a double function here: first, in strengthening the capacity of local FSR teams to prepare proposals and work these into local plans for research and extension, and second, in deciding whether these plans will be approved, as it is the RMU that finally decides which will be financed.

In 1991, the first year, technology validation and transfer projects made up the greatest part of the area plans. Research was directly oriented to crops. Research proposals were based on available literature, without conducting further diagnostic studies. During 1991 and 1992 FSR teams were given in-service training in aspects such as agronomic diagnostics, experimentation by farmers, the farming systems approach, agricultural knowledge and information management, and so forth. A number of specific diagnostic studies were conducted in addition to the on-going crop-related research. Results of research and studies were evaluated, and a synthesis was made at the beginning of 1993. With direct support and technical guidance from the RMU, local teams and NCs organized planning workshops in all selected FSR zones. In addition to farmers, representatives of the NC and researchers who had implemented TR projects in the areas involved participated in these workshops.

In addition to serving as a planning exercise for each area, the planning workshops held in FSR areas provided elements for evaluation related to the impact of PRIAG activities as a whole, as well as the response capacity of both national councils and local teams. The RMU envisaged an increasing broadening of FSR, in four steps. An initial focus on crops (based on agronomic research) would evolve toward the application of a systems approach, including a whole-farm approach and multidisciplinarity; then local development (at above-farm level), including institutional aspects; and finally to strategic, multi-actor planning of FSR and TR. However, the capacity of FSR teams to plan and set priorities for their own research was still limited: it was realized that it was not realistic to expect the development envisaged for FSR to be achieved within one project phase. In other words, these objectives were over-ambitious. Further, PRIAG's need to produce tangible results meant that research had to be cautiously focused on a few major (primarily agronomic) topics.

Integration of FSR and TR: a perspective

The TR projects approved for 1993 offer an important opportunity for the integration of agronomic research: they allow TR and FSR to focus on the same set of regional priorities. This should benefit both. Topics include soil fertility and conservation; integrated pest management and weed control; and seed production. In this way the programme promotes the idea of common themes for TR and FSR, and also systematically promotes direct interaction between TR and FSR and among the actors involved. This has the potential to generate results with regional and national relevance, as well as other visible impacts.

The programme has clearly made progress in integrating agronomic research in Central America. Nevertheless, results to date suggest significant weaknesses on the part of the NARS, in both thematic research and FSR. Not only are the present capabilities of the NARS less than had been hoped, but also the process now under way tends to simply reconfirm traditional relationships (or non-relationships) between thematic research and FSR. Public and semi-public research institutions still prefer to do fundamental research. Local FSR teams continue to do a minimum of research and validation of proposed technologies. They primarily carry out technology transfer and extension. This means that farmer participation and assessment of farmers' demands for technology are weak or non-existent. Thus poor assessment of technology demand is combined with weak backup from research: there is negative feedback in both directions, which encourages the continuation of traditional roles. The presence of this traditional role pattern also explains much of the weakness of local researchers and extension workers in managing and implementing research themselves. Moreover, the resulting lack of information on local conditions, including farmers' needs, has effects at national level: it helps to keep the centralized, supply-driven character of most NARS in place, making change even more difficult. As a consequence, there is still much work to be done to ensure an increasing influence of FSR on national and regional priorities for thematic research.

Conclusions

To strengthen regional agricultural research on basic grains, PRIAG first had to create certain conditions, by establishing mechanisms and gaining credibility. To the authors, the basic elements needed for successful implementation of PRIAG's mission appear to be:

- a basic agreement that includes a clear definition of the mission of the programme;
- an institutional structure, mechanisms and procedures at various levels, with active involvement of many actors, for setting priorities and structuring organizational responses;
- a planning process that reconciles the yearly administrative cycle and the technical or agricultural cycle;
- member countries who guarantee basic technical assistance, especially for FSR teams, and political and institutional support to projects accepted for financing; and
- a regional research management unit (here called the RMU) with enough autonomy, political and technical support to focus TR and FSR projects on the main priorities.

It is too early to know many of the results of this initiative. However, some preliminary conclusions can be drawn.

- Maintaining political accountability is especially important in an environment in which the political and economic context, and the actors as well, may change rapidly. Under these conditions, even a substantial reorientation of basic strategies initiated by policymakers halfway through the priority setting process can turn out to be beneficial: in this case, the Addendum led to an increase in political support. On the other hand, PRIAG must also maintain accountability to farmers. The difficulties presented by this double accountability will continue as long as the target groups or beneficiaries of research are unable to pay for the services they need and, as a consequence, have little weight in decision making. However, the fact that donor agencies tend to be on the side of farmers helps to maintain a balance.

- Focusing TR and FSR on a limited number of priority issues and farmer demands satisfies the minimum conditions necessary to establish a regional agronomic research agenda. This also increases the probability of generating concrete results, including both technological and socioeconomic impact, within the lifetime of the programme. PRIAG's experience shows that even if agronomic research is focused on main priority issues, it will not be possible to meet all technological demands immediately. Real answers cannot be expected quickly enough to be within the currently funded life of PRIAG.

- As noted, the response of the member countries to the PRIAG initiative has not been unidimensional. This differentiation has been due to the variety of institutional configurations and traditional styles of operation in the six countries. Some NARS and other institutions have limited capabilities. Delicate political situations aggravate this situation. As PRIAG's experience illustrates, when NARS' possibilities for responding to short-term local and national demands are drastically limited, they cannot be expected to respond adequately to long-term, strategic regional priorities.

- As the role of the agricultural sector in the national economy diminishes, agricultural research faces reductions in funding. At the same time the complexity of research is increasing, as the necessity to incorporate physical, biological, socioeconomic, and ecological or environmental factors becomes more evident. This presents an even greater challenge for FSR: while thematic research traditionally finds it easier to obtain resources, it appears that FSR must demonstrate the importance of its work not only to politicians and farmers, but also, in many cases, to the entire research and extension community.

- PRIAG's experience demonstrates the widespread weakness of local FSR teams. Sometimes these teams may not even be incorporated in the structure of the NARS. In the past, NARS in some countries have built well-equipped and technically well-trained FSR teams. Initially, PRIAG also followed a strategy of building strong local teams. However, their impact has been moderate. It is therefore necessary to think less of creating heavily equipped teams, and more about FSR as a way of managing agricultural knowledge and information, involving a wide variety of actors and creating synergies. The need for farmer participation in managing and implementing research and extension, for example, leads in turn to a discussion of a redefinition of the role of the state in the delivery of agricultural services, and of the need for a new kind of management and leadership for FSR at all levels.

Note

1   Formerly called the European Community.

15 Getting results: an overview and future agenda

Bram Huijsman and J. Douwe Meindertsma

FSR&D methodology has gradually evolved and grown over time, based on the trial and error experiences of practitioners in the field. This book illustrates a similar learning process, now taking place in research management. The project experiences in the preceding chapters make explicit what FSR&D practitioners have to some extent been doing implicitly: getting to the right research priorities and translating these into workable programmes. These experiences are notable for their frankness in delineating not only successes but also failures and unresolved problems. By systematizing our thinking and exchanging our experiences, we expect to improve our research, and perhaps to help others do the same. The lessons learned are not confined strictly to FSR&D, but apply equally to other types of development oriented research. Three issues identified by several contributors involve areas that at first were seen as easy to address, but in practice have been difficult to deal with. All concern essential features of FSR: farmer participation, interdisciplinary research and involvement of other actors. Before focusing on these issues, first we turn to the central topic of the book: priority setting in the wider context of FSR&D management.

FSR&D management

Why set priorities?

The strength of FSR&D lies in a holistic, participatory approach to farmers' problems, incorporating the knowledge and support of other actors in working to improve agricultural productivity. At the same time, if not properly managed, this perspective can become a major weakness. Throughout this book, team leaders express serious concerns about keeping programmes focused and implementable. FSR&D activities appear to have an inherent tendency to 'mushroom', leading to over-ambitious research programmes that lack focus and coherence. Both internal team dynamics and external forces push in this direction. First, there is a natural tendency to gradually widen research boundaries as FSR&D programmes evolve. This is a logical response to the increasing complexity of the research issues. Having begun from a simple commodity focus, teams soon find themselves faced with a multitude of farm and off-farm enterprises, and dealing with issues including local agricultural support services and local farmer organizations. Without a clear definition of research boundaries, this can easily lead to a 'free-for-all,' a situation that is disorganized enough to leave ample room for individual researchers to follow personal interests. Second, it appears difficult to discontinue ongoing research activities. Over the years, projects show a tendency to add more and more activities to research plans, to avoid a painful cutting back of activities. Researchers often view restructuring of the research plan as threatening. Some find it difficult to change to other topics, feeling less secure in new areas. Others may view it as a personal affront, feeling restricted in their interests and the satisfaction to be gained from their work.

FSR&D teams that actively seek collaboration with other actors or projects are often confronted with a third factor: an increasing external research demand. They may feel obliged to accommodate research demands from other actors – even if these are otherwise of low priority – to maintain their interest in the programme. And even if this does not take the form of demands for specific research, involving more actors brings with it the need to take their general priorities into account. Finally, FSR&D projects are often under pressure from national policymakers and donors to increase the size of the programme in terms of geographical coverage and number of farmers reached.

The penalties for ill-focused, overloaded programmes are severe. Researchers will concentrate on those activities for which they feel responsible, thereby sacrificing essential points: interaction with farmers and interaction within the team; maintaining links with other stakeholders; and analysis, including the synthesis and reporting of results. Because many things are done superficially and none thoroughly, there is little prospect of producing concrete results that can be adopted by farmers. Moreover, half-completed activities that have to be discontinued due to resource constraints represent a waste of resources. Priorities are needed to keep research focused and to make the best use of available resources. The following sections summarize some possibilities for providing structure, followed by a short discussion of cost effectiveness.

Before discussing priority setting further, however, it is important to mention that a focus on priority setting must be seen in context. One of the most important ways to improve priority setting is by strengthening overall programme management, providing a context in which priority setting and implementation interact and support each other in an ever-changing environment. 'Strengthening management' should be understood in terms of the ideas outlined in earlier chapters. The aim is to not to gain 'control' over the research process, but to improve its management, by using a structured, well thought out approach. In fact, encouraging the participation of farmers and other actors, incorporating local knowledge, supporting 'farmer engineering', and working with local organizations makes it necessary for teams to live with the idea of *less* control. This requires management that helps to provide focus while not losing sight of FSR&D as a learning process, evolving iteratively over time.

Strategic and operational plans

Project experiences in a number of chapters indicate the usefulness of adopting a two-cycle process for priority setting and programme design, to structure the iterative FSR&D planning process: a strategic cycle and an operational cycle. The strategic cycle consists of determining in broad terms the major objectives, lines of research, and target groups for a period of perhaps three to four years, based on a critical assessment of past research results. Strategic planning implies a period of reflection; this automatically suggests a review of existing research boundaries and, if needed, their modification. The strategic plan must be carefully formulated on the basis of comprehensive documents, such as earlier review papers, state-of-the-art papers covering main research activities, related policy documents, and so forth. Consultants and evaluation missions can be instrumental in asking good questions and suggesting orientation and strategies for research.

The operational cycle covers the short term. It includes the formulation of annual work plans within the broader themes laid down in the strategic plan. Annual planning exercises preceding or combined with reviews of the results of the previous years' research are important events to consider in reflecting upon and evaluating ongoing research, and in planning new research activities with relevant actors. To arrive at a balanced plan and allow continuity, dividing the plan according to main activities (e.g. diagnostic studies, trials/experimentation, pre-extension) is suggested.

A portion of research resources should be allocated to each of these areas, and their relative importance in different time periods should be indicated in the strategic plan. Specific attention must be given to matching the demand and supply of researcher time. As indicated by the project experiences, management has an important role to play in realistic time planning. This cannot be left entirely with individual researchers, who often underestimate the time required to implement research activities, analyse and report results; and overestimate the amount of work they can do within a given time period.

Periodic planning exercises and syntheses are important in several ways. In particular, they can strengthen both the internal consensus of the team regarding the future direction of the programme, and the team's linkages with other actors – farmers, extension and on-station research, policy-makers and donors – regarding their involvement and commitment. The idea of building in time for reflection, in which data can be compared to results from past seasons and/or other areas or countries, is another important function of periodic syntheses. If this is neglected – if the team is so caught up in operational work that there is no time for proper evaluation – ongoing research may drag on for years even if it is not producing results. Making insufficient use of available research results, whether from the project itself or similar projects elsewhere, leads to duplication of effort and wastes resources. Meanwhile the possibility of adopting new research themes or approaches that might be more promising, or more relevant to the problems at hand, is inadequately considered.

Flexibility and continuity

Well-focused, realistic work plans are a key to successful FSR&D. However, FSR&D programmes should be keenly aware of the danger of focusing research activities too narrowly. In contrast to much other agricultural research, FSR&D must deal with systems and processes that are dynamic. They are affected simultaneously by technical and human elements, as well as seasonal variability and changes in the economy, from long-term trends to short-term market distortions. In a broad perspective, agricultural research is never final. Conditions, whether physical–biological or socio-economic, change continuously, bringing new challenges for research. This has important implications for selecting research themes and designing a research programme. Research plans must be flexible enough to allow adaptation to changes in the farmers' environment; and at the same time they must also give enough continuity to provide useful data.

To meet this challenge, first, research activities must be designed in such a way that the information they yield specifically takes into account the inherent variability in the farmers' environment: changing weather conditions, input availability, price ratios of output and inputs and so forth. This suggests a need for flexible recommendations that incorporate conditional clauses – stating what to do under variable production circumstances. Also, research should not aim at generating monolithic 'technological packages'; thèse take many years to develop, and may become obsolete if production conditions suddenly change. Instead, the aim should be a 'basket' of options, from which farmers may choose and combine elements that fit their own specific conditions. Making this sort of 'farmer engineering' a part of the research plan, and presenting farmers with a range of options, build on the step-wise approach farmers often use in adapting the components of technological innovations to fit their situation.

Next, research plans must be composed of a combination of medium and short-term activities, allowing sufficient flexibility to re-allocate resources in response to a refined diagnosis or changing conditions. When a few research activities claim human and financial resources for considerable periods of time, little room is left for new initiatives. Third, in research planning it is necessary to become more aware of external forces, such as government policies and interventions, and to try to anticipate possible or imminent changes; these can alter production conditions, so that farmers' production decisions change as well. This is particularly relevant, for example, where markets are severely distorted due to subsidies on agricultural inputs or credit, or unreasonably high guaranteed prices for products.

Planning techniques

The contributions in this book show priority setting as an often messy process, well-described by expressions such as 'reconciling conflicting interests', 'arriving at a workable compromise', 'a negotiating process', 'a balancing act'. During the early stages of FSR&D programmes, teams usually arrive at research plans in rather informal ways, as the project experiences indicate. To some extent, this is inevitable and probably appropriate: during information gathering, diagnosis, and data analysis, teams go through an important learning experience. For the several personalities and disciplines involved (and for other actors as well, when they are involved), diagnosis is in large part a process of reaching a common problem definition. In this phase, success may have more to do with how people learn to function together as a team than with the procedures used. But this relatively unstructured phase should not be allowed to go on too long. And in fact, as programmes evolve and knowledge about local circumstances increases, projects tend to adopt more formal procedures to address the increasing complexity of their research issues and to allow more actors to participate in the research process. This leads to a search for methods that will help to structure the process of building consensus and making decisions, both inside the team and with others.

Several of the projects presented here have used the objective oriented project planning (OOPP) technique. The primary strength of this method is that it can increase understanding of complex interrelated problems, because it helps to make cause–effect relationships more visible. However, when projects have not had much experience with OOPP, it may broaden the scope of research rather than focusing it on a few major themes. There is also the planning procedure based on identifying and analysing cause–effect relationships described in Chapter 7. It goes through the various stages of research design, from diagnosis to formulation of concrete research activities, in systematic steps. Thus far, this technique has primarily been used by researchers. While it is argued that the same approach could be used to involve farmers, it would probably need to be fundamentally adapted to make farmer involvement effective.

The value of planning techniques and procedures is not only that they help to structure decision making; they also provide transparency as to why decisions are made, and suggest a built-in system of accountability. However, it would be shortsighted to think that these techniques will make it possible to set priorities simply by following a set of mechanical procedures. This would require quantifiable criteria, which could be used to rank potential research themes according to their contribution to quantifiable objectives or criteria.

In development related research, however, objectives are often complex and difficult to quantify; they may differ substantially among groups of actors. Objectives may concern the farm level – such as number of farmers affected, production and productivity increases, increased farmer income, or decreased risks. Or they could contribute to national priorities – such as attaining national self-sufficiency, generating foreign exchange, stabilizing consumer prices, or protecting the natural environment. Often both types of objectives are involved. Both these objectives and the constraints on the team in terms of mandate, funding, and so forth may contribute criteria to be used in evaluating potential research activities. It is not difficult to make a long list of such criteria for use in selecting research activities; a number of possibilities have been given in Chapter 1. The difficulty lies in reaching consensus – first, on useful operational definitions for project objectives; then on sufficient, suitable sets of criteria; and, hardest of all, with respect to the relative importance of these criteria, including trade-offs between those that conflict or cannot be measured on the same scale. Nevertheless, achieving a common problem definition and consensus on objectives is the key to successful priority setting: when these are obtained, it is usually possible to reach consensus on an initial 'best-bet' plan. Thus consensus building must be a part of the decision making process. Over time, this process is iterative, so that a common base of knowledge can be expected to evolve, making decision making more efficient and leading to better research programmes.

Making the best use of scarce resources

Priority setting is meant to make more effective use of scarce research resources, whether doing more within a given budget, or maintaining existing activities with reduced funding. Earlier chapters cover a number of elements that can contribute to cost effectiveness, including more closely monitoring the progress of individual research activities. In contrast to the attention given to priority setting for new research activities, teams often think surprisingly little about mechanisms to discontinue ongoing research when expected results are not forthcoming, or preliminary data suggests that the results will not be helpful enough to disseminate to farmers. 'State-of-the-art' papers and other ways of taking time to synthesize results and make periodic assessments have been advocated as important mechanisms.

Clustering trials at specific sites or within villages, preferably in areas that are not only representative but also close to FSR&D team headquarters, can improve the efficiency of resource use, simply by reducing research time and other costs, e.g. transportation. Clustering helps to foster closer supervision and better management of trials. It also strengthens field-level linkages with farmers, local extension agents and commodity researchers, as well as among the disciplines represented within the FSR team. Some projects use functional farmer groups to increase the number of farmers involved in research activities. Other ways to improve the cost–benefit ratio of research are to look for high-leverage interventions and to combine research themes, seeking comprehensive research activities.

Further ways to decrease research time are, first, to make use of 'interim best-bet recommendations' and to apply these in pre-extension test programmes, in collaboration with extension agencies. While interim recommendations may be modified by later research results, they can be useful (with one important precondition: farmers must know that these are interim solutions, and be informed about their limitations). Second, researchers (and policymakers) frequently see a need for more data, and often prefer quantitative over qualitative data. However, with more information the subsequent analysis becomes increasingly complex and time consuming. Also, in many cases the wish for 'accuracy' is not justified; sometimes it can be considered a waste of time and resources. Much more attention must be given to the costs versus benefits of data collection. Massive data collection efforts can usurp research resources for long periods of time, without really showing worth for money. Both the degree of accuracy required (what level of uncertainty or ignorance is acceptable in the information to be used as a basis for decision making) and the extent to which alternative, more qualitative methods or procedures can be used must be open to discussion.

Communication, transparency and participation

As earlier chapters indicate, communication, transparency and participation are vital elements of FSR&D. A commitment to working in this way, however, should not be made lightly. Learning to create linkages and work participatively – seeing FSR&D as a node within a network of actors – will require learning new skills and, perhaps even more importantly, new attitudes; it is also time consuming. Participation can only succeed if it begins within the team, and if the team really believes a mutual exchange will be worthwhile. Interest in and openness to others' ideas often require overcoming long-held stereotypes, and learning instead to make realistic assessments of their knowledge and capabilities. Collaboration with other actors on this basis, however, can greatly increase their interest, providing a source of information, commitment, and support.

No matter which actors are to play a part, it is important to involve them early in the process. Either a simple exchange of information or more extensive participation can begin in or before the diagnostic phase. Making a clear decision about the kind of participation the team would like to achieve (and feels it can handle), and stating this honestly, is an important first step; otherwise, expectations may be raised that cannot be fulfilled. Communication, transparency and participation all increase the importance of accountability with respect to decisions that have been made and feedback that has been promised, whether to donors and policymakers or to client groups.

Feedback is clearly an essential part of this process. The mechanisms used to give feedback (formal or informal, oral or written, style, content, and so forth) must be chosen and adapted to fit the actors involved. In reporting results, there is another important consideration: the understandable tendency to highlight exclusively the positive contributions of FSR&D. It should, however, be underscored that properly reported 'negative' results and/or 'failed' experiments can often provide equally important information, and can help to avoid large-scale 'development project' failures. Reporting both sides increases credibility, gives stakeholders a realistic view of the situation, and improves their understanding.

Leadership and strong disciplinary ties

Good internal FSR&D team communication and team coherence are preconditions for developing smooth communication linkages with other actors. A strategy to increase the involvement of other actors can only be effective if the FSR&D team itself is clear about its approach, objectives and strategies. Also, good within-team relationships are very significant to priority setting: they influence the relevance of the research priorities selected, the way research is carried out, and the value of the potential results. In FSR&D, this presents a need for good interdisciplinary cooperation. Sound interdisciplinary work only becomes possible with contributions from strong disciplines. The idea that the FSR&D researcher should be a 'jack-of-all-trades' is a misconception. Foremost, team members must have confidence in and be able to use the analytical tools of their own discipline within a systems perspective. Confidence in one's own background helps make it possible to have a healthy respect for the role of other disciplines, and be willing and able to be a team player. Above all, team members need to be able to listen, understand and accept other's viewpoints, and be prepared to modify their own views. This implies a need for compatible personalities and transparency among team members in terms of job descriptions, communication, responsibilities, distribution of research resources and reward systems. Decision making within the team, too, needs to be transparent and to encourage clear assignment of both responsibility and accountability.

The project experiences make clear that the existence of a multidisciplinary team does not, without further action, ensure an interdisciplinary approach – that is, that different disciplines will have compatible objectives or work together on the same topic. In fact, interdisciplinarity does not come easily; several factors are influential, such as the size and composition of the team; researchers' educational backgrounds and personal interests; training/ experience in farming systems research; and the joint experience gained by the team over the years. Efficient team management and strong but flexible leadership, especially in the early stages, are a prerequisite to bringing team members together in a common research effort: FSR&D management must create conditions that facilitate this process. Opportunities for interaction among researchers, for confronting differences in approaches and terminology, and for conducting joint research activities should be built in. This is particularly important when disciplines are organized in separate sections. Competence and personality, rather than a specific disciplinary background, and a capacity to build on the strengths and minimize the weaknesses of individuals, are important characteristics of team leaders. Encouraging sensitivity to cultural backgrounds and personalities is essential, especially in teams composed of both local and expatriate researchers. For example, ways of reaching decisions may differ substantially across cultures: some are accustomed to spelling out differences openly in group discussions, whereas others try to achieve consensus through bilateral discussions before group decisions are made.

A variety of specific ways in which project management can encourage interdisciplinarity are suggested by the project experiences. Examples include stimulating joint project activities; having researchers present proposed research in 'research protocols' that spell out justification, objectives and links to other research; organizing workshops or seminars annually, to define the research programme; and taking time at regular intervals (every two to three years) to evaluate past research and review orientation and strategies.

Farmers first: beyond romance and rhetoric

Virtually all of the project experiences in this book suggest that research is being done on the real problems of farmers; but the extent to which farmer participation has had an actual impact on the orientation of research and research activities is often not clear. The issue is not whether we are working with farmers, but one of the farmer's role. Potentially, farmers – the final end-users or clients of the research process – should have tremendous leverage regarding the orientation and content of FSR&D programmes. The ultimate success of these programmes is determined by the extent to which farmers adopt agricultural technologies or other interventions meant to improve agricultural production and/or incomes. Using indigenous knowledge as a basis and properly communicating new information are important; the interest and commitment of farmers are vital.

Farmer involvement is thus not only a central tenet of FSR&D, it is also essential to its success. However, romanticism and rhetoric aside, the situation is not that simple. First, farm households and farm communities across the world are highly heterogeneous, both in terms of resource endowments and in access to external resources. Hence, interests among farmer groups will differ; they may even be in conflict. The tendency for farmers with high social and economic status to be disproportionately represented at meetings, field days and other project events is well known. It usually takes a conscious effort – at times even positive discrimination – to get resource-poor farmers, women, or other disadvantaged groups into the foreground and actively involved in the research programme. Second, notwithstanding the emphasis on farmer participation in priority setting and the clear need for incorporation of farmer's knowledge, there are several reasons research cannot be determined by farmer needs alone:

- farmers are part of a society; the needs, interests and priorities of other groups (including regional and national) must be taken into account as well. Sustainability and equity are among the important concerns;
- farmers, with good reason, focus on immediate needs. Too strictly following farmers' priorities and research demands puts FSR&D programmes at risk of becoming overcautious and may curtail innovative long-term thinking;
- some farmer problems and priorities cannot be translated into researchable issues, or do not fall within the mandate of the FSR&D team.

It is important to recognize that even though their direct participation in priority setting exercises may be uncommon, farmers do influence priorities. Many teams have found ways to assure significant farmer input. Still, information flows between teams and farmers could be improved. Researchers have not been very creative in finding ways to harness the research potential of farmers. The desire to 'put numbers on things' puts a major barrier between researchers and farmers; some feel that quantitative social science methods based on questionnaire-driven surveys have failed to make use of the potential inherent in the idea of true farmer participation. More use could be made of non-conventional, participatory research methods, as a supplement to conventional techniques: these alternative methods can pull farmers more into the centre of decision making processes, including priority setting. When well used (and contrary to common belief), they can yield quantifiable results for large numbers of farmers, and often much more quickly than conventional tools. However, none of the projects described here report using these methods; on the other hand, almost all made use of rapid rural appraisals, farmer meetings and group interviews, some of which may have incidentally included similar techniques.

Thus some techniques are available now, but further development is required: to encourage farmers to participate in decision making, appropriate linkage mechanisms, modes of communication, and methods of data collection must be used. That is, they must suit both the interest and the ability of farmers. The physical presence of farmers during critical decision moments does not guarantee that their viewpoint will be taken into account. The ways farmers interact with researchers may take various forms, according to the knowledge and expertise of the FSR team and the type of research activity. In any case, an open, honest dialogue is needed with farmers, based on mutual respect and sharing information. Researchers need to be honest about what they know and do not know! Achieving real farmer participation requires communicating through concrete, specific examples; establishing a common knowledge base; and organizing groups of farmers around the testing of specific techniques. Understanding and building on indigenous knowledge and local organizations, recognizing farmer experimentation, packaging recommendations with farmer engineering in mind, and defining areas of local responsibility and authority can all serve to increase relevance, interest and participation.

The need, then, is to find ways to integrate a realistic perspective while working to realize the great potential impact of farmer participation. In this process, researchers need to think about transparency and accountability to farmers. Working with farmers – increasing communication – raises expectations; this in turn makes it particularly important to be clear about the objectives and potential for results. While the process is not easy, it is rewarding: with support and encouragement, farmers can fill many roles, including those of advisor, colleague, student, extension worker and friend.

Increasing exposure: interaction with the environment

Throughout this book, linkages and good communication with a variety of agricultural development actors are advocated. In addition to farmers, these include thematic researchers, policymakers and planners, marketing boards, development agencies and extension services, but also private sector actors such as rural banks, commercial suppliers of inputs, marketing boards and policymakers, NGOs and, of course, funding agencies. In part, this emphasis is a reaction to the relative isolation of many FSR&D projects in the past from the wider institutional and policy environment: it has clearly been much easier for FSR&D teams to receive inputs from other stakeholders than to influence their priorities and strategies. In the early phases of an FSR&D project, as teams go through a process of building a team and establishing credibility, this is understandable. In the long term, however, exposure to the wider decision making environment and interaction with other actors are essential to sustaining FSR&D programmes. The number of short-lived projects that never gained momentum and so vanished into obscurity is great. As suggested in earlier chapters, influence does not have to be direct; but neither direct nor indirect influence will be possible without carefully built relationships with other actors.

These chapters should encourage FSR&D teams to increase their exposure, actively interact with their environments, and seek collaboration or linkages. The need for FSR&D teams, and especially team management, to actively invest in creating opportunities to work with and involve others has been amply illustrated. Other actors have important contributions to make in terms of:

- representing societal needs related to e.g. distribution of benefits and ecological sustainability;
- providing supplementary skills and knowledge in defining and finding solutions to agricultural problems;
- supplying information about future developments;
- determining policies and providing support services for sustainable agricultural development;
- disseminating results emanating from FSR&D activities; and
- directly or indirectly, helping to ensure continued support for the programme.

An FSR&D team needs to think carefully about who should be involved during various stages of priority setting, and how. Who is involved in decision making (and how) has an effect on both the decisions reached and the ease of implementation. But 'involvement' does not always mean joint priority setting; nor does it mean everyone must be equally involved at all times. Sometimes priorities may be set within the team. Decisions can be made about crucial moments to involve particular actors, information flows to particular groups of actors, and what issues should be left undiscussed. Also, involving others, including setting priorities jointly, does not mean all must agree completely. It does mean that seeking common problem definitions and finding points of agreement – in short, consensus building – must be a part of the decision making process. And, as this process is iterative, a common knowledge base will gradually evolve, and decision making will become more efficient.

Information flows are decisive factors. For example, FSR&D may need specific contacts at specific times, to have the required information on hand. Too, other actors need appropriate feedback from FSR&D, given at the right time. In addition to providing information, this helps to increase commitment and, not incidentally, to assure others that their resources (whether time, money or something else) are being used well. This implies a need for projects to learn to tune their communication, whether written or verbal, to the information needs, interests and capabilities of different actors: the amount and intensity of feedback given should be adapted to match the group. It is important to assess and appreciate the reasons partners (or potential partners) might want to be involved. Knowing their interests and seeking common ground, it is possible to improve communication and interaction, so that other actors may come to recognize that they, too, have a stake in the results.

One aspect of such interactions seems particularly in need of emphasis, since it does not come naturally to FSR&D practitioners. In many project areas, external factors have become major barriers to agricultural development. Under such conditions, continued investment in problem-solving research may not be effective: a policy and institutional environment that is at least minimally supportive is a necessity for success. Yet it appears that projects do not often put themselves in a position to create/use leverage with agricultural policymakers, in an attempt to influence priorities and strategies. The capacity of FSR&D teams to influence policy, even at the delivery level, is usually weak. At the least, teams need to be aware of what is happening in this part of their environment. But they can in fact go further. While FSR&D programmes should certainly not be co-opted by political factions, they can establish more leverage and become more creative if they begin to draw upon other actors, including policymakers, as partners rather than adversaries. Proper packaging of information and more active participation in decision making (not only getting others to take part in FSR&D-defined processes, but finding ways to contribute to their decisions as well) can become important elements in strengthening the research–policy interface. The aim should be to contribute to formulation of policy by making field-level insights available and interesting: for example, what makes rural communities tick, and what triggers can be used to stimulate their development.

Future agenda

Looking into the future of FSR&D, we see a period that is apt to be difficult but challenging. Difficult, because it is not likely that the restricted funding situation will ease; challenging, because there are new areas in which FSR&D can make important contributions. The sustainability issue presents a formidable challenge to all actors in agricultural development. FSR&D has a major potential role, because of the location specificity of most environmental issues. However, FSR&D programmes' orientation to farmers tends to emphasize a near-term horizon; in fact, FSR&D programmes have often been criticized for an inherent conservatism. In the future, ecological stability – and thus a long-term perspective – needs to be incorporated. This will require moving from a focus on improved productivity for individual farm enterprises, and towards a broader perspective on land use systems and natural resources management. A stronger sense of trends and dynamics will be needed. At the same time, this will require more, rather than less, attention to local information and the participation of farmers. FSR&D teams must become familiar with processes of resource degradation and their underlying causes, as well as the wider issue of livelihood systems. A number of projects included in this book are already working along these lines. Nevertheless, a great deal of work is still to be done with respect to methodologies that allow diagnosis of the non-sustainable features of land use systems, evaluation of interventions based on sustainability criteria, and so forth. Applied environmental economics is a field in particular need of development. Sustainability of another sort is also an issue: the institutional sustainability of the structures established and built up by the research programme, whether at village level, with the extension service, or with other actors.

Many of these topics suggest new complexities and new demands on FSR&D teams: thus there will be an ever-increasing need for attention to research management, particularly to priority setting. To achieve sustainability, work must continue on development of tools and techniques that can help move FSR&D teams towards focused activities, leading to results that will be adopted by farmers. Techniques that facilitate transparent priority setting and work well in a setting with multiple actors and interests are required, including participatory tools that pull farmers more into the decision making process. However, because of the many ways FSR&D can be implemented, it would be futile to seek standard recipes for procedures and tools. What is needed is a cafeteria of formal and informal tools and techniques, from which FSR&D teams can select according to their needs.

   The cost-effectiveness of FSR&D is and will remain an important issue. The current climate of donor withdrawal and financial curtailment makes it essential to look for improved returns from research resources. Discussions of cost effectiveness also point up the need to find ways to measure the impact of farmer-oriented approaches, to back up the message that a participatory approach is apt to be the most sustainable one, and therefore the most efficient and cost effective in the long term. Getting this message across is another vital matter.

One way for FSR&D teams to move toward the future is, as several authors suggest, to become more proactive, to play what some have called a more 'entrepreneurial' role. This does not suggest a move away from the goals of farming systems research, but that living in isolation is no longer affordable. As outlined in the preceding section, it is necessary to become more aware of the environment in which FSR&D takes place, constantly being alert to new opportunities and potential constraints. This could mean increased political awareness – for example, awareness of the political leverage linkages can provide, and attention to the integration of FSR in the national research system, at whatever level. It could mean recognizing the increasing importance of NGOs and private companies, and the need to build linkages for the future. But it could also mean closer attention to farmers' needs, understanding how and where new demands are being articulated, and working toward demonstrable sustainability, via a responsive research system. All of these possibilities call for communication, transparency and accountability – in short, they involve opening up the priority setting process.

Experimentation with new ways to embed FSR&D in agricultural research systems is another potential area for change. Making concepts such as the use of indigenous or local knowledge, farmer engineering, and local organization a reality could lead to research that is more relevant, and more sustainable. At other levels too, many FSR&D programmes – especially in Africa – are likely to be confronted in the future with changing institutional environments. The overriding importance of the public sector is likely to weaken, in favour of a stronger private sector presence. The existing roles of actors will change; new research-funding actors (such as NGOs and private enterprises) will emerge. FSR&D will have to accommodate these changes by creating new linkages, for example seeking opportunities to incorporate local NGOs and farmer cooperatives in research planning – and perhaps working to attract funding from non-conventional sources. In short, the tendency of FSR&D to be somewhat isolated from both local and national structures (with team members as the lead actors in FSR&D at local level) needs to change.

Thus, in summary, FSR&D needs to develop research management and priority setting compatible with working with others, and a proactive approach to interaction with its environment. This requires a more assertive and less defensive stance, and suggests making conscious choices about what will be done; developing strategies; learning to communicate; building linkages; working toward common definitions of the problems faced; plus finding ways to manage a creative, sometimes messy, iterative learning process. We hope that the future of FSR&D will include acting together with other stakeholders, sharing not only the difficulties but also the satisfaction of meeting these challenges – and getting results.

About the authors

James Bingen, based at Michigan State University, East Lansing, Michigan, USA, is a faculty member in the Department of Resource Development.

Agronomist *Chris Bosch,* a Royal Tropical Institute (KIT) staff member, has worked within the Lake Zone FSR project in Bukoba area, Tanzania, since 1989.

Keija F. Bunyecha, an economist and Zonal FSR Coordinator for the Lake Zone project, has been based in Ukiriguru, Mwanza, Tanzania, since the inception of the FSR&D programme in 1988.

Wim van Campen is a soil conservation expert and KIT staff member. From 1986-1991 he was teamleader of the *Projet Lutte Anti-Erosive dans la zone Mali-Sud* (PLAE).

Agronomist *Amadou Diarra* is the former head of the Department of Farming Systems Research within IER (l'Institut d'Economie Rurale) in Bamako, Mali.

Driek Enserink, agronomist and KIT staff, was teamleader for the Tanzania/Netherlands Farming Systems Research Project Lake Zone, in Mwanza, Tanzania, from its inception in 1988 to 1992.

Thomas Eponou is a research fellow at the International Service for National Agricultural Research (ISNAR), The Hague, The Netherlands.

Bram Huijsman, an agricultural economist, is director of the Agricultural and Enterprise Development group at KIT.

KIT sociologist *Rita Joldersma* worked as a member of the DRSPR technical assistance team in Sikasso, Mali, from 1989 to 1993.

Margo Kooijman, KIT agroeconomist, was teamleader of the Technical Assistance Team for the Department of Farming Systems Research (DRSPR), Sikasso, Mali, 1989–1992.

Simone Kortbeek has been teamleader of the Women and Development Project (*Projet Femmes et Développement,* PROFED) since 1991.

Valentin Koudokpon is an agronomist and researcher on the staff of the Directorate for Agronomic Research (DRA) of Benin. He is coordinator of the FSR&D team on the RAMR project in Mono Province.

Agronomist *Bert Meertens* worked on assignment from SNV to the FSR project Lake Zone in the Maswa/Meatu area, from 1989–1992.

Douwe Meindertsma, a KIT agroeconomist, was from 1990–1992 FSR coordinator for the ATA-272 project within MARIF, in Malang, Indonesia.

Since 1981 *Mukelabai Ndiyoi,* an agronomist, has worked in FSR in the Western Province, Zambia; currently, he is ARPT coordinator in the Western Province.

David Norman is professor of agricultural economics at Kansas State University, Manhattan, Kansas, USA.

Agronomist and KIT staff member *Petra Penninkhoff* works in the area of on-farm trials and gender issues in FSR.

Robert Rhoades is professor and chairman of the Department of Anthropology, University of Georgia, Athens, Georgia, USA.

Stephan Seegers worked from 1990–1992 as a research associate at KIT, where he was involved in issues related to research management in FSR including the organization of the conference on *Priority setting in farming systems research and development.*

Antonio Silva is an agricultural economist; he has been a member of the Regional Management Unit of the *Programa Regional de Reforzamento a la Investigación Agronómica sobre los Granos en Centroamérica* (PRIAG/CORECA-EEC), Central America, since 1990.

Fred van Sluys, a rural sociologist and KIT staff member, has been co-director of the Regional Management Unit of the *Programa Regional de Reforzamento a la Investigación Agronómica sobre los Granos en Centroamérica* (PRIAG/CORECA-EEC), Central America, since 1990.

Leendert Sprey is an economist on the staff of KIT. He has been team leader and economic advisor to the RAMR project (Benin) from 1989.

Willem Stoop is senior agronomist at KIT, in charge of agronomic and research management aspects of field projects.

Soil scientist *H. Suyamto* is a senior researcher and FSR coordinator of the Malang Research Institute for Food Crops (MARIF), Malang, Indonesia.

Klaas Tamminga, a socioeconomist, has worked with the FSR project Lake Zone in Mwanza, Tanzania, since 1991.

Robert Tripp is the director of the economics programme at the International Maize and Wheat Improvement Centre (CIMMYT), Mexico, DF.

Gerben Vierstra, rural sociologist and KIT staff member, worked from 1987–1991 within the Adaptive Research Planning Team (ARPT) of the Western Province, Zambia.

Tri Wibowo, head of the Department of Food Crops of the West Nusa Tenggara Province (DIPERTA-NTB), Indonesia, took part in the FSR&D programme in Lombok from 1990–1992.

Jonathan Woolley is senior economist at the International Maize and Wheat Improvement Centre (CIMMYT), Mexico, DF.

KIT staff member *Lida Zuidberg* was teamleader of the women's extension project *Projet d'Appui à l'Animation Féminine,* or PAAF, during its first phase, 1987–1990.